Married in Mission:
A Handbook for Couples in Cross-Cultural Service

Alexis C. Kenny

Chicago: Paul Bechtold Library Publications
Catholic Theological Union
2015

Grateful acknowledgment is made for permission to reprint the following selections in this book:"Re-entry" by IES Abroad, © 2014. Adapted by permission of organization. *Survival Kit for Overseas Living: For Americans Planning to Live and Work Abroad* by L. Robert Kohls, ©1984. Adapted by permission of Nicholas Brealey Publishing. Adaptations from *The Seven Principles for Making Marriage Work* by John M. Gottman, Ph.D., © 1996 by John M. Gottman, Ph.D., and Nan Silver. Used by permission of Crown Books, an imprint of the Crown Publishing Group, a division of Penguin Random House LLC. All rights reserved. Adaptations from *Ten Lessons to Transform Your Marriage: America's Love Lab Experts Share Their Strategies For Strengthening Your Relationship* by John M. Gottman, Ph.D., © 2006 by John M. Gottman, Ph.D., and Joan DeClaire. Used by permission of Crown Books, an imprint of the Crown Publishing Group, a division of Penguin Random House LLC. All rights reserved. *The 5 Love Languages: The Secret to Love That Lasts* by Gary Chapman, © 1992. Adapted by permission of Moody Publishers. "Five Questions with Forgiveness Expert, Dr. Everett Worthington" by Ryan Martin, © 2011. Adapted by permission of Ryan Martin. "Types of Infidelity" by Cathy Meyer, © 2015. Adapted by permission of Cathy Meyer. "Do You See What I See?" by Thirty-Three Ministries, © 2011. Reprinted by permission of organization. "How to Create a Timeline: The Power of Re-working Your Life's Story, 1 of 2" by Athena Staik, © 2013. Adapted by permission of Athena Staik.

LC call number: BV2094.6 .K46 2015
OCLC Number: (print) 922895849
　　　　　　(ebook) 922895993
ISBN: (print) 9780963665942
　　　(ebook) 9780963665935

Published 2015 by Paul Bechtold Library Publications, Catholic Theological Union

Paul Bechtold Library Publications
Catholic Theological Union
5401 S. Cornell Ave.
Chicago, IL 60615
pblpubs@ctu.edu

Focus and Scope: Paul Bechtold Library Publications is a Catholic online, open-access publisher of theology and pastoral ministry monographs at the Catholic Theological Union through the Paul Bechtold Library. Its mission is to serve the Church by providing a forum for theologians and pastoral ministers to engage the Catholic tradition in respectful, constructive, and critical dialogue. Its primary intent and direction is to promote a deeper understanding of the Christian faith and the mission of the Church.

The mission of Catholic Theological Union is to prepare effective leaders for the Church, ready to witness to Christ's good news of justice, love, and peace.

Table of Contents

Many thanks to this handbook's readers:
Joyce Dombrouski, Rich Dombrouski, Gerry Doran, Vic Doucette, Dorcie
Kafka Dvarishkis, Laura Mae Gardner. C.R. Murphy, Roger Schroeder,
SVD, Alyssa Sickle, and Ken Wiggers.

In partnership with:
Catholic Theological Union
Catholic Volunteer Network
From Mission to Mission
Paul Bechtold Library Publications

"This is dedicated to the one I love"

To Pat . . .

from me and The Shirelles

Preface
Introduction

Men and women—even man and wife are foreigners. Each has reserves that the other cannot enter into, nor understand. These have the effect of frontiers.

—Mark Twain, *Notebook, 1904*

Personal Background

My name is Ali Kenny. I started my Master of Arts in Intercultural Ministry at Catholic Theological Union (CTU) in the fall of 2012. After one year of studies, I took a sabbatical of sorts. Patrick Kenny and I were married near Glacier National Park on June 22, 2013. Following our Hawaiian honeymoon, the two of us flew to Honduras—not as an extension of our post-wedding vacation (although many people jokingly referred to it that way), but rather, to begin our thirteen-month commitment as volunteers working at an orphanage. If I were to describe our mission experience in one word, that word would be "intense." Serving in a rural, hot, and notoriously dangerous environment was intense, being the primary childcare providers for abused children was intense, and doing it all as newlyweds was … you guessed it … intense. While Pat was (and continues to be) a self-contained and internal processor, I remember feeling like it would have been helpful to have had some guidance in navigating through my cross-cultural experience in Honduras as a *wife*—someone part of a dyadic unit.

After returning back to the United States, I sought out literature specifically for married couples transitioning home from international ministry, and came up relatively empty-handed. I had one semester of coursework to finish at CTU and a thesis to write before my graduation. Seeing that I had the time, academic means, background, and aspiration, I decided to fulfill my thesis requirement by creating a resource for other volunteer husbands and wives. *Married in Mission: A Handbook for Couples in Cross-Cultural Service* is an informally formative manual meant to accompany spouses through the highs and lows of the complete overseas mission experience—the realities faced *before, during,* and *after* service abroad.

Project Overview

Catholic mission work, originally a vocation taken up by men and women belonging to religious orders, has been an expanding form of ministry since the Second Vatican Council. A greater involvement of lay people (non-clergy) is a significant part of the development of Catholic international outreach. While resources exist for Protestant missioners—both single volunteers and missionary families—similar material for their Catholic counterparts is lacking. Though *Married in Mission* aims to be accessible across denominational boundaries, it is dedicated to closing the literary gap that exists in the Catholic mission world, specifically in regard to the unique issues married individuals confront while engaged in cross-cultural service.

This handbook functions as a compilation and consolidation of topics and subjects that have already been taken into account by other authors and experts. That being said, *Married in Mission* is unique in the fact that it addresses all "stages" of international service work in one volume. Moreover, this guide contains a total of twenty-one exercises relevant to topics present at each missionary stage, making it both interactive and practical. Sources for this guide consist of books, periodicals, and articles about cross-cultural encounters, my own research, and effective techniques that can enhance spousal relationships as proven by the marital psychology generated by Dr. John Gottman, one of the most influential therapists of the past quarter-century.

In the fall of 2014, I created two surveys: one for program staff members who work directly with married missioners serving abroad, and the other for married individuals who volunteered for at least nine months at an international ministry site with their spouse. The program staff survey was comprised of 15 questions; three of which were short-answer questions. The married missioner survey was comprised of 126 questions; 27 of which were short-answer questions. These two surveys were disseminated to member organizations of Catholic Volunteer Network in January 2015. Additionally, these questionnaires were distributed to several Protestant missionary institutions. The following is a list of how survey participants self-identified in terms of religious affiliation: Anabaptist, Anglican, atheist, Baptist, Christian, Evangelical Free Church of America, Independent Bible Church, Lutheran, Mennonite, Presbyterian, nondenominational, Quaker, Roman Catholic, Southern Baptist, United Church of Christ, United Methodist, unsure, and Wesleyan. It is difficult to say how many individuals with the desired background were reached in the promulgation of these two surveys, but my best guess is somewhere around 400 people. Out of these 400 people, 119 participants completed all or parts of the surveys: 30 program staff members and 89 returned married volunteers.

In analyzing the completed surveys, I was able to make informed inferences based on the comments in the short-answer sections of both questionnaires. I have also incorporated some anecdotal data into the handbook text, adding authenticity and credibility to its content. To help further fill out certain parts of my research, I conducted additional interviews via email correspondence with eighteen individuals (single and married, international missioners and service program staff members) in the spring and summer of 2015.

Disclaimers

Limitations. As a human being in general, and as a budding author expressly, I have undeniable biases and constraints—limitations I would like to share with you. I am young—27 to be exact. Thus, my knowledge and experience concerning international mission work is germinal, yet ever growing. The volunteer commitment that my husband and I completed together would be considered by professionals in this field as a short-term, highly specialized contribution to the greater good of this planet. I am newly married with no children (yet). I am a practicing Roman Catholic, but I feel comfortable engaging in secular, interreligious, and ecumenical dialogue.

Acknowledgments. There are a number of wonderful individuals, of all spiritual persuasions, who have devoted many, many years to various aspect of cross-cultural service: extended work with particular communities, research and resolutions, direct member care, inculturation and evangelization, etc. A few of these people were instrumental in the creation of *Married in Mission,* and I would like to recognize their efforts. A sincere thanks to Dr. Gerry Doran for his exploration of the interface between theology and psychology; to Vic Doucette for his attention to issues of social justice and program leadership; to Dr. Laura Mae Gardner for her expertise in making international ministry a healthy and effective pursuit; to Colin Murphy for his commitment to enhancing preparatory development and care for first-time/multi-term missioners; to Alyssa Sickle for her ability to promote multi-organizational collaboration; to Fr. Roger Schroeder for his faithfulness to the Society of the Divine Word charism and academic progress; and to Ken Wiggers for his managerial excellence and on-the-ground ventures.

Terminology. I use the words "missioner" and "volunteer" (and their derivatives) synonymously in this handbook. My simple definition of these terms is *an individual who freely offers himself/herself in service for the betterment of others.* I know that there exist differences between these words, religiously driven motivations, job types, and length of commitment being main points of contrast. However, for several reasons, I have chosen to focus more on the terms' similarities, allowing for their interchangeability. You and your partner can identify with whichever label most accurately reflects your role and work abroad.

Audience. This resource was created for married couples who (a) are departing from and returning to a Westernized society, and (b) have committed to an extended, international ministry assignment. I am intentionally using "extended" so as to allow for greater audience engagement. I believe that spouses doing six months of mission work together—or those doing decades of it—can both benefit from the topics and exercises put forth in this manual. That being said, I see *Married in Mission* being especially suited for couples serving anywhere from nine months to four years abroad.

Scope. I wrote this guide with a focus more on marriage than on family, more on the relationship between husband and wife than on the dynamics among father, mother, and child. While this publication will touch upon some obstacles faced by parents, it is by no means a how-to book on raising third culture/missionary kids. See References for those kinds of resources.

Perspective. There exists much material that specifically deals with various themes inherent to international work (e.g., approaches to studying a language, intercultural learning in relation to local contexts, or multi-cultural methods of sharing one's faith with others). While matters such as language, learning, and approach will be taken up, they will be done so from the perspective of married individuals and how those matters can affect one's marriage.

Timeline

We must start looking at extended, international mission work as more than just the time spent in a foreign location. How you prepare for (insert host country) and how you process your experience of (insert host country) directly impacts the relationship you have with your ministry in (insert host country). With that in mind, I have opted to break down the overseas service experience into seven phases. *Stages of Cross-Cultural Transition* (located and labeled on the following page as **Figure Preface.1**) is representative of an *individual* moving through his/her volunteer commitment. This timeline is to be read as a flexible model, not an immutable prototype. Not everyone's "adventures" abroad will be accurately reflected in **Figure Preface.1**, for creating an outlined timetable that incorporates all experiences of this nature is impossible. However, I anticipate that you and your spouse will be able to identify with parts of this illustration and find it useful as you make your way through the handbook.

<u>Timeline Explained</u>

My conception of a missioner's cross-cultural experience is informed by both literal geography ("home," "abroad," "home") and Arnold van Gennep's theoretical stages of transition (renamed here as "separation," "liminality," "incorporation").[1] (These stages of transition are analogous to William Bridges' delineations: "ending," "neutral zone," "new beginning.")[2] In reference to the *Stages of Cross-Cultural Transition* timeline, I have identified and separated extended, international service into seven different phases: the pre-departure processes of (1) discernment and (2) preparation; the (3) beginning, (4) middle, and (5) end of the abroad experience itself; and finally, the post-service stages of (6) re-entry and (7) integration. Each chapter of *Married in Mission* is dedicated to one phase of your ministry together: Chapter 1 = Discernment, Chapter 2 = Preparation, and so on.

The following questions will give you and your partner an idea of the kinds of concepts that are to be covered in each chapter:

> **Chapter 1:** Whose motivations are being taken into consideration when we think about committing to a ministerial assignment?
> **Chapter 2:** Are we sharing decision-making power equally in preparing for our time in mission?
> **Chapter 3:** Is it "normal" for our expressions of intimacy to be noticeably different at the beginning of our overseas placement?
> **Chapter 4***:* Will we be able to manage the opposing emotions we may feel during a temporary visit to our home country?
> **Chapter 5:** How is each of us to construct meaningful goodbyes in hopes of creating a sense of closure for ourselves and for those we have come to love at our volunteer site(s)?
> **Chapter 6:** What should I do if my significant other is processing our service experience differently than I am?
> **Chapter 7:** How can we both meaningfully honor our past missionary work within our marriage today?

<u>Reading Tips</u>

This handbook is intended to be utilized over the course of *a year or more*. Because each chapter is devoted to a particular period within your and your partner's cross-cultural service, they are to be read concurrent with your shared experiences. For example, couples will

---

1   Victor Turner, "Betwixt and Between: The Liminal Period in Rites of Passage," in *Betwixt and Between: Patterns of Masculine and Feminine Imitation,* eds. Louise Carus Mahdi, Steven Foster, and Meredith Little (La Salle, IL: Open Court, 1987), 5.

2   William Bridges, *Managing Transitions: Making The Most of Change* (Cambridge: Da Capo Press, 2003), 4–5.

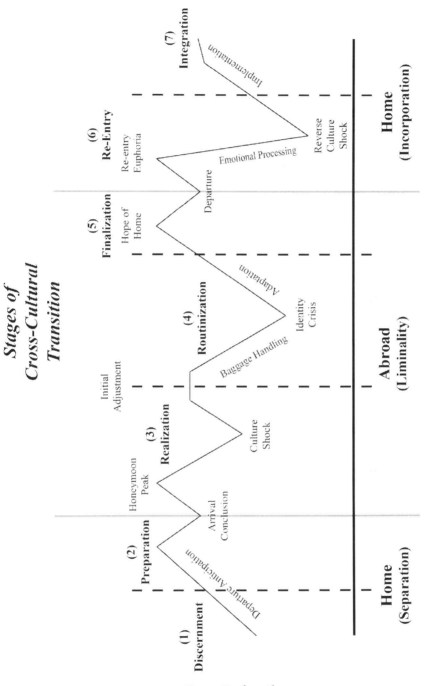

Figure Preface.1[3]

3 Adapted from "Re-entry," *IES Abroad,* accessed October 15, 2014, http://www.iesabroad.org/study-abroad/parents/re-entry.

want to read Chapter 3 during the first few months after arriving to their host country, as material within this section takes up issues which are *likely* to surface at that time. I emphasize "likely" here because each marriage and each individual within it will have a completely unprecedented experience of international mission work. The purpose of this handbook is not to assume and project, but rather, to suggest empathy, education, and communication. Some couples will not undergo significant gender role reversals, need time to reflect theologically, or struggle with mutual integration. Thus, subject matter in each chapter is divided into titled sections, so that you and your partner can engage with topics pertinent to your relationship at whatever level the two of you choose.

Additionally, you will find three activities in each chapter. These exercises are meant to help partners resolve some of the common issues that can arise in each phase of an international mission experience. For example, a conflict resolution activity is located in Chapter 3 because many survey participants reported an increase in the number of arguments had with their spouse during the beginning of their time overseas. These activities are to be completed over a period of several months, and only if their purposes will be beneficial for your marriage. Some exercises will be relevant and useful for you and your partner, and others, maybe not so much. Ergo, complete these activities at your own discretion.

Culture, Marriage, and Mutuality

According to Dr. John Gottman, when we think of "culture," most of us think in terms of large ethnic groups or even countries where particular civilities and cuisine prevail.[4] But "culture" can be more accurately defined as "a system of shared symbols and meanings."[5] In this sense, each couple creates their own micro-culture. Like other cultures, these small units have their own customs (large, home-cooked dinners every Sunday), rituals (the recitation of wedding vows on each anniversary), and myths (the true, false, and slightly embellished stories spouses share with others). And like cultures, each couple's own customs, rituals, and myths are symbolically meaningful, and representative of their marriage.[6] The construction of one micro-culture by two individuals should be a *mutual* process. To more clearly understand this, let us turn to the word "mutuality."

"Mutuality" stems from the Latin derivative, *mutuus*. *Mutuus* has an ethical and collective connotation that communicates a "simultaneous exchange" or a "concurrent crossover." Mutuality stretches beyond equality and complementarity. Moreover, mutuality stands outside of reciprocity; for in reciprocal relationships, each person does something for the other, while in mutual relationships, individuals "do something together that neither one of them could do separately."[7] A good analogy of this is the coming together of two musical notes. If you play a D on a piano and, at the same time, play an F, you get a harmony—a completely new sound that consists of two notes; notes that still remain differentiable. Likewise,

---

4   John M. Gottman and Nan Silver, *The Seven Principles for Making Marriage Work* (New York: Crown, 1999), 244.

5   Gerald A. Arbuckle, SM, *Culture, Inculturation, and Theologians: A Postmodern Critique* (Collegeville, MN: The Liturgical Press, 2010), 7.

6   Gottman and Silver, *Seven Principles*, 244.

7   Quoted in Michelle Maiese, "The Life of Dialogue," Conflict Research Consortium, article summary of Abraham Kaplan, "The Life of Dialogue," in *The Reach of Dialogue: Confirmation, Voice, and Community*, eds. Robert Anderson, Kenneth N. Cissna, and Ronald C. Arnett (New Jersey: Hampton Press, 1994), http://www.colorado.edu/conflict/peace/example/lifeofdialogue.htm.

marriage consists of two "I's," forever unique unto themselves, that mutually join to form a completely original "we."

Mutuality is a part of all Christian marriages, for husbands and wives are called to "be subject to one another out of reverence for Christ," to "be submissive to one another in fear of God," to "submit to each other out of respect for Christ" (Eph 5:21). Each of these translations points toward the same idea—that spouses are to mutually love one another as part of their faith commitment. Catholic couples specifically, are meant to hold mutuality at the forefront of their covenantal communion, for "this mutual inward moulding of husband and wife, this determined effort to perfect each other, can in a very real sense, as the Roman Catechism teaches, be said to be the chief reason and purpose of matrimony."[8] Catholic or not, mutual growth inspired by each partner and undergone by both spouses can be a fulfilling part of any marital relationship.

Crisis

So, back to the top, Christian marriage, as the mutual creation of a shared micro-culture, involves the merging of two separate paradigms of living into one new partnership. "Priorities and values," "energies and enthusiasms," "patterns of emotional responsiveness and sexual expression" are all collectively challenged and affirmed.[9] As all married couples know, confronting and, often times, changing your perspective on any one of these aforementioned elements of reality can be difficult. In "becoming married," both husband and wife can expect to encounter many crises—moments of instability that encourage a response. A crisis is often a situation of paradox: a time of danger and opportunity, of vulnerability and heightened potential. When we experience a crisis, in our marriage or otherwise, we are alarmingly deprived of our predictable life patterns. In this state of deprivation, we are nearly forced into discovering or recovering other values and insights.[10] Though ambiguous and vexatious, crises can transform a person into more of what God intends him/her to be. The unrealized can be made known, and when it has, a move in the direction of transcendence may be taken. So instead of categorizing crises as panic-inducing debacles that always seem to occur too frequently in your marital relationship, try to view—and literally read—"crisis" as *Christ-is*. Christ is. He is there in the unclear soreness that constitutes personal and joint development in your marriage, ever stepping up and forward with you and your partner.

Married in Mission

"How does this relate to living in a thatched hut with my spouse while working 70 hours per week at a makeshift clinic in Malaysia?" you may ask. Marriage is a permanent and intimate state of being with a person from a culture not your own in which you form a shared system of meaning despite your differences. Marriage, like foreign missions, is all about giving, receiving, and making something new. A local family teaches you Malaysian, you provide healthcare for their children, and together your mutual acts of ministry will create a better world. In marriage, you and your partner adapt and transition to constant change. Volunteering abroad is based on the same kind of adaptation and transitioning: *"I heard that we*

---

8 Pius XI, *Casti Connubii* (1930), no. 24, http://w2.vatican.va/content/pius-xi/en/encyclicals/documents/hf_p-xi_enc_31121930_casti-connubii.html.

9 Evelyn Eaton Whitehead and James D. Whitehead, *Marrying Well: Possibilities in Christian Marriage Today* (Garden City, NY: Doubleday, 1981), 101.

10 Whitehead and Whitehead, *Marrying Well,* 428.

do not have running water anymore … The directors need us to share our living space with a group of short-term, missioners next week … I always thought that my home country was the only place we could raise our family, but now … " As a married couple, you and your spouse (assumedly) already know how to be flexible in times of shifting uncertainty. Thus, when you experience similar themes of fluctuation in serving internationally, you both have the ability to navigate through those changes with veteran-ed success. You have been deeply trekking about in your spouse's expansive frontier for _____ years, so lace up those hiking boots for yet another terrain to be explored.

Christian marriage is both a private and a public covenant. In the Catholic Church, marriage is a sacrament; meaning that "the love and faithfulness husbands and wives have for each other are not simply the sign and symbol of the love of God—they are the effective sign, the fulfilled symbol, and the real epiphany of the love of God that has appeared in Jesus Christ."[11] In actualizing this sacrament, and more generally, the vocation of marriage, couples are called to share with the global community the effects that their marriage has on their visions and actions.[12] Spouses are meant to continue ministering beyond the single ritual of their wedding into a lifelong, Christian modus operandi. Some couples do this by raising children, while others do it by spending time at the local soup kitchen. But if you and your partner are still reading, it appears as though one or both of you wants to fulfill, at least some aspect of your marital ministry, through international service—a decision, if made, that will alter the courses of your lives in ways both imaginable and surprising.

C. S. Lewis will now poetically (and, perhaps, hyperbolically) direct you and your significant other from this page to the next. All your life in this world and all your adventures have only been the cover and the title page: now at last you are beginning Chapter One of your Great Story which no one on earth has read: which goes on forever: in which every chapter is better than the one before.[13] And so to Chapter 1 of this Great Story we now turn.

---

11 Walter Kasper, *Theology of Christian Marriage* (New York: Crossroad, 1981), 35.

12 Mark Searle, "The Journey of Conversion," *Worship* 54 (1980): 54.

13 C. S. Lewis, *The Last Battle* (New York: MacMillan, 1956), 184.

Discernment

Chapter 1
Pre-Commitment

A soul without reflection, like a pile
Without inhabitant, to ruin runs.

—Edward Young, *Night Thoughts*

Discernment

The start of your and your spouse's service experience begins with the phase of discernment. The length of this particular stage varies, as each couple's consideration of international ministry is different. That being said, this handbook (according to its presumed context) defines **discernment** as the period of reflection *before* your joint commitment to a mission organization has been made. If you refer to the *Stages of Cross-Cultural Transition* timeline in the Preface, you will notice that the line of "departure anticipation" within this phase moves upward. As you and your partner continue to deliberate, one or both of you may experience an increase in positive and or negative anticipatory emotions.

"Discernment" comes from the Latin word *discernere,* which means "to separate," "to distinguish," or "to sort out." From a Christian perspective, discernment is an "interior search that seeks to align our own will with the will of God."[1] In this context, discernment is the decision-making process that honors God's place and presence in determining whether you and your partner are called to overseas volunteer work. For married persons, this spiritual contemplation is threefold.

I–You–We

Married couples discerning whether or not to serve abroad should be able to answer three distinct questions:

> (1) What are my intentions in pursuing international ministry?
> (2) What are the intentions of my spouse?
> (3) What are our shared intentions?

The first question takes into account your own perspective (**I**), the second, the perspective of your partner (**You**), and the last question, that of your marriage (**We**). My conception of this tri-processing will be referenced throughout the handbook, so it might do you well to remember: **I–You–We** = Me–My Spouse–Our Marriage.

Back to discernment, as each of you begins to reflect on your personal motivations and goals in the contemplation of overseas mission work, you are likely to feel a variety of emotions: uncertainty, excitement, hesitancy, spiritual drive fervor, confusion, confidence, anx-

---

1   Joe Paprocki, "Discernment: Making Inspired Choices," *Loyola Press: A Jesuit Ministry*, http://www.loyolapress.com/discernment-making-inspired-choices.htm.

iety, and/or hopefulness. One day you may be thrilled at the idea of sharing an extended, cross-cultural experience with your spouse, and the next you could be thinking that leaving behind your family and friends for years at a time sounds rather difficult. Your partner is likely to be whizzing up and down on the same emotional yo-yo. Put the two of you together and you end up like some kid with three Duncan Butterflies knotted around his hands, sniffling a bit as he tries to sort out the mess (I–You–We). In trying to avoid such an entanglement, let us take a look at the most common challenges couples face during the discernment period and how you and your spouse might overcome them.

Vocational Dreams

Marriages are places of multiple dreams: his dreams, her dreams, his dreams of her, her dreams of him, collective dreams, etc. Becoming husband and wife is to implicitly agree "to live in terms of another person's story,"[2] both the dreamt-up chapters as well as the nonfictional ones. Vocational dreams play a significant role in your partner's story. For Christians, a vocational calling is "an invitation to live a certain kind of life, one shaped by two powerful influences—the values of Christian faith and the gifts we find in ourselves."[3] As theologian Frederick Buechner once said, "Vocation is the place where our deep gladness meets the world's deep need."[4] Each individual's vocational dreams are as unique as his or her own personhood. With whom you choose to be in relationship can be one of your most important callings. Some people are part of a religious community, others are married, and still others remain single. While vocations are often driven by the public and private commitments made to particular people, they can also be further realized in our works. In reading this handbook, you and your partner are taking your vow to married life and pairing it with the potential and distinct vocation of mission work.

From a more psychological perspective, Dr. John Gottman, marital therapist and research analyst, outlines the various levels in which spouses can honor each other's dreams (vocational or otherwise). The first level of supporting your partner's dream is to express an understanding of the dream and an interest in learning more about it, even though you may not necessarily share it. ("*You like learning about other cultures? That is great! Is there a particular country you want to explore more in depth?*") The second level is to offer financial support for your spouse's dream. ("*You should start taking an Amharic language course. It would not be too hard to make adjustments to our budget so you could do that.*") Finally, the third level is to become part of your significant other's dream.[5] ("*We are doing it! We are going to be volunteers in Ethiopia for two years!*") It is likely that you and your partner are trying to figure out if a particular level-three dream is one you can pursue together.

Motives

All couples in the discernment phase should be reflecting on whose vocational calling is prompting the contemplation of cross-cultural mission work, and what objectives both spouses have in regard to service abroad. Here are a few of the motives with which survey

---

2   William Bridges, *Transitions: Making Sense of Life's Changes* (New York: Addison-Wesley, 1980), 71.
3   Whitehead and Whitehead, *Marrying Well*, 199.
4   Frederick Buechner, *Wishful Thinking: A Theological ABC* (San Francisco: Harper San Francisco, 1973), 95.
5   Gottman and Silver, *Seven Principles*, 233–34.

participants identified and shared in their desire to pursue an international service experience:

- "We wanted to learn how to serve the poor."[6]
- "Life has been good for us, so we had a desire to give back. No doubt a calling from God."[7]
- "Our journey began when my wife was profoundly affected by American complicity in the horrors of the Guatemalan civil war."[8]
- "I wanted to serve alongside my spouse."[9]
- "Our family's personal response to 9/11. We wanted our (then seven-year-old son) to not grow up afraid of different cultures, skin colors, etc., and wanted our actions to align with our values."[10]
- "A promise made many years before."[11]

As you can see, there is a wide range of motivations and inspirations that can be at play in the discernment of this particular kind of ministry.

Motivation Examination[12]
Duration: 20–35 minutes

If either one of you feels the need to further explore your own motivations and/or your spouse's motivations, the following exercise can help you do so. Even if you have already discussed the objectives each of you holds, completing this activity may reveal intentions that neither of you has yet to formally discern nor articulate.

STEP 1: Roles. Each partner will need a pen or a pencil. Designate one partner to write on the left side of the exercise (*Spouse #1*) and the other on the right (*Spouse #2*).

STEP 2: Identification. Following is a list of common objectives that motivate many individuals in making the decision to live and work abroad. In private, *Spouse #1* will place an X next to all the motives that apply to him/her under the "I" column. Next, *Spouse #1* will place an X alongside all those he/she feels apply to his/her partner under the "You" column(Markings may be the same for you and your significant other.) Once *Spouse #1* has finished, cover the left-hand side of the page, and have *Spouse #2* repeat this step.

---

6   Alexis Kenny, "Married Missioner/Volunteer Survey,"(master's thesis survey, Catholic Theological Union, 2015), 15.

7   Kenny, "Married Missioner/Volunteer Survey," 15.

8   Kenny, "Married Missioner/Volunteer Survey," 15.

9   Kenny, "Married Missioner/Volunteer Survey," 15.

10 Kenny, "Married Missioner/Volunteer Survey," 15.

11 Kenny, "Married Missioner/Volunteer Survey," 15.

12 Adapted from L. Robert Kohls, *Survival Kit for Overseas Living: For Americans Planning to Live and Work Abroad* (Yarmouth, ME: Intercultural Press, Inc., 1984), 35–36.

Spouse #1

(I) (You)

Spouse #2

(I) (You)

(I)	(You)		(I)	(You)
____	____	Advancement in job or profession	____	____
____	____	Response to vocational call from God	____	____
____	____	Desire to expand perspectives of family/children	____	____
____	____	Desire to experience an exotic, foreign place	____	____
____	____	Hope that new setting will solve a stressor	____	____
____	____	Desire to learn a language and/or explore another culture	____	____
____	____	Desire to experience the challenges of overseas work	____	____
____	____	Desire to keep up with others who have been abroad	____	____
____	____	Response to vocational call from members of faith community	____	____
____	____	Desire for personal growth	____	____
____	____	Mission work aligns with beliefs and values	____	____
____	____	Pressure from superiors	____	____
____	____	Desire to get away from life in home country	____	____
____	____	Desire to have unique, life-changing experiences	____	____
____	____	To accompany spouse in pursuit of his/her vocation	____	____
____	____	Hope that different setting will give life new direction	____	____
____	____	Desire to obtain a sense of achievement	____	____
____	____	Chance to make a difference in the world	____	____
____	____	Desire to help those less fortunate	____	____
____	____	Desire to meet like-minded people	____	____
____	____	Opportunity to learn new kinds of specialized skills	____	____
____	____	Gain a renewed sense of appreciation for life in home country	____	____
____	____	Affiliation with a certain organization church	____	____
____	____	Desire to serve alongside spouse	____	____
____	____	Other:_____	____	____
____	____	Other:_____	____	____
____	____	Other:_____	____	____

STEP 3: Rank. Once finished, each partner should go back through the list and circle the top three motives in their own "I" columns. Next, number the motives you circled in order of importance, with "1" being the most important.

STEP 4: Discussion. *Spouse #1* can begin the conversation. Share the top three motivations you have identified for yourself with your partner. Dialogue about the implications such intentions could have in regard to serving abroad (*"I want to develop my counseling skills, specifically concerning kids with emotional problems. How do you think that will affect our own children's experience overseas?"*). After both partners have talked through *Spouse #1's* three objectives, *Spouse #2* is to share his or hers. Respond to the same prompts above.

STEP 5: More Dialogue. Next, discuss the objectives you two have identified for one another. *Spouse #1* can begin the conversation once more. Were your assumptions correct? Incorrect? Consider the differences between the motives you guessed your partner to have and his/her actual motives. How do you think your spouse's ambitions affect you? Once the conversation naturally concludes, *Spouse #2* is to answer the same questions.

STEP 6: Final Review. Re-read the motives outlined in STEP 2. Are there objectives on the list (or other desires internally held) that either of you may be unwilling to recognize (*"I am secretly competing with my older sister. She is a former Peace Corps volunteer and the family has never stopped talking about her service in the Philippines."*)? If they exist, <u>gently</u> explore these kinds of "hidden agendas" together.

Most people who choose to live and work abroad have a mixture of motives that inspire them to do so. The point of this exercise is to acknowledge the objectives that are held by you and your spouse, because they will inevitably influence your mission experience. It is best to name these intentions and share them with your partner before making a commitment to cross-cultural ministry.

Spousal Dynamics

Once you have discussed the motivations that drive your discernment of overseas service, the next step is acknowledging what roles you and your spouse have taken on in this first phase. There are three roles partners can adopt: co-spouse, leading spouse, or accompanying spouse. Co-spouses are equally interested in committing to international mission work. A leading spouse is the partner who is actively interested in committing to international mission work. An accompanying spouse is the partner who follows his/her significant other in committing to international mission work. While partners can switch from one role to another throughout the entire ministerial experience, each spouse should determine what role he/she fits into at this time.

As you may have guessed, co-spouses often have an easier time discerning a future cross-cultural volunteer commitment together. The contemplation and decision-making processes tend to be more balanced, as both partners are pursuing a similar kind of vocation. One co-spouse survey participant wrote in agreement, "Because we were both 'called' to service and had our own future responsibilities ... we were one and continually encouraged and strengthened each other."[13] Dynamics between leading and accompanying spouses can be more tenuous, complex, and uneven, especially during the pre-departure stages. An accompanying spouse survey participant shared, "When my husband began talking about going away to do mission work for a few years, I was very reluctant. I was comfortable with my life, and though I enjoyed doing short-term trips of a week, I did not want to move away."[14] Program staff also recognize the potential difficulty of this tension, "It's a challenge when one member of the couple is more motivated to be in mission than the other, who may be acquiescing to suit the spouse. Related to this is that one member may be more qualified for this type of service than the other."[15] In the most simplified, worst-case scenario, a leading spouse may force their partner into a volunteer commitment by making a one-sided decision. This can leave the accompanying spouse feeling bitter and resentful. Not only is an overseas ministry likely to fail when committed to in this manner, but more importantly, a marriage is apt to suffer.

---

13 Kenny, "Married Missioner/Volunteer Survey," 20.
14 Bridget Studer, personal e-mail, March 28, 2015.
15 Alexis Kenny, "Program Staff: Married Missioners/Volunteers Survey," (master's thesis survey, Catholic Theological Union, 2015), 13.

General Considerations

There are many factors that impact a couple's ability to discern a cross-cultural service commitment. Some of the more obvious and straightforward considerations include age, length of marriage, number of children, general health, non-negotiable familial obligations, etc. Knowing where you are in your marriage life cycle is important. What a young couple with children will be concerned about in regard to international living will be different than that of a husband and wife who have just retired and are looking to re-channel their energies, gifts, and interests. You and your spouse should make time to survey your marital life course and see where you both are situated in relation to responsibilities with which you are currently charged.

Some service organizations will not admit couples who have recently undergone significant changes in their relationship. One volunteer director remarked, "We do not accept those who are newly married (less than two years) or newly divorced—it takes time for people to adjust to marriage before the additional commitment of joining our community and difficult overseas mission situations."[16] Another staff member shared a similar kind of policy: "Married couples need to have been married for more than one year in order to participate in our program."[17] Have you or your spouse experienced semi-current and/or substantial relational changes? If so, it would benefit you both to have a conversation about the implications of such change and its potential impact on your processes of discernment.

It is best not to put your marriage in a situation that you and your partner may not be able to handle. A former missioner wrote in agreement, "It is imperative that both spouses be compatible with limited marriage issues that need to be dealt with. This is extremely important when being far away from family or friend support systems."[18] "Marital and other family problems which exist prior to departure will rarely improve under the strains of living overseas. … Even the most stable of families can expect new stresses."[19] Couples should work to communicate about present-day conflicts and try to resolve lingering issues before leaving home. It can also be advantageous for spouses to brainstorm what potential stressors they may be prone to experiencing when serving abroad. The upcoming sections will explore apprehensions commonly felt by married individuals, providing more topics that may be helpful for you and your partner to discuss.

Finances

Financial instability was a theme that drew many comments from survey participants. One former missioner explained, "It was hard being married on such a low monthly stipend. It doesn't set you up financially for your future."[20] Program staff members also recognized this stressor: "Financial support—especially when volunteers have children—is challenging because their needs are significantly different than single volunteers."[21] In terms of finances, there are several points to consider. The first is your fundraising commitment. Most service organizations strongly suggest or require that missioners raise funds in order to offset their

16 Kenny, "Program Staff: Married Missioners/Volunteers Survey," 20.
17 Kenny, "Program Staff: Married Missioners/Volunteers Survey," 10.
18 Kenny, "Married Missioner/Volunteer Survey," 263.
19 Kohls, *Survival Kit,* 55.
20 Kenny, "Program Staff: Married Missioners/Volunteers Survey," 32.
21 Kenny, "Program Staff: Married Missioners/Volunteers Survey," 13.

living costs. This can be a one-time responsibility or a continuous precondition. You and your spouse should decide if you feel comfortable fundraising and discuss how you will go about doing it. Communicate with your program about what expenditures are covered by your mission appeal efforts (i.e., room and board, travel to and from your host country, health insurance, etc.). Most organizations do not reimburse its members for spending associated with visiting home during time off. Practical decisions that may need to be made in regard to your house, car(s), and other possessions will be addressed in Chapter 2.

Many mission institutions are only able to offer its employees minimal monetary compensation. Most volunteers spend more money than they make. Language school, in-country vacations, purchasing specialty food items, and unforeseen trips to the hospital are just a few things you could be paying for during your overseas ministry. It can be difficult to put together an accurate budget plan for your time abroad, but attempting to do so with the assistance of your sending program may be helpful. The last consideration to take into account is the financial obligations the two of you could be coming back to after your service experience concludes. Student loans, auto payments, mortgages, professional training workshops, or graduate school tuition may be waiting for you at the airport, without flowers and without a "welcome home" sign. If you are interested in reading about expenses you may be dealing with upon your return to your passport country, see sections *Anxieties* and *Anxieties Continued* in Chapter 5. It would be expedient for you and your partner to assess your financial situation as you continue to discern this type of commitment.

Children

If you have children, choices to be made about their well-being and care will probably be your biggest sources of deliberation. There is much material available on raising kids across cultures (again, see References), so not much time will be spent in addressing this subject. Nevertheless, here are a few practical generalizations:

Mobility. Many young families leaving their passport country do not experience a tremendous amount of difficulty doing so, as they have yet to establish roots in a particular community and tend to be more open to relocating. Older families who have already made life-defining arrangements may encounter more serious challenges in creating a new home overseas.[22]

Adjustment. A major reason for the early return of missioners with children is their family's inability to adapt to the conditions of living abroad.[23] It is prudent that the choice to move to another country is one made as a family, and a choice that involves your kids in the decision-making process as much as possible.

Foresight. It is necessary to spend some time troubleshooting certain realities that may be a part of your child's overseas experience: the significant disruption of their education, limited medical access and its potential impact on their health, how relocation can alter

22 Sidney L. Werkman, "Coming Home: Adjustment of Americans to the United States after Living Abroad," in *Cross-Cultural Reentry: A Book of Readings,* ed. Clyde N. Austin (Abilene, TX: Abilene Christian University, 1986), 7.

23 Nessa P. Loewenthal and Nancy L. Snedden, "Managing the Overseas Assignment Process," in *Cross-Cultural Reentry*, 32.

their personal development, etc. One survey participant affirmed the existing difficulties of such matters: "Two of our greatest challenges were health and education. We had numerous bouts of malaria and other lesser tropical illnesses. I felt responsible for exposing my kids and wife to those hardships. Our son was entering high school when we arrived in Africa and finding suitable schooling for him was an effort."[24] Parents should be thinking ahead in terms of how this experience will inevitably impact their children, especially taking into consideration the variables of age and maturity.

Adolescents. Former missioners strongly suggest that families with teenagers, especially young teenagers, wait a few years before serving abroad. Teens tend to have an especially tough time adjusting to a new lifestyle, as they have already begun to cement peer relationships and develop an adult identity within their home country environment.[25]

Specialized Education. Couples may want to reevaluate their interest in international work if there are any indicators that their child has or could develop a learning disability. These children need continuity in their educational careers and assistance from experienced professionals; such individuals are, in most instances, not available at mission sites or schools.

Site Specifics

In regard to selecting the right program for you and your spouse, two complications immediately present themselves: (1) identifying service jobs that both of you would find fulfilling, and (2) finding an organization with those specific positions that accepts married couples. My husband and I talked for a long time about what we did and did not want in a volunteer experience. After our discussion, there were only two programs that met our list of "requirements"! One survey participant wrote: "Finding meaningful positions for both wife and husband in the same ministry site requires time and compromise."[26] Service program employees share similar sentiments. One staff member commented, "I would say that placements are our toughest challenge in working with couples, mainly because we need to find placements where both people will be utilized."[27] Beyond providing volunteer positions for both spouses, mission organizations often find it difficult to offer ideal living spaces for couples. One program director noted, "The majority of our participants are single, young adults. Therefore, our housing is geared toward this demographic. As a result of this arrangement we sometimes have a hard time securing housing for married couples."[28] Several other staff members shared comparable opinions. As a result of inadequate lodging options, many former missioners reported that lack of privacy was a significant stressor they had to deal with during their service commitment. One survey participant admitted, "I felt like we couldn't deal with our conflicts and issues, but had to ignore them as we lived with others."[29] Yet another conceded, "It was difficult to have intimate times as we lived in group accommodations with little privacy."[30] This point leads us to the last major consideration for couples selecting a mission organization.

---

24 John Studer, personal e-mail, March 24, 2015.
25 Coralyn M. Fontaine, "International Relocation: A Comprehensive Psychosocial Approach," in *Cross-Cultural Reentry*, 46.
26 Kenny, "Married Missioner/Volunteer Survey," 80.
27 Kenny, "Program Staff: Married Missioners/Volunteers Survey," 13.
28 Kenny, "Program Staff: Married Missioners/Volunteers Survey," 13.
29 Kenny, "Married Missioner/Volunteer Survey," 119.
30 Kenny, "Married Missioner/Volunteer Survey," 119.

Institutions that work with married individuals are often tasked with the challenge of facilitating the integration of a couple within the greater intentional community of volunteers. An intentional community is a planned, residential living situation where members typically hold similar values, and are dedicated to maintaining relationships of cohesion and teamwork. Some programs create primary focal points or goals for their intentional communities (e.g., simplicity, hope, hospitality, or nonviolence). Out of all the topics that surfaced in both the program staff and married missioner surveys, the intentional community lifestyle was what drew the most remarks. One volunteer director wrote, "Incorporating a married couple can be uncomfortable for the community. It needs to be handled very carefully for placement. The combination can often result in a us-them dynamic."[31] Another staff member confessed, "Married couple missionaries do not always integrate well into the larger missionary community."[32] Yet another shared, "Couples may be less interested or involved in their community due to their focus on their relationship."[33] Similarly, married couples themselves retrospectively reported adversities and anxieties that such a lifestyle invoked:

- "I wish I had known how hard and difficult it would be to live in community. There were eight people (four marriages) living in one house and I didn't expect the conflicts and stressors as a result of that."[34]
- "I was nervous about any perceived alienation in a community that my marriage might cause the other community members."[35]
- "I was worried about intentional community distracting me from my marriage."[36]

While not specifically addressed in the quotes above, the reality of living in a cross-cultural intentional community can be an even more complex experience for reasons that will be addressed in Chapter 3. Whether multicultural or not, community living is a factor that should definitely be discussed in your discernment-phase conversations.

Finding Common Ground[37]
Duration: 45–60 minutes

The following activity will help to facilitate the exploration of the many variables that exist within international ministry. You and your spouse can use this exercise to communicate about the three main considerations for married couples discerning service abroad (placements, housing, and community), as well as other, more specific aspects of this decision. Finally, engaging in this activity will help you and your partner distinguish which parts of this future commitment are negotiable, and which are less so.

---

31 Kenny, "Program Staff: Married Missioners/Volunteers Survey," 13.
32 Kenny, "Program Staff: Married Missioners/Volunteers Survey," 13.
33 Kenny, "Program Staff: Married Missioners/Volunteers Survey," 13.
34 Kenny, "Married Missioner/Volunteer Survey," 16.
35 Kenny, "Married Missioner/Volunteer Survey," 18.
36 Kenny, "Married Missioner/Volunteer Survey," 18.
37 Adapted from Gottman and Silver, *Seven Principles,* 182–84, 237–39 and John M. Gottman, Julie Schwartz Gottman, and Joan DeClaire, *Ten Lessons to Transform Your Marriage* (New York: Crown, 2006), 145–47.

STEP 1: Circle Drawing. Each spouse will need a sheet of paper and a pencil with an eraser. On your respective pieces of paper, draw two circles—a smaller one inside a larger one. Make sure these circles are big enough in which to write.

STEP 2: Factors. Complete this step as individuals. Referring to the bulleted considerations, write what aspects "must" be part of your ideal overseas experience in the *smaller* circle. In the *larger* circle, list the variables with which you can be more compromising. For a simplified example of what your finished product should look like, please see **Figure 1.1**.

- **Geography:** international, domestic; urban, suburban, rural
- **Climate:** hot, cold, rainy, dry, humid, etc.
- **Language:** English, Spanish, Arabic, etc.
- **Institutional Affiliation:** religious, secular; political, social, etc.
- **Living Situation:** private, shared; on-site, off-site
- **Length:** months, one year, years
- **Demographic of Population Served:** children, teenagers, adults, families, individuals with special needs, the dying, the sick, etc.
- **In-country Support:** authority on site, language school, retreats, etc.
- **Type of Service:** teaching, general labor, childcare, evangelization, community organizing, etc.
- **Fundraising Commitment:** amount; costs covered; one-time, continuous
- **Financial Support:** stipend, health insurance, loan deferment, etc.
- **Amenities:** potable/running water, medical access, electricity, heat, air conditioning, transportation, schooling for children, etc.
- **Technological Access:** cell phones, Internet, community computers, etc.
- **Organizational Structure:** general handbook, multi-themed orientation(s), job evaluations, exit interviews, etc.
- **Post-experience Support:** re-entry retreat(s), literature provided about transition and/or integration, etc.
- **Visitor Policies:** possible dates, space to host, assistance with transportation, etc.
- **Option for Ministry Renewal:** availability, decision-making timeline, extension process, etc.
- **Furlough/Vacation Time:** specified or flexible; frequency, traveling guidelines, etc.
- **Gender Ratio:** balanced, more women, more men
- **Average Missioner Age:** younger, older, mixed

STEP 3: Discussion. Once you have both completed your circles independently, come together and designate one partner as the speaker and the other as the listener. The speaking spouse is to explain to the listening spouse what variables he/she placed in the smaller, inner circle.

The listener's job is to draw more information out of the speaker. The listening partner should not try to debate issues that may arise in regard to the speaking partner's inner circle selections. In fact, neither spouse should be trying to persuade the other. Use a sampling of the questions on the next page to engage in a content-gathering conversation:

Figure 1.1

- What is important to you about the variables in your small circle?
- What are the most important variables?
- Why are they the most important?
- What would your ideal service experience be?
- How do you imagine things would be if all your variables were met?
- Is there a deeper purpose or goal here for you?
- Does your small circle relate to some of your beliefs or values?
- Do you have a fear about not experiencing some of these variables? If so, what is it?

STEP 4: Role Reversal. When the speaker is finished sharing, spouses are to switch roles, with the new speaking partner revisiting and completing STEP 3.

STEP 5: Negotiation Process. Once you have both discussed the variables in your smaller circles, dialogue about what each of you has written in your larger circles. What factors do you both have in common? Has one partner placed a significantly lesser or greater number of variables in the outer circle? If so, explore this.

STEP 6: Variable Movement. Brainstorm how each of you can honor your inner circle variables in different ways (*"I want to volunteer outside my home country, but my partner does not want to learn a new language. Let's research programs that serve English-speaking locations like New Zealand or South Africa."*). As you are able to, work together to each move variables from your smaller circles into your larger circles. What do your circles look like now? Do you both feel that your more non-negotiable factors are being respected?

STEP 7: Volunteer Organizations. Now that you and your spouse have a clearer idea of what kind of service opportunity you would like to pursue, you can start to investigate and see what mission placements are available. Below are a few websites dedicated to matching future volunteers with well-suited ministry sites:

- Catchafire: www.catchafire.org
- Catholic Volunteer Network: https://catholicvolunteernetwork.org/
- ChristianVolunteering.org: http://www.christianvolunteering.org
- Cross-Cultural Solutions: www.crossculturalsolutions.org
- Foundation for Sustainable Development: www.fsdinternational.org
- Global Volunteers: http://www.globalvolunteers.org
- Go Eco: www.goeco.org
- International Volunteer Programs Association: http://volunteerinternational.org
- Omprakash: www.omprakash.org
- OXFAM International: www.oxfam.org/en
- Peace Corps: www.peacecorps.gov
- Projects Abroad: www.projects-abroad.org
- UVolunteer: www.uvolunteer.net/project-destination.php
- Volunteers For Peace: www.vfp.org

Miscellaneous

As we conclude with the most common obstacles couples face in contemplating a cross-cultural service experience, here are a few more matters to consider during your shared discernment process:

Strive for a 5:1 ratio. What often separates contented husbands and wives from those who are unhappily married is the difference between the number of positive and negative interactions had between spouses. Dr. Gottman's studies reveal that couples who were most satisfied in their marriages maintained a ratio average of five positive encounters to every one negative encounter. Examples of how partners can show one another positivity include: demonstrating interest and concern; being affectionate, appreciative, caring, empathetic, and accepting; joking around; and sharing joy.[38]

Do an evaluative self-assessment. Generally speaking, the most successful overseas worker is an individual who is comfortable with failure, has a sense of humor, possesses effective interpersonal skills, is self-aware, and can express himself or herself appropriately without disregard for others.[39] Does this sound like you? If not, in what ways can you develop the aforementioned personality traits?

Be a persuadable spouse. What is your "influence-ability"? Some husbands and wives have trouble accepting their partner's perspectives or requests because they believe that in doing so, they may lose "power" in their relationship. However, research conducted by Dr.

---

38 John M. Gottman and Nan Silver, *Why Marriages Succeed or Fail* (New York: Simon & Schuster, 1994), 56–61.
39 Loewenthal and Snedden, "Managing the Overseas Assignment Process," 32–33.

Gottman shows the opposite to be true. Married individuals who allow themselves to be influenced by their spouses are more satisfied with the dynamics in their marriage than those who do not. That is because spouses who feel empowered and respected in their relationship are able to show more flexibility and support for their partners' ideas and suggestions. Married persons who allow themselves to be influenced by their spouse, stop creating barriers in communication and learn how to compromise.[40]

Connect with returned married missioners. If available to you, find a couple who has served abroad or who is currently involved in ministerial work with whom you can have a conversation. One former volunteer shared the benefits of such correspondence: "I was in touch with a woman who was in Panama with her husband and three children by mail. Her letters to me were a tremendous help. She was able to answer many of my questions, and speak as a mom to me about the experience she was having with her family in mission. Her children even exchanged letters with my kids."[41] Having access to the perspective of spouses who have worked overseas together may open your eyes to aspects of this opportunity not yet considered.

Prioritize institutional health. When trying to find a program that honors the objectives and variables the two of you identified in exercises *Motivation Examination* and *Finding Common Ground*, it would do you well to pay attention to each program's form and condition. Dr. Laura Mae Gardner, cross-cultural missions consultant and author, shares her own perspective on the topic:

> One of the convictions I hold is that not all humanitarian and religious cross-cultural organizations are the same! All are not equally healthy, nor are they necessarily good institutions with which to serve. This pushed me to try to define for myself and others, what is a healthy organization? In today's world, the question that now arises in new recruits is—Is this organization going to be good for me and good to me? Are they reputable? Do they manage their assets well—finances? Do they care well for their people? Do they have a personnel structure that aims to follow best practice? What do workers serving with this organization say about it? Do they live up to their promotional material? Do their people have training in their areas of expertise—that is, are leaders trained in leadership principles and practices? Do they have an HR department or a personnel department, and are those staff specifically trained in their area of ministry? If I have a problem, do resources exist to help? How do I access those resources?[42]

Such questions are important to ask and get answers to during the beginning stages of program exploration. The theme of organizational stability and reliability will be further discussed in Chapter 2.

---

40 Gottman, Gottman, and DeClaire, *Ten Lessons*, 180.
41 Kenny, "Married Missioner/Volunteer Survey," 82.
42 Laura Mae Gardner, personal e-mail, August 27, 2015.

Marital Skill Building

Though complicated at times, discerning an international service experience with your partner can be exciting! Married persons may feel more engaged with their own values, beliefs, and faith traditions. Spouses are able to more deeply explore each other's perspectives on issues and principles that might not have otherwise been explored. Individuals learn about the origin and depth of their partner's dreams. A healthy discernment period will also test each spouse's ability to effectively communicate and compromise. This testing of accommodation can lead to a fuller understanding of the concept of sacrifice and contentment. All of this, in turn, has the potential to create a renewed sense of emotional intimacy between husband and wife. In spirit of this closeness, you and your significant other should think about writing your own marriage mission statement.

Marriage Mission Statement[43]
Duration: 45–60 minutes

A *personal* mission statement identifies an individual's unique purpose, and how he or she goes about fulfilling it. Your personal mission statement defines the values that motivate what you do and how those values impact your relationship with others. Though *marriage* mission statements take into account the specific objectives of each spouse, they reach beyond particular intentions and convey a mutually conceived sense of meaning. This exercise is meant to guide you and your partner through the necessary steps in order to construct your very own marriage mission statement.

STEP 1: Past Achievements. Each spouse will need a pen or a pencil, two individual pieces of paper, and one sheet to be shared. Together, spend some time identifying three examples of how your marriage has been successful in balancing the needs and wants of each member in your family system. These achievements could have occurred at work, in your faith community, or at home. Please write a short description of each one below:

•

•

•

---

43 Adapted from Randall S. Hansen, "The Five-Step Plan for Creating Personal Mission Statements," *Quintessential Careers*, http://www.quintcareers.com/creating_personal_mission_statements.html and "Mission Statement Builder," *Franklin Covey*, http://www.franklincovey.com/msb/missions/family.

STEP 2: *Talents.* Determine three natural talents/gifts each spouse possesses that played a role in the achievement of the aforementioned successes.

<u>**Spouse #1**</u>   <u>**Spouse #2**</u>

-
-
-

-
-
-

STEP 3: *Core Values.* Circle the qualities listed (or create your own) that best describe your marital relationship. These descriptors can also be representative of each individual within your marriage.

Active	Exhilarating	Peaceful
Affirming	Faithful	Playful
Alive	Fascinating	Poised
Appealing	Focused	Proud
Ardent	Funny	Quiet
Assured	Generous	Realist
Affectionate	Gentle	Relaxed
Balanced	Grateful	Romantic
Bold	Happy	Satisfying
Brave	Hardy	Secure
Buoyant	Heroic	Sincere
Carefree	Hopeful	Social
Comfortable	Humble	Spirited
Confident	Inquisitive	Strong
Contented	Inspired	Sympathetic
Cooperative	Interesting	Thoughtful
Courageous	Joyous	Trusting
Creative	Kind	Trustworthy
Determined	Loving	Warm
Eager	Loyal	Wild
Earnest	Mutualistic	Wise
Economical	Open	Other:_____
Encouraging	Optimistic	Other:_____
Enthusiastic	Outgoing	Other:_____
Exciting	PassionatePatient	Other:_____

STEP 4: Top Five. Once you have both finished reviewing the characteristic list, try to narrow down the marital qualities you circled to the five most important. Write those descriptors below:

1. _____

2. _____

3. _____

4. _____

5. _____

STEP 5: Top Value. Choose the one value-trait in your marriage that is most meaningful and significant to the both of you. Write down this descriptor:

_____

STEP 6: Contributions. Brainstorm ways in which your marriage can make a difference. In an ideal situation, how could your partnership contribute best to ...

- the world in general?

- your family?

- your employer or future employers?

- your friends?

STEP 7: Goals. Spend some time thinking about the goals you have for your marriage. Make a list of these goals; three short-term (up to five years) and three long-term (beyond five years).

Short-Term Goals

•

•

•

Long-Term Goals

•

•

•

If you and your spouse have the time and energy to continue constructing your marriage mission statement, please continue to the following step. If either one of you needs a break—take it here. You can come back to STEP 8 within the next few days.

STEP 8: *Statements.* As individuals, using your own pieces of paper, begin writing phrases and sentences to create your marriage mission statement. Refer back to the first seven steps for inspiration. If necessary, complete/answer the prompts to help jump-start this process:

- If we had unlimited time and resources, we would …
- Imagine your marriage as an epic narrative featuring you and your spouse as the hero and heroine of the story. What do you imagine your shared journey to be about? What are you doing? Why are you doing such things? Whom do these actions benefit? What are your journey's results?
- Our most important contribution(s) to others has been/will be …
- The significant experiences that God has used to shape our marriage are …
- Think of balance as a state of fulfillment and renewal in each of the following four dimensions: physical, spiritual, mental, and social/emotional. What are the most important things you do as an individual in these four areas that have the greatest positive impact on your marital relationship?

STEP 9: Marriage Mission Statement. By completing STEPS 1–8, you and your partner are now ready to construct a marriage mission statement. On the last piece of paper, use what you have written as individuals to make a rough draft of your shared marriage mission statement together. Once you have a final draft ready, transcribe it inside of the heart on the next page. (Leave the second heart blank—an explanation as to why will follow in a later chapter.)

Conclusion

As we come to the end of this chapter and, presumably, to the conclusion of your discernment period, you and your partner should know whether or not you have decided to serve overseas (a decision mutually made, equally determined, and jointly agreed to!). If both of you feel led in joy and peace to pursue an international volunteer experience—congratulations! If the two of you have realized that this particular vocation is not a good fit for you as a couple, continue on the journey in which God accompanies you both. He will guide you to a place where only you and your partner will be able to fill the unique need that exists there. As for those of you who have chosen to follow your "deep gladness" in committing to cross-cultural mission work as husband and wife, may God go with you on your way! No one can say with 100 percent certainty that your lives will be changed for the *better*. But as most couples who have embarked on this kind of an adventure together can agree, each of you will be changed for *good*.

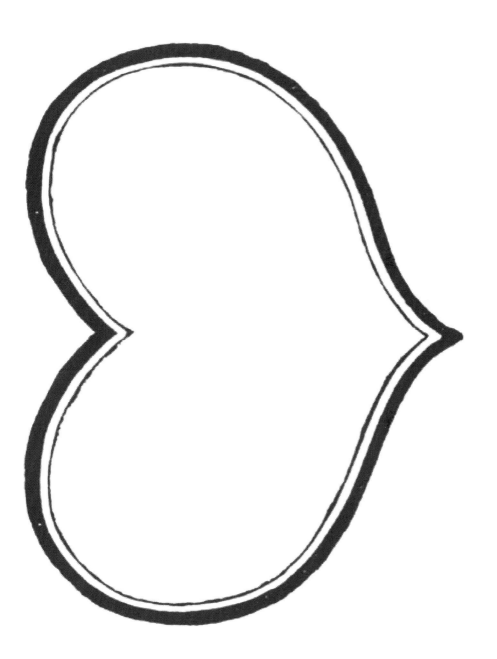

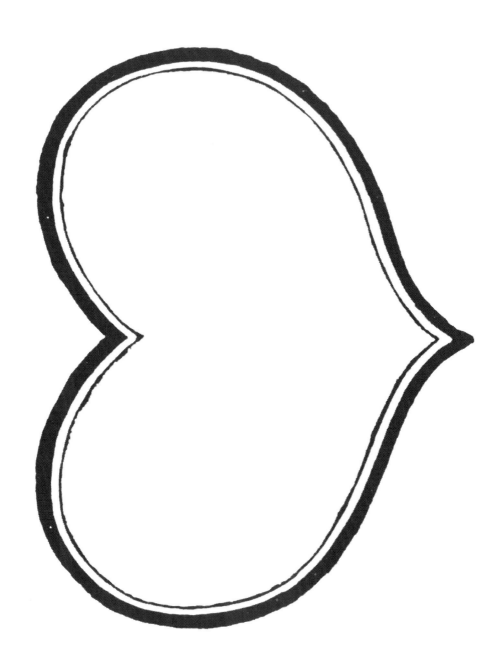

Preparation

Chapter 2

Post-Commitment—Pre-Departure

The more that you read,
The more things you will know.
The more that you learn,
The more places you'll go.

—Dr. Seuss, *I Can Read with My Eyes Shut*

As you and your spouse make your way through *Married in Mission*, one or both of you may not be able to relate to particular experiences, emotions, or situations that were presented in the previous chapter (or in material that will constitute the chapters following this one). Every person, marriage, and service commitment is unique, and even more so are the combinations of those three factors. Thus, feel free to skip over sections, flip back to pages read, or move forward to new thoughts and topics. As written in the Preface, the purpose of this handbook is not to assume and project, but rather to suggest empathy, education, and communication.

<u>Preparation</u>

By saying "yes" to serving abroad, you and your partner have entered into the second phase of your shared ministerial experience. Like each of the seven stages, there are no hard-set time delineations. Nearly every organization with overseas placements for married couples operates on different calendars and chronologies. For purposes here, **preparation** is defined as the period of anticipation and readying *after* your joint decision to international mission work has been made, but *before* your actual departure. (Assumed acceptance into a program occurs between the two.) If you and your spouse refer back to the *Stages of Cross-Cultural Transition* timeline in the Preface, you will notice the "departure anticipation" line continues its upward reach. Common anticipatory emotions felt by individuals during this period include: uncertainty, anxiety, preparedness, confusion, excitement, frustration, release, resistance, apathy, and/or insightfulness.

Some of these emotions are similar to those of the discernment phase, but several are exclusive unto this stage. Many couples reported experiencing emotions more pronouncedly during preparation. For it is during this period that you and your significant other will start to fill out program applications, line up phone interviews, schedule Skype/in-person meetings, etc. These additional tasks may feel taxing in the context of your already busy lives. (Thankfully, each of you can use reflections from exercises in Chapter 1 to answer some of those application questions.) A continued increase in the intensity of emotions felt can occur when you and your partner finally determine to which mission institution you want to commit.

If you have children, try to involve them in as much of your decision-making processes as possible. When the two of you select a particular program, share the news with your children in a way that conveys the importance of this event, even if they may be too young to fully comprehend its significance. Be prepared to answer questions your older kids may have about school, housing, culture, climate, and general information about your future host country. As you and your spouse prepare for your family's departure, allow your children to participate: have them pack their rooms, plan their own farewell parties, write letters to family members, etc.

Organizational Health

While many service organizations do a great job of providing their members with ample preparation material and assistance, there are some institutions that do not. One survey participant wrote, "When we volunteered, the program was not as developed as it is now, so we received little support before service. We did all our own preparation."[1] Another former volunteer shared, "I wish I would have known how little supportive structures there would be in our sending organization."[2] Staff members within your mission institution may be unsure of how to properly ready you and your spouse for your life abroad. One survey participant disclosed his own experience in regard to such uncertainty: "Our program director (the one who directly supervised us) had no previous experience working with a married couple in the context of the volunteer program. He was not able to help us before we came down, and couldn't help us with some of the problems we had during our year."[3] Many service organizations are underfunded and, as a consequence, underdeveloped. As individuals *choosing* to be part of a program's ministry, you both need to be aware of the commitment you are making to existing conditions ahead of time.

As you survey what kinds of organizations are available to you and your partner, look for actual structures that signify the institution's dedication to taking care of its missioners/ staff members:

- **Handbook.** An up-to-date handbook with information about housing arrangements, jobs, medical access, safety and security, emergency protocols, time off, visitor policies, etc.
- **Buddy System.** A buddy system that pairs you up with a current volunteer during the application process, so you can ask questions and get a better idea of what day-to-day life looks like at the service site.
- **Orientations.** Thorough pre-departure and in-country orientations.
- **Language.** Option to attend language school or partake in language learning services offered by the organization itself.
- **Authority.** A clear structure of oversight in program and personnel management.
- **Assessments.** Job assessments and personal check-ins to ensure accountability on the part of all missioners, external colleagues, and supervisors.
- **Flexibility.** Institutional flexibility in providing adequate housing, schooling for children, an extended food budget, or other such issues specifically concerning married couples.
- **Retreats.** In-country retreats hosted (and paid for) by sending program.
- **Evaluations.** The opportunity to give feedback (in the form of exit interviews and/

---

1   Kenny, "Married Missioner/Volunteer Survey," 81.
2   Kenny, "Married Missioner/Volunteer Survey," 16.
3   Kenny, "Married Missioner/Volunteer Survey," 17.

or written observations) as departing volunteers that will be reviewed by in-country and homeland-based administrative staff members.

- **Re-entry Support.** Post-service guidance in aiding returned missioners in the navigation of the re-entry phase (i.e., retreats, workshops, literature, etc.).
- **Networking.** Assistance in helping reentrants find jobs, housing, graduate school programs, other service opportunities, connections to nearby alumni, etc.
- **Continued Involvement.** The ability for former missioners to mentor new volunteers, participate in fundraising events, write articles for the organization's newsletter or website, visit overseas ministry site, etc.

A service institution is a living system and, hopefully, one with a spirited pulse. Each mission program is characterized by the complex interaction of power, structure, leadership styles, goals, vision, history, individual members, policies, culture, and practices.[4] An appraisal of the health of the organizations to which you and your spouse are applying should be a key part of your preparation phase.

Spousal Dynamics

As you and your partner complete and submit your program application(s), it is important to keep in tune with each other's feelings and how those continue to affect your marriage. Do you still have a co-spousal dynamic? If so, wonderful! If the two of you began as co-spouses and now sense some dissonance in your relationship, it would be wise to address this shift and talk about why it has occurred. If both of you initially identified with the leading and accompanying spousal dynamic, things may have changed for the better. During the preparation phase, the leading spouse can become more adaptable, start to take into account his/her partner's vocational dreams, and/or be inspired to strive for greater balance in decision-making processes. Similarly, the accompanying spouse can opt to be more open to the idea of overseas mission work, come to be truly involved and invested in the situation at hand, and/or further research ministerial assignments that appeal to him or her.

A leading spouse survey participant shared how this kind of role shift took place in her marriage during the preparation period:

> Initially, I was more enthusiastic about finding a service experience than my husband. At the onset, I was seeking the experience, but it was a non-specific pursuit. However, as we learned of the specific opportunity that would become our mission (developing water and sanitation systems, which is a mutual passion of ours), my husband grew in his interest and excitement.[5]

In this real-world example, the leading spouse demonstrated a healthy amount of flexibility. Meanwhile, her husband, the accompanying spouse, actively identified a project about which he was animated. The result: a co-spousal dynamic. Unfortunately, the opposite of this scenario may occur—the negative tendencies of both the leading and accompanying spouses can persist or increase during this second stage. If this is what you and your part-

---

4   Lois A. Dodds and Lawrence E. Dodds, "Caring for People in Missions: Just Surviving—or Thriving? Optimal Care for the Long Haul," in *Heartstream Resources for Cross-Cultural Workers* (Liverpool, PA: Heartstream Resources, 1997), 11, http://www.heartstreamresources.org/media/Membercare.pdf.

5   Kenny, "Married Missioner/Volunteer Survey," 80.

ner are experiencing, reviewing exercises in Chapter 1 may be helpful in alleviating some of those tensions.

Loss

One of the reasons for continued resistance on the part of the accompanying spouse may be the realization of how a commitment to international mission work will not only change his/her external realities (job, residency, relationships), but will also deeply impact him/her as a person, as a marital partner, and possibly as a parent. With any significant life change comes loss. In *All Our Losses, All Our Griefs,* authors Kenneth Mitchell and Herbert Anderson identify six major types of losses not occasioned by death:

(1) **Material**—loss of object or familiar surrounding
(2) **Relationship**—loss of ability to relate to a particular person or persons
(3) **Intrapsychic**—loss of an emotionally important image of oneself
(4) **Functional**—loss of muscular or neurological operation of the body
(5) **Role**—loss of accustomed place in a social network
(6) **Systemic**—loss of belonging to some interactional structure[6]

An individual moving from a predictable and known environment to a foreign and unfamiliar locale will most likely experience several of the aforementioned losses. Leaving behind the house in which you and your spouse currently live can be categorized as a material loss. You or your partner may feel a sense of systemic loss in moving on from an accustomed workplace or faith community. In most cases, material and systemic loss are easier to identify and work through than the loss of relationship, role, and/or an intrapsychic perspective. Because loss of relationships, roles, and a particular self-image are consequential, they have the potential to negatively impact one's future adjustment to another country if not acknowledged and properly managed. Relationship, role, and intrapsychic losses are intricately linked. The people with whom you are in relationship define who you are and what you do. This, in turn, impacts the image you have of yourself. Parents are only parents because they have children to raise; teachers are only teachers because they have students to instruct; and doctors are only doctors because they have patients for whom to care. For Christians, the interconnectedness between self and other is framed within our belief in a Trinitarian God. The Trinity is fundamentally relational. We can look to God's relationship with God's Selves (Father, Son, and Holy Spirit) as a theology that is par excellence a theology of communion: "God to us, we to God, and we to each other."[7] From this standpoint, it is clear that loss of relationship, role, and intrapsychic conception are powerfully substantial.

While both partners can expect to experience various types of losses upon moving abroad, the accompanying spouse may feel those losses more acutely. Because his/her involvement with the decision to relocate is often minimal and/or passive, an accompanying spouse may see little satisfying compensation or incentive for giving up homeland, job, and identity. To the leading spouse, is not that perspective understandable on some level? Be gentle with your significant other if he or she begins to grieve for future losses at this time. If you or

---

6 Kenneth R. Mitchell and Herbert Anderson, *All Our Losses, All Our Griefs: Resources for Pastoral Care* (Philadelphia: Westminster Press, 1983), 36–44.
7 Catherine Mowry LaCugna, *God For Us: The Trinity & Christian Life* (New York: HarperCollins,1973), 243.

your partner feels like your marriage needs extra support, you may want to consider working with a marriage therapist or counselor.

Relational Strain

The preparation phase can be trying, even for co-spouses. It is in this stage that you will ultimately commit to the program that will, essentially, *be* your international mission experience. When this formal step in the process has been taken, both partners will be able to more vividly imagine what it will be like to fulfill the responsibilities of their service work. While one spouse may be grinning from ear to ear from daydreaming about a Cambodian classroom replete with bright-eyed students, the other's forehead creases may be deepening as he/she worries about having to learn Khmer. Partners can undergo the same kinds of mood swings they had during the discernment phase. (On Tuesday, *"This is such an exciting time in our lives! Let's read over the volunteer handbook again!"* On Thursday, *"I don't know if I can do this. Leaving my job seems like a really stupid decision to make right now."*) With the potential of such varied responses in reaction to selecting your sending organization and host country, it is no wonder that unresolved marital issues and/or family concerns may surface at this time. If you or your spouse feels strained in preparing for this experience, then you may need to work on your marital *friendship* by strengthening your fondness and admiration for one another. Happily married couples behave like good friends, so maintaining that relationship of solidarity will ultimately keep your marriage joy-filled and healthy.[8]

Fondness and Admiration[9]
Duration: 20–35 minutes

According to Dr. Gottman, "Fondness and admiration are two of the most crucial elements in a rewarding and long-lasting romance."[10] This next activity is binary. The first section is an interactive acknowledgement and exchange of affection and appreciation. The second section of the exercise will not be shared between partners at this time. An explanation as to why will be given in STEP 7.

STEP 1: Characteristics. Each partner will need three sheets of paper, an envelope, and a pen or a pencil. As individuals, review following the list of characteristics. Both spouses are to circle <u>three</u> qualities that describe their significant other. There are also spaces for partners to write in their own brainstormed traits. You will (hopefully) be able to identify more than three characteristics, so feel free to come back to this exercise at different points throughout your ministry.

---

8   "Research FAQs," *The Gottman Institute,* http://www.gottman.com/research/ research-faqs/.
9   Adapted from Gottman, Gottman, and DeClaire, *Ten Lessons,* 116–17.
10   Gottman and Silver, *Seven Principles,* 63.

Active	Kind
Adventurous	Lively
Affectionate	Loving
Athletic	Loyal
Attractive	Nurturing
Beautiful	Organized
Brave	Playful
Calm	Powerful
Caring	Practical
Cheerful	Protective
Committed	Receptive
Communicative	Relaxed
Considerate	Reliable
Coordinated	Reserved
Creative	Resourceful
Decisive	Responsible
Dependable	Sensitive
Elegant	Sexy
Energetic	Spiritual
Exciting	Strong
Expressive	Supportive
Flexible	Sweet
Fun	Talented
Funny	Tender
Generous	Thoughtful
Gentle	Thrifty
Graceful	Trustworthy
Gracious	Truthful
Handsome	Understanding
Honest	Vulnerable
Imaginative	Warm
Intelligent	Witty
Interesting	Other:_____
Involved	Other:_____

STEP 2: Descriptions. On one of your pieces of paper, each spouse is to copy the text below <u>three</u> times. For each copied text, write down one of the characteristics that you have identified, and some notes about a situation during which your partner displayed this trait and it pleased you.

Characteristic:_____

       Situation:

STEP 3: Discussion. Come together and take turns sharing the characteristics and situations you identified concerning each other. Describe to your partner why you appreciate these three traits and how the situations you wrote about demonstrated something valuable to you.

STEP 4: Self-Compliments. Let us move on to the second part of the activity. On one of your two remaining sheets of paper, each of you is to write five of the most flattering/complimentary statements you can come up with for yourself. You are basically completing the sentence: *"The nicest thing anyone could say to me is ... "*

STEP 5: Envelope. Once each of you has written your five complimentary statements, fold up and place those pieces of paper in your respective envelopes, leaving them unsealed. Write your name on your envelope.

STEP 6: Spouse's Compliments. Next, on your final sheet of paper, both of you are to write five complimentary statements about your partner.

STEP 7: Envelope Exchange. Upon completion, fold up the piece of paper with the five statements of admiration about your spouse and place it in the envelope that has his/her name on it. At this point, each partner should have an envelope filled with two sets of complimentary statements.

Exchange envelopes, so that you have each other's envelope. Put these in a safe place, for each of you is going to bring it with you on your overseas assignment. Later in this handbook you will be prompted to open your envelope and start putting those compliments to good use.

Family and Friends

Now that you both are feeling very fond of one another, let us tackle another issue that can surface during the preparation phase: the lack of encouragement from friends and/or family. For most married individuals, positive support from these people matters. Some couples are fortunate enough to receive an ample amount of assurance and enthusiasm from loved ones. One former missioner shared, "Our desire to serve became very clear and focused. Accepting our mission position united us with our support community. The spiritual peace, surety, and passion made it easy to move into international service."[11] Other couples may face a very different kind of situation. One survey participant confessed, "We felt a total lack of support from all family members and friends. Our isolation started before we left the country."[12] Yet another returned volunteer reported, "Not all family members were supportive. One of my husband's siblings shared more warnings than support."[13] If the latter two examples sound familiar to you, here are a few strategies that Member Care consultant Dr. Ronald Kotestky has developed to help everyone cope with your and your spouse's upcoming relocation:

---

11 Kenny, "Married Missioner/Volunteer Survey," 82.
12 Kenny, "Married Missioner/Volunteer Survey," 82.
13 Kenny, "Married Missioner/Volunteer Survey," 82.

Communication. Tell your family and friends about your choosing to serve abroad early on. No one likes surprises such as these. Moreover, explain to your loved ones *why* you want to volunteer overseas. Sharing your personal motivations may open their eyes to the depth and sincerity of your decision.

Dialogue. Invite the input of your parents, adult children, and/or friends. Such an invitation does not mean you have to take their advice, but at least give these people a means to be heard and understood.

Grief. Let those you are close to grieve the future loss of your relationship as it exists now. Although their anger, confusion, and/or sadness may be difficult to accept, allow your loved ones to express their emotions.

Information. As you and your partner prepare for your mission commitment, share the materials you are receiving and the information you are finding through research with family and friends. The more they know about what it is you are going to be doing, the more comfortable they are likely to feel.

Contact. Talk about how you will communicate abroad, if and when you will be able to make a trip home, and the possibility of individuals coming to visit your ministry site.

Farewells. Ritualize your goodbyes and actual departure. Write notes to family members, take the time to visit good friends, host a farewell party for yourself or for your children, etc. These concrete acts of letting go can help everyone prepare for the life change at hand.[14]

Variance. As a final note, your and your spouse's families may be offering different levels of support. This reality will likely impact your relationships with particular family members, but the effects of such disparities in encouragement do not need to be negative. Allow the assurance from some individuals to act as yet another positive piece of your relationship, and work to see the lack of enthusiasm from others as an area of potential growth.

Logistics

It is during the preparation phase that to-do lists are created, and boy can they be long! One of the biggest contributors to higher levels of stress during this phase is pure logistics. What should you do with all of your material possessions? (Most resources advise not selling your house, especially if your mission assignment is only for a few years.) How will volunteering abroad impact your concrete familial dreams and commitments (*"Are we deciding to have children later in life? How do we make sure that our ailing parents will be taken care of during our absence? What will being a grandparent look like now?"*)? How is your fundraising commitment going? What shots do you need? Does your sending organization offer you health insurance? Should you buy one-way or round-trip airline tickets? How many bags do you want to check/carry-on? Do either of you need an international driver's license? Do you have enough medical supplies for the amount of time you will be without easy access to clinics/hospitals? Are you interested in creating a blog so as to keep friends and family informed? (See the Appendix for some of the top, free blogging platforms.) Are there spe-

---

14 Koteskey, "Missionary Marriage Issues," in *Missionary Care: Resources for Missions and Mental Health,* January 2010, http://missionarycare.com/ebooks/Missionary_Marriage_Book.pdf, 108-110.

cific places you want to travel to while you are overseas? If so, do you need to make plans or reservations now?

Make lists. Writing down tasks, ideas, or concerns can help you and your partner keep everything organized, while also clearing out some headspace. For several thorough packing checklists, refer to the Appendix once again. The following points are a few of the more obscure concerns and pieces of advice to consider that are not mentioned in most checklists:

- **Snail Mail.** If you are able to receive cards or packages at your ministry site, or if your program sends mail with visitors, give your address to loved ones, perhaps on the back of a recent family photo.

- **Education.** Research the transferability of your children's educational curriculum and what paperwork you will need to fill out in order to enroll them into a local school. Make and retain a hard copy of your children's school records, even if you have sent electronic copies to the appropriate persons.

- **Documentation.** Ensure that you have all the travel documentation needed for yourselves *and* your children. Even minors need their own passports. Some countries require specific paperwork or letters of permission for particular situations, such as traveling as a single spouse with your children. Do the appropriate research on matters such as these. The U.S. Departments of State and the Health and Human Services' websites have helpful information in regard to proper documentation, as may your service program. Seek out guidance as necessary.

- **Contingency Plans.** Create contingency plans for unpreventable situations like political unrest, natural disasters, or experiences of trauma. Under what circumstances would you and your partner return to your home country? What would you do, heaven forbid, in case of a kidnapping or a death? Investigate what policies your sending organization has on the aforementioned matters as well. Lastly, be sure your loved ones are aware of such policies.

- **Pregnancy.** Decide whether or not you need an insurance plan that covers prenatal care, pregnancy services, or postnatal care. A surprising number of married couples and program staff members commented on the complexities of unexpected pregnancies abroad. One organization director wrote, "It could be a problem for the program and the couple if they get pregnant during their year of service, because of the commitment and sometimes the area of service."[15] Another staff member explained, "We cannot cover kids with insurance, so if a couple gets pregnant and are due to have a baby during term, we'd have to make arrangements for their service to end."[16] It would be smart for you and your spouse to have a conversation about the possibility of getting pregnant overseas. If you already have children, does your sending institution offer health insurance plans that cover them?

- **Wedding Rings.** You may want to consider finding a simple band substitute if your engagement/wedding rings appear expensive. Visibly "downgrading" can help you

---

15 Kenny, "Program Staff: Married Missioner/Volunteer Survey," 14.
16 Kenny, "Program Staff: Married Missioner/Volunteer Survey," 13.

avoid potential theft. You would never want to put your local neighbors in a situation where providing for their family includes taking something valuable from you. Moreover, a lot of international mission work is dirty, rough, and often done with one's hands. (This tip should be taken into account concerning all kinds of jewelry.)

•   **Homeland Snacks.** Specialty food items (or even run-of-the-mill products) may not be readily available in your host country. Leave room to pack those treats that you, your spouse, and/or your children particularly appreciate. However, be prepared for the day when supplies run out. You and your partner may have to get creative and scour for foreign alternatives. But do not worry—there will be many traditional dishes you will all come to enjoy.

Once each of you feels ready to fill those suitcases, remember to prioritize your packing. Keep medicines and certain toiletries in a carry-on bag, maybe even an extra set of clothes in case of a delayed flight. Ensuring that your luggage is thoughtfully stocked with all the recommended supplies necessary for extended, cross-cultural service can help ease some of your pre-departure nerves.

Well-Being

As you and your partner prepare for your departure by crossing off items from your to-do lists, you should also be emotionally equipping yourselves. Awareness and understanding of your own self (I), your partner (You), and your marriage (We), are the best ways to protect them all from the inevitable stressors inherent to international ministry. Marriage is a reality that requires both adjustment and stability. Spouses are to honor past commitments made and recognize the ever-changing context in which those commitments remain alive today. Similarly, cross-cultural mission work enjoins individuals to adapt, while still remaining true to their own selves. A person creates an identity through constructing habits, routines, and outlets in order to balance individual tendencies, work and family responsibilities, and the unpredictabilities of the surrounding environment. Even Jesus needed to assess his own sense of well-being, and engage in some self-nurturing when his ministry had stretched him too thin. (See Mt 14:23; Mk 1:35-36; 6:31–32, 46–47; 7:24b; 8:13; Lk 5:16; 6:12; 9:18.)

I-You-We-Care Stars[17]
Duration: 30–45 minutes

This exercise will assist you and your partner in determining what constitutes your own self-care regimens. The two of you will also create a "we-care" star diagram, outlining the ways in which to best tend to your marriage.

STEP 1: Star Diagram. Each spouse will need a pen or a pencil. Designate a *Spouse #1* and a *Spouse #2*. *Spouse #1* will fill in **Figure 2.1** and *Spouse #2* will fill in **Figure 2.2**. Please refer to your respective figures on the following page in completing the next step.

---

17 Adapted from Julie Lupien, "Self-Care Stars" (presentation, From Mission to Mission Workshop, Chicago, Illinois, October 24–26, 2014).

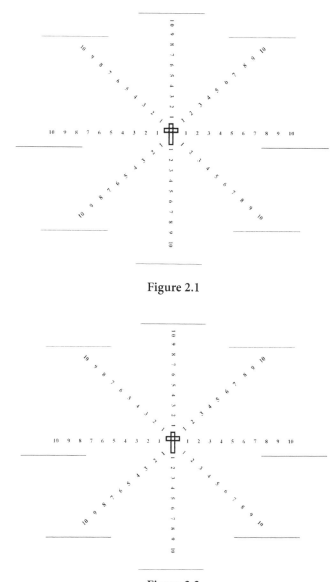

Figure 2.1

Figure 2.2

STEP 2: Fill-In Diagram. For each of the eight spaces at the ends of the number lines in **Figures 2.1** and **2.2**, both of you is to identify a routine, habit, or outlet that must be in place for you to feel like you have a balanced life. Here are a few examples: exercise, fellowship/worship, communication with your family, downtime to relax, reading Scripture, playing a musical instrument, or journaling.

STEP 3: Assign Numbers. After the two of you have written down your eight methods of self-care, circle the number that corresponds to how you are <u>currently</u> doing in regards to each method—with "1" being poor and "10" being excellent (*"I have been going to bed early this past week. I am going to circle '9' for 'adequate rest.'"*).

STEP 4: Routine Revealed. Lastly, connect the numbers from one line to the next to see how balanced (or not) your circle of care appears. See **Figure 2.3** below for an example of how I am doing with my own self-care routine.

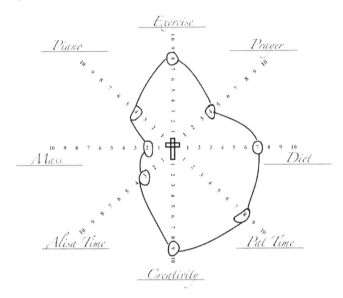

Figure 2.3

As you can see, my care circle is a little lopsided. The goal is for your self-care star to be a large, even circle. It is important to pinpoint what keeps you functioning at a healthy level before going abroad; when you and your spouse arrive to your host country, one or both of you are likely to experience discomfort, confusion, and insecurity. As individuals, you will instinctively want to refer back to established routines and forms of stress reduction so you can regain a sense of control and self-worth.

You may find it helpful to review your self-care star as you begin to settle into your home away from home. Feel free to modify your regimen according to your new context, and as you come across new methods of personal care in your life overseas.

STEP 5: Star Diagram. The second part of this activity is meant for both spouses. The two of you are going to create a shared "we-care" star diagram for your marriage. Together, identify eight routines or habits that must be in place for your marriage to be at its best. Write those care methods atop the number lines in **Figure 2.4**. Here are a few examples: date nights, spiritual time together, frequent expressions of intimacy, shared household responsibilities, spontaneity, or effective communication.

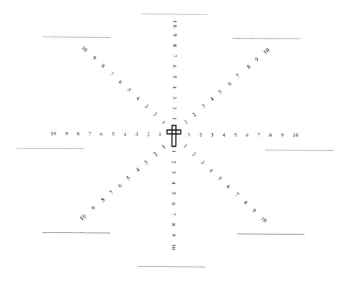

Figure 2.4

STEP 6: Fill In Diagram. Decide where your marriage is at <u>right now</u> in regard to the eight care methods you identified together. Circle the respective numbers in each line. After connecting the numbers, discuss the shape of your "we-care" star. Why are certain points so high? Low? In what ways can you both better care for your marriage so that your circle looks rounder and fuller? Referring to your "we-care" star once you and your spouse are abroad can help each of you recapture stability in your marital relationship as you both undergo your own cross-cultural transitioning.

<u>Miscellaneous</u>

Preparative foresight is good. Thinking ahead is natural and can be constructive, so let your minds and hearts actively anticipate your departure. Here are a few more tips to help further ready yourselves:

Leave your assumptions behind. No matter what precautions you and your partner are taking, your time overseas will fall below, meet, and surpass your expectations. One survey participant agreed with this sentiment in writing: "Service experiences like we had in Guatemala cannot be planned for, nor can the type of experience or value realized from the experience be anticipated."[18] Thus, focus on renouncing any preconceptions that you may have about your future ministry. Doing so will allow you to more fully enter into and appreciate the upcoming opportunity.

Do not lower your marriage standards. Even though adapting to another culture may be difficult, you and your spouse should not reduce the expectations you have for your marital relationship. Studies by marriage researcher Donald Baucom "show that couples who have high expectations for romance and passion in their relationships are more likely to have these qualities in their marriage than those who have low expectations; and those with high

18 Kenny, "Married Missioner/Volunteer Survey," 36.

expectations have happier marriages as a result."[19] Leave behind assumptions you may have for your pending international experience, but not for the kind of marriage for which you both are striving.

Help your children prepare. Just as for adults, information is key to your children's readiness for life overseas. Letting your kids help with preparations for the big move allows them to get more accustomed to the idea of this major change.[20] Have them box up their rooms, pack their own suitcases, create personal to-do lists, etc.

Do some research. It is a good idea to investigate what customs exist in your host country concerning married persons. What are appropriate public signs of affection? How do local husbands and wives interact in formal settings? Are there any laws or traditions surrounding purity mores? Do married men and/or women have to dress a certain way as to indicate their relationship status? You do not necessarily have to adhere to all of the customs you come across, but knowledge about such conventions is important.

Bring a memento. Some of you have probably already thought of this, but in case it has not made the official checklist, both of you should pack an object that reminds you of home. Bringing along pictures of family members, friends, and places you love in your passport country is also a good idea. Such tangible reminders can help you get through challenging days.

Make room for Providence. In all your measure taking, remember that the unfolding of your service experience is not solely under the control of you or your partner. One former missioner concurred in sharing:

> Before my wife and I got married, we did not fill out any paperwork, do psychological testing, or examine each others' profiles. We fell in love and headed into life. Along the way, we ended up in Papua New Guinea for ten years. We had kids. There was not a great deal of planning or forethought involved in our lives. (This was probably stupid.) But we did it, and we actually did it pretty well. My point is to allow for some serendipity. Allow for some spontaneity. Allow for unplanned, unexpected divine appointments.[21]

Making space for God's presence and involvement in this journey is what will get you both through it in two whole and healthy pieces.

Deepening Your Relationship

If you and your spouse are handling the preparation period productively, you both will be exercising your abilities to dialogue effectively, reach balanced compromise, and articulate your values and beliefs. In moving through this second phase successfully, you will be able to more fully understand the strengths and areas of growth in your own self and your partner. Thus, each of you is getting to know the other on a distinctly deeper

---

19 Gottman, Gottman, and DeClaire, *Ten Lessons to Transform Your Marriage*, 45.
20 Robin Pascoe, *Culture Shock! Successful Living Abroad: A Wife's Guide* (Portland: Graphic Arts Center Publishing Company, 1992), 20.
21 Colin Murphy, personal e-mail, May 15, 2015.

level. Improving and finessing these kinds of skills ultimately enhances your marriage. Another way the two of you can further develop your marital relationship is by identifying your personal love language(s) and the love language(s) of your significant other.

In his book *The 5 Love Languages: The Secret to Love That Lasts,* Dr. Gary Chapman explains how our most basic emotional need as humans is to be genuinely loved by another—"to know a love that grows out of reason and choice, not just instinct."[22] Spouses need to be loved by a partner who consciously decides to love them, who sees in them something worth loving.[23] Thus, it is important for individuals to understand exactly how they themselves, and their significant other, give and receive love. It is possible that Jack truly loves Jill, but she feels undervalued because he does not express giving and receiving love in the same way that she does.

Generally speaking, everyone has a primary love language for giving love and for receiving love. Those languages may be the same or they may be different. Here is an example: Jill may show Jack love by physical touch (hugging him when he gets home from work), and performing acts of service (baking him chocolate chip cookies after dinner). However, Jill prefers receiving love from Jack in the form of words of affirmation (*"Wow, Jill, your violin playing sounds great. You must be practicing a lot."*) and in the form of small, thoughtful gifts (a surprise bouquet of flowers on an ordinary weeknight). The point here is that husbands and wives should be aware of and in tune with the ways in which his/her spouse feels most respected and appreciated.

Love Languages[24]
Duration: 30–45 minutes

This activity is meant to help each of you identify your own love language, as well as that of your partner. Engaging in this exercise can increase the intensity and frequency of feeling loved and cared for within your marriage.

STEP 1: Website. Each spouse will need access to a computer, a sheet of paper, and a pen or a pencil. Designate a *Spouse #1* and a *Spouse #2*. As individuals, visit Gary Chapman's *5 Love Languages* website at http://www.5lovelanguages.com.

STEP 2: Complete Profile. Allow ten to fifteen minutes to complete the online profile. Take it when both of you are relaxed, and try not to rush through it. Fill in the necessary pre-profile information and then begin answering the questionnaire.

---

22 Gary Chapman, *The Five Love Languages: The Secret to Love that Lasts* (Northfield: Northfield Publishing, 1992, 2015), 33.

23 Chapman, *The Five Love Languages*, 33.

24 Adapted from "Love Languages Personal Profile," *The Five Love Languages,* https://s3.amazonaws.com/moody-profiles/uploads/profile/attachment/1/CHP_5LoveLanguagesSingles_Quiz_Rev3-26.pdf and "Love Languages Study Guide," *Utah Education Network,* http://www.uen.org/Lessonplan/downloadFile.cgi?-file=28905-2-35976-Love_Language_StudyGuide.pdf&filename=Love_Language_StudyGuide.pdf.

STEP 3: Tally Score. Once the two of you have finished your profiles, a summary page will appear on your screen. (This page will also be sent to your email.) As individuals, write in the scores of each love language under the respective columns below.

The highest score in your profile is your primary love language. If point totals for two love languages are equal, you are "bilingual" and have two primary love languages. If you have a secondary love language, or one that is close in score to your primary love language, this means that both expressions of love are important to you.

Spouse #1   **Spouse #2**

_____   *WORDS OF AFFIRMATION*   _____

You feel most cared for when your partner verbalizes his/her love for you. Positivism expressed by your spouse about your character gives you the confidence to believe in your own self-worth and abilities.

_____   *QUALITY TIME*   _____

You feel most cared for when you are with your partner in a situation where both of you can be fully present to and engaged with one another. In your mind, time spent together—no matter how the time is spent—indicates that your spouse genuinely enjoys being around you.

_____   *RECEIVING GIFTS*   _____

You feel most cared for when your partner demonstrates the foresightedness, romance, and thoughtfulness that is involved in gift-giving. This act illustrates the desire your spouse possesses in wanting to take the time to externally convey his/her appreciation for and understanding of you.

_____   *ACTS OF SERVICE*   _____

You feel most cared for when your partner does something helpful for you. Having your spouse relieve you of a task, being especially kind to you, or making an extra effort for your benefit, is evidence of his/her love and willingness to sacrifice.

_____   *PHYSICAL TOUCH*   _____

You feel most cared for through physical affection: a good hug, holding hands, a deep kiss, etc. Physical intimacy, initiated or warmly received by your partner, makes you feel attractive and loveable.

STEP 4: Prompts. Keeping your primary (and secondary) love language(s) in mind, you and your spouse are going to prepare for a guided and in-depth conversation about the communication of love. On your respective pieces of paper, each of you is to respond to the prompts on the next page:

- Do you feel like the love language(s) that your profile generated is/are accurate? Why or why not? With which other love language(s) do you identify?
- When you look back at your childhood, do you feel that you were adequately loved by your parents? How did they primarily express love? What impact did your parents have on the way you convey love to your partner?
- Make a list of all the circumstances, locations, and types of appropriate touch that you believe enhance your marital relationship.
- What are the differences in the emotional, psychological, physiological, and spiritual components of both the "falling in love" experience and the more mature kind of mutual and lasting love that can follow such a phase?
- Note a few specific examples of when you have felt loved by your partner in the past year.
- Brainstorm ways in which you could honor your spouse's love language in a new and foreign setting.

STEP 5: Dialogue. *Spouse #1* can begin the conversation by sharing his/her responses to the first prompt from above. Once the two of you feel like you are able to move on, *Spouse #2* is to communicate his/her answer to the same question. Move through the prompts in the same alternating style and engage in the discussion that these questions invoke.

Marriage and Mission

From a Catholic perspective, each individual is a mission. Pope Francis writes about the implications of such a concept in *Evangelii Gaudium*:

> My mission of being in the heart of the people is not just a part of my life or a badge I can take off; it is not an "extra" or just another moment in life. Instead, it is something I cannot uproot from my being without destroying my very self. I am a mission on this earth; that is the reason why I am here in this world. We have to regard ourselves as sealed, even branded, by this mission of bringing light, blessing, enlivening, raising up, healing and freeing.[25]

As spouses, your call to mission is defined by your covenantal relationship. You have been commissioned as a wife and as a husband to mutually love one another. Though common enough, the decision to marry and dedicate your life to someone as equally complex and as much a "work-in-progress" as yourself is a challenging ministry. "If you want to be free to serve Jesus, there's no question—stay single. But if you want to become more like Jesus, I can't imagine any better thing to do than to get married."[26] Married individuals help one another become the men and women God has intended them to be. The mission of marriage is the constant and continual cultivation of the sacredness found within yourselves and in your shared, familial culture.

In deciding to become international volunteers, both of you have chosen to commit to a second kind of mission. "The Christian family is thus called upon to offer everyone a witness of generous dedication to social matters, through a 'preferential option' for the

25 Francis, *Evangelii Gaudium* (2013), no. 273, http://w2.vatican.va/content/francesco/en/apost_exhortations/documents/papa-francesco_esortazione-ap_20131124_evangelii-gaudium.html.
26 Gary Thomas, "The Transforming Miracle of Marriage," *Psychology for Living: Narramore Christian Foundation*, http://www.ncfliving.org/miracle_marriage1.php.

poor and disadvantaged … we must have special concern for the hungry, the poor, the old, the sick, drug victims and those who have no family."[27] Preferential option for the poor is one of the seven principles within the tradition of Catholic social teaching. It is based on the Christian understanding of Jesus becoming poor himself (2 Cor 8:9) and his closeness to the poor and the outcast throughout his earthly ministry. While we are responsible for taking care of the marginalized in our home countries, we are also called to live out that responsibility within our global society. For "an authentic faith—which is never comfortable or completely personal—always involves a deep desire to change the world, to transmit values, to leave this earth somehow better than we found it."[28] By saying "yes" to overseas mission work, you and your significant other are following Jesus' lead in challenging your own prejudices, expectations, and life of First World comforts, in order to transcend those boundaries in making present God's Kingdom in the here and now.[29]

As "global spouses," you and your partner are *being* missions twice over—in both your marriage and your future service. These vocations embody the Christian approach to mission: "that life is attained and matures in the measure that it is offered up in order to give life to others."[30] Your newly committed-to purpose is to nurture and enliven not only your mutual communion, but also the universal community in which you are pursuing your marriage; in which some of you will leave your children, and your children's children.[31] You and your significant other are living out this faith of service by fulfilling your baptismal call to Christ by his sending of you in a unique way, as missioners and as married persons—as mission-marries! Like marriage, what your overseas ministry will make the two of you is not necessarily happier (although sometimes that, too, will be the case), but "wholier."

---

27 Pius XI, *Casti Connubii* (1930), no. 47, http://w2.vatican.va/content/pius-xi/en/encyclicals/documents/hf_p-xi_enc_31121930_casti-connubii.html.

28 Francis, *Evangelii Gaudium*, no. 183.

29 Anthony J. Gittins, *Bread for the Journey: The Mission of Transformation and the Transformation of Mission* (Maryknoll, NY: Orbis, 1993), 10.

30 Fifth General Conference of the Latin American and Caribbean Bishops, *Aparecida* Document, June 29, 2007, no. 360, http://www.celam.org/aparecida/Ingles.pdf.

31 Michael G. Lawler, *Marriage and Sacrament: A Theology of Christian Marriage* (Collegeville, MN: Liturgical Press, 1993), 104.

Realization

Chapter 3

Beginning of Abroad Experience

Take the Adventure, heed the call, now ere the irrevocable moment passes! Tis but a banging of the door behind you, a blithesome step forward, and you are out of the old life and into the new!

—Kenneth Grahame, *The Wind in the Willows*

Realization

Realization is the beginning period of your experience serving in a different country. This phase typically lasts from three to six months after arriving at your ministerial site. (Several couples with longer mission commitments reported feeling that realization continued beyond the six-month mark.) While it is possible for you and your spouse to transition at the same rate with the same ease at certain moments, it is likely that there will be more points of disparity in how each of you responds to living in a foreign culture than not. One survey participant shared, "I think us both reacting differently to situations caused a lot of confusion for me. I didn't know how to be okay with us being at different places and having other views."[1] This chapter can help you and your partner adjust your initial perspectives and approaches (if necessary) to volunteering overseas as husband and wife. By becoming more adaptable and aware, both of you can manage the realization stage as successfully as this former missioner, as indicated by her reflection, "We learned to be patient with ourselves and be supportive of each other, recognizing that—while we were a couple—our experiences were the experiences of two individuals."[2]

Culture Shock

Many of you have probably heard the term culture shock. According to its most basic definition, culture shock refers to an individual's personal reaction to being in a different environment. Oftentimes, this response is one of disorientation, anxiety, and agitation. These distressing emotions can negatively affect a person's physical, emotional, mental, and spiritual well-being. It is imperative to note that your reaction, as well as your spouse's reaction, to this new situation is in response—not necessarily to the culture at large—but to the conduct of those within the culture. In order to cope with this internal chaos, individuals must allow themselves to become accustomed to the behavior of the local people—behavior that may originally come off as annoying, confounding, or otherwise unsettling. Likewise, the same individuals must adjust their own behavior so that it does not annoy, confound, or otherwise unsettle the local people.[3] Constructing a comfortable and meaningful lifestyle overseas is a balancing act of responsive adaptability; an attitude that you as missioners are invited to initiate.

---

1   Kenny, "Married Missioner/Volunteer Survey," 157.
2   Kenny, "Married Missioner/Volunteer Survey," 24.
3   Craig Storti, *The Art of Crossing Cultures* (Boston: Intercultural Press, 1989), 15.

If you refer to the *Stages of Cross-Cultural Transition* timeline in the Preface, you will see a small dip at the point where a volunteer reaches his/her host country. "Why the drop?" you may ask. Here is why: as you deplane, back aching from your overpacked carry-on, you feel a blanketing of sticky humidity, followed by several unidentifiable and pungent odors. A hoard of men loudly try to convince you to *"Take taxi with me!"* and your stomach starts to gurgle in halted digestion of whatever free and exotic food the flight attendants gave you. End scene. Your spouse may be feeling equally uncomfortable and overwhelmed, and if you have kids, then you are likely to have an even lower "arrival conclusion" downtrend. Fast-forward a few days later, and you and your partner may be experiencing the initial feelings of travel euphoria: curiosity about the culture, excitement about the newness of the geography and people, and open-mindedness to local customs and traditions. These feelings of novelty and adventure are what is behind the rise in spirits as illustrated by the "honeymoon peak" in the *Stages of Cross-Cultural Transition* timeline.

If you fast-forward another month or two, the infamous plunge of culture shock begins. You may feel confused, conflicted, embarrassed, irritable, bitter, fearful, homesick, insecure, and/or lonely. The following bullet points are common manifestations—in response to experiencing the aforementioned emotions—of a person who has chosen to relocate internationally for a significant period of time:

- Social withdrawal
- Physical exhaustion
- Trouble sleeping
- Expressions of grief
- Chauvinistic tendencies
- Inability to work effectively
- Unexplainable fits of weeping
- Compulsive behavior (eating, drinking, cleanliness, etc.)
- Stereotyping others (both locals and fellow compatriots)
- Hostility toward others (both locals and fellow compatriots)
- Somatization (headaches, fatigue, colds, muscle pain, etc.)[4]

My husband and I definitely exhibited some compulsive behavior regarding cleanliness during our first few months in Honduras. Who am I kidding? Our community mates will tell you that our obsession with bottles of bleach and systematic dishwashing was a year-long culture shock symptom. Each individual's experience of culture shock will be different; with different emotions felt and different responses had. While this bulleted list includes the more commonly reported manifestations of culture shock, please remember that you and/ or your partner may have other kinds of feelings and reactions to living in another country not accounted for in this handbook.

Enculturation

As encultured beings, humans first learn how to behave by watching and imitating others in early childhood. Personal development continues as individuals begin to assign and re-assign meaning and value to particular people, events, actions, emotions, etc.—what psychologists call "meaning making." The unfolding of this process is usually informed by one's

---

4   Kohls, *Survival Kit,* 65–66.

caretakers, along with other figures of authority (e.g., teachers, coaches, or religious leaders) and surrounding social institutions (e.g., interest groups, schools, or faith traditions). As the years pass, we come to create for ourselves a world of relative predictability, based on established internal and external habits and expectations. According to multicultural communications expert and author Craig Storti, when in our home countries, we feel in control much of the time and are able to relax; we can trust our instincts and be ourselves. Routines enhance our perceptions of well-being and security and thereby can contribute to higher impressions of self-confidence.[5] When moving to a foreign environment, initially, your cultural know-how is minimized, and your meaning making abilities are significantly strained. During the realization phase, your sense of self-worth may be low, for self-esteem is directly proportional to cultural know-how and meaning making.[6]

For example, a seemingly simple trip to get ingredients for a family meal can actually leave you physically and emotionally drained. After several crowded and bumpy bus rides, you find yourself wandering around an open market madly trying to calculate the conversion rate for dollars to naira, as you struggle to remember the Hausa translation for "*How much do these matches cost?*" while cringing in nervous apprehension as you select vegetables from under the gaze of a nearby stray dog. So when you return home, red in the face with a ripped bag of six eggs, brown rice, and a few unidentifiable pieces of produce, it is understandable that your self-esteem has been slightly diminished. When what you have always known and assumed to work does not deliver the same results in your unfamiliar locale, you are forced to reconstruct responses for various encounters—the number of which depends on the difference(s) between your passport and host cultures.

In the first few months abroad, you must consciously pay attention to interactions that were once dealt with subconsciously in your life back home (e.g., the proper way to eat a meal or how to interact with elders). For each event, try to observe objectively—that which is objective according to the perspective of the local people—what is happening, and take into account the customary responses (e.g., eating only with your right hand or bowing your head slightly when greeting an older person). Adjusting your behavior to reflect what is culturally appropriate in your host country is similar to the process of enculturation you underwent as a child. You are socially re-grooming yourself, so that when you eat dinner or meet an aged individual, you do so in a way that is congruous with what is considered normal or conventional in your new home.

Family Culture Shock

In addition to the individual experience of adapting to the realities of international relocation, married couples must address another type or dimension of culture shock—the communal piece:

> Family culture shock [analogous to couple culture shock] is a collective experience. … It is initially about loss of control over new surroundings and then, later, over each other's behavior. As each person struggles with the shock of

---

5   Craig Storti, *The Art of Coming Home* (Yarmouth, ME: Intercultural Press, 1997), 22.
6   Kristen Thogersen, "Afterword: Self-Esteem and a New Environment," in *Homeward Bound: A Spouse's Guide to Repatriation,* ed. Robin Pascoe (Vancouver: Expatriate Press, 2000), 183–84.

regaining equilibrium, family culture shock also includes feelings of losing control over the actions and reactions of other family members.[7]

As an interconnected system, a couple will be mutually impacted by the responses of its members. If one string of your love *erhu* is plucked (yes, there exists a two-stringed instrument called an *erhu* and it now represents your marriage), the resonance of its twang will reverberate and vibrate through its neighboring string. Remember, your entire service experience is comprised of how you are handling your transitioning to life overseas (I), how your partner is managing his or her reactions to this change (You), and how your marital relationship is coping with it all (We). If applicable, do not forget to add a couple of "Me, Me, Me's" to this illustration to symbolize your children. (In that case, you will have to come up with your own stringed instrument analogy.) Family culture shock is a collective process of several people and many factors, so being "in tune" with your loved ones and empathetic to their experiences is crucial.

Grief and Loss

Grief can be a major aspect of adjusting to a new lifestyle in a foreign land.[8] You and your spouse have just said good-bye to a comfortable world of meaningful relationships and established roles. Mourning these kinds of losses is natural, no matter how much both of you prepared for your overseas ministry. Coping with the grief that often accompanies international relocation begins in acknowledging what has been lost. Once again, here are the six major types of losses as defined by Mitchell and Anderson:

(1) **Material**—loss of object or familiar surrounding
(2) **Relationship**—loss of ability to relate to a particular person or persons
(3) **Intrapsychic**—loss of an emotionally important image of oneself
(4) **Functional**—loss of muscular or neurological operation of the body
(5) **Role**—loss of accustomed place in a social network
(6) **Systemic**—loss of belonging to some interactional structure[9]

Both partners can expect to feel the impact and grief of more than one of these losses. No two occasions of grief are ever exactly the same. "Grief is always a particular response to the particular loss of a particular object" at a particular time.[10] Thus, you and your partner will have different encounters with grief and will, most likely, handle such grief using various types of coping mechanisms. One survey participant attested to this when she wrote, "My husband was very laid back and didn't stress about much. I had a lot of anxiety and I didn't know how to be okay with change sometimes. We reacted very differently to situations we faced."[11] Try to be sensitive to your spouse's grief over the absence of certain relationships and systems in your new life abroad. Proper mourning is a proven avenue in assisting people to move on from experienced loss in a healthy manner, so allow each other to do so.

---

7   Robin Pascoe, *A Moveable Marriage* (North Vancouver: Expatriate Press Limited, 2003), 130.
8   Kenneth R. Mitchell and Herbert Anderson, *All Our Losses, All Our Griefs: Resources for Pastoral Care* (Philadelphia: Westminster Press, 1983), 53.
9   Mitchell and Anderson, *All Our Losses*, 36–44.
10 Mitchell and Anderson, *All Our Losses*, 53.
11 Kenny, "Married Missioner/Volunteer Survey," 160.

A person who links his/her own self-image with a particular role or structure may have a more difficult time acclimating to a world without such a role or structure. Roles, and what people do while they are in them, help individuals to define themselves; roles also elicit the opportunity for recognition from others. Who Jack understood himself to be as a high school guidance counselor in Oregon will change as he takes on the role of a parish minister in Zimbabwe. What Jill did as a nursing student from Texas and how her classmates acknowledged her work will be different from the way local colleagues will affirm Jill in her role as the primary healthcare provider in a rural Japanese community. Like Jack and Jill, you and your significant other must work to be aware of how the loss of a specific home country role or interactional structure may be affecting your individual self-concepts and/ or feelings of personal worth.

Role Orientation

Directly related to loss is the challenge of possible shifts in gender roles. Gender roles are socially constructed positions that a society holds in dictating what behaviors, activities, and attributes are generally acceptable, appropriate, or desirable for a person based on his/ her perceived gender.[12] A shift in gender role orientation can affect your or your partner's performance as a spouse, as a parent, or both. You will find yourself processing how locals view you as a wife/husband, a woman/man, and a missioner. At the same time, you could also be adapting to a spousal/parental role that you may not have had at home. Your partner could have certain expectations of you, knowingly or not, that were not a part of your marriage before this life change.[13] Here is an example: Jack and Jill wanted to volunteer in China. Jack quit a high-paying job to move overseas, while Jill was able to take a year-long sabbatical from her teaching position. Jill spoke Mandarin, which played a big part in their decision to pursue a mission opportunity in China. Jack did not know Mandarin. Even after language school, Jack was still unable to relate to others effectively. Therefore, Jill had to interpret many important conversations for Jack, and witnessed many situations in which Jack could not function at a competent level because of his language barrier. Jill found herself feeling annoyed with Jack's inability to communicate. It created more work for her to do, work that Jack had been in charge of back home. Similarly, Jack was discouraged. He did not like depending on his wife in such an exaggerated way. Jack felt that he could not contribute to his marriage at the same level he could in his passport country. Conclusion, Jack and Jill were dissatisfied with their new spousal roles.

If you and your partner feel a similar kind of negative tension between yourselves, it can be helpful to determine why this strain has surfaced. One survey participant commented on the reasoning behind her marital stress: "At the beginning I was frustrated with my husband because I didn't understand why or what he was doing. As time went on, I realized that he was going through identity exploration and became more okay with him exploring that."[14] Generally speaking, your spouse's change in behavior is not a permanent one. In fact, it is likely a reactive one. Moreover, such a behavioral change is probably one they do not particularly like themselves! What is the lesson learned here? Be empathetic and flexible. Knowing your closest ally in a new culture is not satisfied with how you are acting as a

---

12 "Gender," World Health Organization, http://www.who.int/gender-equity-rights/understanding/gender-definition/en/.

13 Pascoe, *Culture Shock! Successful Living Abroad,* 85.

14 Kenny, "Married Missioner/Volunteer Survey," 116.

spouse and/or parent is painful—for it is what we want to do our best at more than most things in life.

As touched upon earlier, you and your significant other may be experiencing a shifting of unspoken agreements—the more emotional spouse becomes less reliant, or work and childcare responsibilities switch from one partner to the other. Each of you will need to be able to give up, suspend, and/or modify previous expectations and hopes. Instead of solving problems superficially, you and your spouse should try to learn how to be more comfortable with the personal changes each of you may be undergoing at this time. Be open to letting your partner adjust and grow. Disallowing such growth means that not only is the vitality of your relationship at stake, but also the ongoing development of you and your spouse.[15] In order to strengthen your selves and your marriage, consider reflecting on the following two questions: *What can I do for my partner so that he/she can be a better spouse or parent? What do I need from my partner in order to be a better spouse or parent?*

Spousal Dynamics

Let us return to the topic of spousal dynamics. In this chapter, we will focus primarily on the perspective of the accompanying spouse. Why? Because, as a gross oversimplification, those who are leading spouses or co-spouses are where they have wanted to be since the start of this process—in a different country as a volunteer—so undergoing culture shock for them is, assumedly, worth the initial discomfort. The accompanying spouse may not see the viability in this tradeoff, which can potentially make his/her experience of transition longer and more labored. While both partners have lost part of their identities, it may be that the accompanying spouse does not find the same joy—at least not yet—in replacing it with the new self that is associated with and partly defined by his/her ministerial commitment.

Reducing the leading and accompanying spousal dynamics to such a flat archetype ignores the larger spectrum across which this relationship can span. However, simplifying it in this way gives you both a clear point from which to begin. Here are some of the more extreme reactions an accompanying spouse may have during the realization phase:

- Resistance to suggestions
- Critical of authority
- Willful incompetence
- Forgetful of missionary obligations
- Feelings of resentment and bitterness
- Sullen sarcasm
- Generally accusatory[16]

If either of you sees these kinds of attitudinal and behavioral expressions in your own self or your significant other, make time to communicate about the issues that underlie such symptoms using the exercise *Conflict Resolution* in this chapter.

While both partners may be engaged in some type of service work, couples with children may have to designate one parent as the family's primary caretaker. If this task falls upon the

---

15 Bridges, *Transitions*, 72.
16 Koteskey, "Missionary Marriage Issues," 14–15.

accompanying spouse, understand that being homebound can intensify his/her emotional "down cycles" and, consequently, disrupt his/her adaptation to the surrounding culture.[17] It is usually helpful for partners to share household responsibilities in a balanced manner, so as to ensure that each person feels that he or she has the time and energy to be involved in meaningful activities beyond the home. Accompanying spouses who spend the majority of their day without adult interaction should take initiative in creating social relationships. Whether the accompanying spouse is the principal childcare provider or has a volunteer position within the community (or both), being aware of and in conversation with his/her partner about how he/she is adjusting to this life change is important.

On the other hand, the two of you may experience the opposite of what has been described. It could be that you, as the leading spouse, are not transitioning as expeditiously to your host country as your partner, the accompanying spouse. Perhaps your significant other is picking up the language more quickly as grammar, intonation, and pronunciation come more naturally to him/her. Or perhaps your extroverted spouse is winning over the locals with his/her friendly and welcoming demeanor. While it may feel unnerving for the leading spouse to experience such a shift in dynamics, the accompanying spouse's growing interest in and passion for your overseas ministry indicates that you are both on your way to becoming co-spouses. Be patient with each other's styles of adaptation, and have confidence in the fact that in a few more months, you and your partner will have found your individual niches within the community at the pace that was right for you both.

Physical Realities

For many, serving abroad involves a *physical* readjustment to a notably different kind of climate. "To one unaccustomed to it, the heat of the tropics can be debilitating. For the first few weeks, even months, one feels a marked loss of energy, a need for more sleep, and any number of symptoms commonly associated with dehydration, such as headaches and low-grade fevers."[18] Unrelenting downpours during your host country's rainy season can make you feel like a prisoner in your own living space. If you and your spouse are volunteering in the far north or south, cool temperatures and minimal sunlight may also result in a lot of time spent indoors. Weather is an uncontrollable variable present in relocation, so relax into it the best you can. Give yourselves plenty of time to acclimate, and be open to new and creative ways of doing things.

An undersupply of basic amenities is another factor that comes into play while getting accustomed to life as an international missioner. Figuring out how to take an effective bucket shower requires hand-eye coordination and lots of practice! Lack of running/potable water, unreliable electricity, limited household supplies, little or no access to technology, and other such challenges are realities of many ministry sites abroad. Learning how to go without some of the more superficial luxuries—normal cheese, peanut butter, good thread, hand soap, duct tape, and English books—is often an overlooked part of your volunteer commitment. While, in the scheme of things, such sacrifices are fairly insignificant, an accumulation of such can take their toll, especially as you confront other and more impactful changes. Remember how you were supposed to pack that specialty food item for yourselves or your kids? Well, make sure that when you eat it, you give yourself plenty of time to do

---

17 Fontaine, "International Relocation," 44.
18 Storti, *The Art of Crossing Cultures*, 3–4.

so. I took at least thirty minutes to eat a single Fiber One bar from my stash of US goodies. I allowed each tiny chocolate chip to melt in my mouth before moving onto the next bite. It was nuts, but that was something that kept me sane on a certain level, and always made the tougher days a little sweeter.

Your sleeping routines will most likely shift, as will your diets, and you may be more generally exposed to bacteria new to your immune system. These kinds of factors have the ability to alter your body: weight gain, weight loss, blemished skin, unsightly rashes, more body hair due to less shaving, tons of mosquito bites, etc. It can be hard to see your once fit and muscular spouse lose pound after pound because of limited access to food. Likewise, it can be frustrating to look into the mirror and see only a mop of frizz and a face with clogged pores. (Can you tell what happened to my husband and me?) The appearance of your body can fluctuate throughout your time abroad, and sometimes you will be annoyed with those changes. But at the end of the day, you married your significant other for his/her personal qualities, characteristics more important than physical attributes, and your spouse would undoubtedly say the same. So focus on your overall health, and try to leave the body image issues behind.

This final note is in regard to the wildlife that literally pops out of every nook and cranny in your new home: clouds of flies, scorpions, rats, snakes, head lice, spiders, giant grasshoppers, worms, maggots, etc. If you and your partner are serving in a warmer climate, ready yourselves for the constant battle against such creatures. I never got used to having to scan the grass for giant toads on my walk to work. One survey participant shared her own story of distress caused by such pests:

> I had a terrible allergy to fleas, which were rampant in the host family home where we stayed, making me quite miserable. My husband did not have this allergy, so for the first two months, I was more miserable and tired than him. (I could not sleep soundly with fleas.) I was wishing that I could sleep without feeling the fleas like my husband![19]

Hopefully your run-ins with critters will not last for months, but be prepared for a few creepy crawlies to wiggle their way into your beds … I mean life … but probably beds as well.

This section of the handbook is not meant to alarm you, it is merely meant to acknowledge the fact that you are not alone in experiencing physical discomfort. No matter how small the hardship, it *is* impactful, because it is just one of the many difficulties you and your spouse are going through. Although it may sound like a small consolation prize at this point, all your stories of "simple" living will make for some truly hilarious and unique anecdotes to share at future social gatherings back home.

Increased Conflict

As written in Chapter 1, marital and other family problems that exist prior to your departure will rarely improve under the strains of overseas living. Indeed, there is a high probability that those issues could worsen. Even the most stable of families can expect new stresses

---

19 Kenny, "Married Missioner/Volunteer Survey," 164.

while serving abroad.[20] Let us suppose that you were not able to solve all your marital and family problems before coming to this foreign place. (How did that not make the to-do list?) With all of the changing and transitioning involved at the beginning of an international mission experience, it should not come as a surprise if you and your spouse find yourselves arguing more than usual. Before we review the best method with which to approach conflict, it is important to understand that the key to reviving or cultivating a healthy relationship "is not in how you handle disagreements, but in how you are with each other when you are not fighting."[21] Therefore, focus first and foremost on nurturing your marital friendship. Refer to the first part of the exercise *Fondness and Admiration* in Chapter 2 if either of you feels that you could be more affectionate and tender toward your partner.

Developmental psychologist Evelyn Whitehead and husband pastoral theologian James Whitehead believe that when managed appropriately, conflict can make a constructive contribution to your marriage. It can bring you both to a more nuanced appreciation of each other, and it can deepen your capacity for mutual trust.[22] Similarly, the experience of facing together the conflicts that arise between you as spouses "can give greater confidence" and "increased security in the strength and flexibility of the commitment" you share.[23] As one survey participant wrote, "Working through the initial and subsequent difficulties we faced has helped us to value each other more, communicate better, and know how to best support one another."[24] Simply put, the presence of conflict in a marriage indicates that something in that relationship is worth fighting for. Dr. John Gottman affirms that couples who avoid conflict "don't get to know each other as well as couples who are more open to exploring their emotional differences. ...The hazards of conflict-avoiding relationships often become apparent when a husband and wife face a crisis" and lack the practiced knowledge of dispute-handling.[25] Exercising your capacities to disagree effectively will give you and your significant other blueprints that can guide you through addressing contentions that may surface during the realization stage.

Interestingly enough, anger is scientifically regarded as a positive emotion. "Images from brain scans show that we experience anger on the left side of our brain, the same region that experiences feelings of amusement and intense interest. Unlike sadness or fear—which are experienced on the right side of the brain and cause us to withdraw from the world—anger can stir us to engage with others, to take action, and to get involved."[26] Engaging with anger as a positive emotion can help you learn how to better express it. By expressing your anger in a healthy way, your partner is more likely to understand your perspective, which leads to less resentment and a greater chance at solving disagreements.[27]

---

20 Kohls, *Survival Kit,* 55.
21 Gottman and Silver, *Seven Principles,* 46.
22 Whitehead and Whitehead, *Marrying Well,* 317.
23 Whitehead and Whitehead, *Marrying Well,* 318.
24 Kenny, "Married Missioner/Volunteer Survey," 30.
25 Gottman, Gottman, and DeClaire, *Ten Lessons,* 55.
26 Gottman, Gottman, and DeClaire, *Ten Lessons,* 210.
27 Gottman, Gottman, and DeClaire, *Ten Lessons,* 211.

> **Conflict Resolution**[28]
> *Duration: 45–60 minutes/ongoing*

The following exercise is meant to help couples facilitate their problem-solving processes. Getting good at productive arguing takes time and repetition, so try to use the approaches in this activity whenever you and your partner have a difference of opinion.

STEP 1: Checklist. Each spouse will need a pen or a pencil. Designate a *Spouse #1* and a *Spouse #2*. Research shows that individuals with the highest expectations for marriage usually wind up with the highest-quality partnerships. One way to hold your marriage to a high standard is by regularly assessing it. In doing so, you and your partner can detect small issues in your marital relationship before they grow into big ones. Below is a list of questions that you should ask yourself if you feel emotionally distant from your significant other.

This step is to be done as individuals. *Spouse #1* is to review the checklist and then place an X next to as many statements as he/she believes apply to what he/she is currently experiencing. Once finished, cover up the left-hand side of the page and have *Spouse #2* review the checklist and place their Xs as prompted above.

Spouse #1		Spouse #2
_____	I have been feeling irritated.	_____
_____	There has been a lot of tension between us.	_____
_____	I find myself wanting to be somewhere else.	_____
_____	I have been feeling lonely.	_____
_____	My partner has seemed emotionally unavailable to me.	_____
_____	I have been angry.	_____
_____	We have been out of touch with each other.	_____
_____	My partner has little idea of what I am thinking.	_____
_____	We have been under a lot of stress, and it has taken a toll on us.	_____
_____	I wish we were closer right now.	_____
_____	I have wanted to be alone a lot.	_____
_____	My partner has been acting irritable.	_____
_____	My partner's attention seems to be somewhere else.	_____
_____	I have been emotionally unavailable to my partner.	_____
_____	My partner has been angry.	_____
_____	I have little idea of what my partner is thinking.	_____
_____	My partner has wanted to be alone a lot.	_____
_____	We really need to talk.	_____
_____	We have not been communicating very well.	_____
_____	We have been fighting more than usual.	_____
_____	Lately, small issues escalate.	_____
_____	We have been hurting each other's feelings.	_____
_____	There has not been much fun or joy in our lives.	_____

---

28 Adapted from Gottman and Silver, *Seven Principles,* 159, 164–66, 173–75, 178, 181, 263 and Gottman, Gottman, and DeClaire, *Ten Lessons,* 172–75, 193–94, 217.

STEP 2: *Results.* If either you or your spouse placed an X by more than <u>four</u> statements, plan on discussing why each of you did so within the next few days. The subsequent steps will help facilitate your conversation.

STEP 3: *Soft Startups.* This step is for the individual who initiates an issue-resolving conversation. Softening your intro, or startup, in the beginning stages of conflict resolution is extremely important; as discussions invariably end on the same note they begin. A startup should be devoid of criticism, contempt, or defensiveness. Here are a few specific suggestions to help ensure that your startup is soft:

- **Complain but do not blame.** Go from this: *"You're always coming home from work way too late. It's like you do not even care about your own family"* to this: *"Hun, you have been working a lot. The kids miss you. I miss you. Can we talk about your schedule?"*

- **Make statements that start with "I" instead of "You."** Go from this: *"You make me do all the housework here. There are always ants everywhere"* to this: *"I feel overwhelmed with household chores. Can we take the compost outside after every meal? Doing so will give us a fighting chance at keeping bugs out of the house."*

- **Describe what is happening, do not evaluate or judge.** Instead of accusing or blaming your partner, describe what you see happening in your relationship. Use the X-Y-Z Statement: "When you did (or did not do) X in situation Y, I felt Z." This will help prevent your spouse from feeling attacked and retaliating in response.[29] Here is an example: *"When you spent money on those souvenirs (X) when we were on vacation (Y), I felt angry (Z)."*

- **Be clear.** Tell your partner what you want rather than what you do not want. Express your needs openly and suggest certain courses of action your significant other could take to meet your needs. Go from this: *"You are not as much fun as you used to be"* to this: *"I feel like we have been having less fun together. Maybe we could play a board game sometime this week."*

- **Be polite.** Go from this: *"Kiss me darn it"* to this: *"Could you <u>please</u> be more physically affectionate with me when we are alone together?"*

- **Be appreciative.** If your spouse has, at some point, handled a situation better, then couch your request with a statement of gratefulness that acknowledges what your partner did right in the past and how much you miss that. *"Remember how you used to wait for me to get ready for bed so we could go to sleep together? I always thought that was so nice of you. Can we start doing that again?"*

- **Do not store things up.** It is hard to be gentle when you are ready to burst with recriminations. So do not wait too long before bringing up an issue, otherwise it can intensify in your mind. *"I know you need to prepare for work right now, but can we figure out a time when we can talk tomorrow? I have something I need to discuss with you."*

---

29 Gottman and Silver, *Why Marriages Succeed or Fail*, 191–92.

STEP 4: Questions. This step is for the individual on the receiving end of the startups. Try to respond to your spouse's statement(s) of need with open-ended questions. This will encourage the idea of "anecdotes before antidotes." In other words, it is better to let your significant other communicate his/her feelings and for you to understand those feelings before either of you begins brainstorming solutions. Below are examples of phrases you may consider utilizing in order to facilitate this process:

- What are all your feelings about this issue?
- Tell me why this is so important to you.
- I may not be looking at it in the same way you are. Tell me how you would like to approach this.
- What are your goals around this issue?
- Help me understand why you feel so strongly about this.
- What are your needs here?
- What do you want to see happen?
- What is frustrating for you in this situation?
- What obstacles are in the way of getting what you want?
- What is painful about this situation?
- What are some other things that we can do to accomplish this same goal?
- How can I help you?

STEP 5: Repair Attempts. A repair attempt is anything either partner can do in order to de-escalate tension in a problem-solving conversation. Repair attempts range from suggesting a timeout (*"I need a break. Can we talk about this in twenty minutes?"*) to expressions of acknowledgement (*"Shoot, I should not have said that."*) to personal requests (*"Do you think you can communicate more positively?"*). In conflict, both spouses need to learn how to make and receive repair attempts. Below you will find a list of neutralizing phrases. These are specific statements you can say to each other as to reduce the stress-filled energy often present in disagreements. By using them when arguments get too negative, you will be better able to keep your discussions from spiraling out of control.

- I feel defensive. Can you reword that?
- I need things to be calmer right now.
- I need your support right now.
- I need to finish what I was saying.
- My reaction was too extreme. I am sorry.
- Let me try again.
- I can see my part in all of this.
- How can I make things better?
- Can we compromise?
- I never thought of things that way.
- Your point of view makes sense.
- I might be wrong here.
- Hang in there. Please do not withdraw.
- We are getting off track.
- I know this is not your fault.
- Thank you for …
- This is not your problem, it is *our* problem.

Some of these repair attempts may sound unnatural. That is because they offer a very different way of speaking with your spouse when you are upset. Formalizing repair attempts by using set phrases can help to defuse disagreements by ensuring that both you and your partner are paying attention to the situations that give rise to these attempts. Once you have incorporated these types of de-escalators consistently into your conflict-resolving conversations, other, more personalized attempts will organically appear. Be patient with yourselves as you adopt and adapt to this new way of communicating.

STEP 6: Self-Soothing. Knowing how to calm down is a skill that will help prevent unproductive fighting or running away from discussions that need to be had. If your disputes tend to physically agitate and/or mentally exhaust you or your spouse, taking a break during such disagreements may be necessary. Work to give yourselves twenty-minute breaks, since it will take that long for your bodies to relax. It is crucial that during this time you avoid thoughts of righteous indignation or innocent victimhood. Instead, spend your break doing something therapeutically distracting. Here are several self-soothing techniques:

- **Space.** If you feel like it would be helpful, leave the room you are currently in and find a different place to calm down.
- **Breathe.** Sit up straight in a chair, or lie on your back on the floor. Focus on regulating your breathing. Take slow, deep breaths.
- **Relax your Muscles.** Do this exercise in a comfortable position. One at a time, tightly squeeze the muscle group(s) that feel tense, usually your forehead, jaw, neck, shoulders, arms, and back. Hold for two seconds, then release. Repeat as needed.
- **Imagery.** Many people find it effective to think of a scene they associate with peacefulness, like a forest, a lake, or a beach. Imagine this place as vividly as you can. Keep focused on this vision for thirty seconds. Repeat as needed.
- **Pray.** Recite memorized prayers, say a rosary decade, or read your favorite Scripture passages. If you would find it therapeutic, pray for your spouse during this time.
- **Mindless Chores.** Some individuals like completing simple tasks in times of stress. Such tasks can include: washing or folding laundry, sweeping, doing the dishes, or organizing personal space.
- **Music.** Sing, whistle, hum, or listen to a familiar and uplifting tune. Redirect and quiet your thoughts while doing so.

STEP 7: Compromise. Negotiation is easier after having completed the previous steps: softening startups, candidly exploring the topic at hand, repairing discussions, and creating/re-creating soothing situations. Following these steps prime you and your partner for compromise by making your conflict healthy and accessible. Before you try to resolve any issues, remember that the cornerstone of compromise is being able to accept influence from your spouse. This means that, for compromise to work, you cannot have a closed-minded attitude toward your partner's opinions or desires. You do not have to agree with everything your significant other says or believes, but you have to be honestly open in considering his/her position. Refer to the exercise *Finding Common Ground* in Chapter 1 to help facilitate further negotiations.

Forgiveness

Not all your disagreements can be resolved. Some arguments will end, not only without positive conclusions, but also with harsh words said and feelings hurt. It is here that forgiveness as the ultimate "Christian relational skill" becomes important.[30] For Jesus, the apex and highest expression of mercy is the commandment to love one's enemies through forgiving them. At times, our spouse can be our worst enemy, as he/she has both the know-how and ability to cause us great pain. If the person with whom we most intimately share our life's experience hurts us in some way, the wound of their failure is piercing and down-reaching. Yet it is in this injury that God invites us to forgive. Forgiving your partner (and others) is making manifest God's mercy in the here and now. As theologian Walter Kasper explains, "If God treats us mercifully and forgives, then we too must forgive and show mercy to one another. In our acts of mercy, God's mercy for our neighbor becomes concretely realized. In our acts of mercy, our neighbors experience something of the miracle of God's royal dominion."[31] In marriage, your spouse is not just your neighbor, he/she is *the* neighbor. Thus, ensuring that you and your significant other each have developed your capabilities to forgive is paramount.

Dr. Everett Worthington, professor of psychology at Virginia Commonwealth University and expert on forgiveness, has made a distinction between two types of forgiveness: "decisional forgiveness" is a statement of the victim's intentions about future behavior, in that they will not seek revenge, but rather aim to treat the offender as a person of value. One can make a decision to forgive and still harbor negative emotions toward the offender. "Emotional forgiveness" is the victim's emotional replacement of negative, unforgiving emotions (i.e., resentment, hostility, anger, and fear) with positive-oriented emotions (i.e., empathy, sympathy, compassion, and love).[32]

As a married couple, you and your spouse must look to forgive one another both on a decisional and an emotional level. Dr. Worthington has developed a five-step process in attaining such multileveled forgiveness. This process is called REACH:

- **R**ecall the hurt caused by your partner objectively, without feeling victimized
- **E**motionally replace negative feelings had toward your spouse with empathy and compassion
- **A**ltruistic gift-giving—remember a time when your significant other forgave you, and offer that same gift of forgiveness in return
- **C**ommit to forgiveness by saying to your partner, "*I forgive you*"
- **H**old on to and honor the choice you made to forgive your spouse[33]

Work to turn this process into a habit. If you and your partner are able to make your approach to forgiveness receptive and authentic, your marital relationship will be strengthened in mercy.

---

30 David M. Thomas, *Christian Marriage: The New Challenge* (Collegeville, MN: Liturgical Press, 2007), 11.

31 Kasper, *Theology of Christian Marriage,* 133.

32 Ryan Martin, "Five Questions with Forgiveness Expert, Dr. Everett Worthington," *All the Rage: Commentary and Resources on the Science of Anger and Violence,* April 29, 2011, http://blog.uwgb.edu/alltherage/five-questions-with-forgiveness-expert-dr-everett-worthington/.

33 Martin, "Five Questions."

Ministry

Nearly all international service can be described by the maxim "Always doing, never done." The work you have committed to is good, hard work. From teaching underserved populations, to sharing your faith, to sustainable farming, to all other types of life-giving ministries—each will have its own difficulties. Below are several variables concerning your service commitment that can become stressors if not properly managed and that can then, in turn, negatively affect your marital relationship:

Location. If you live on the same property as your site (or very close by), you may find it hard to establish clear boundaries between your work and home life—as regards both time and relationships. Spending time and creating meaningful friendships with locals and other community members is fruitful only when done in a balanced manner. If your home is farther away from your volunteer site, a longer commute to work naturally constructs relational boundaries. However, more time spent in transit means less time serving and being with your spouse/family. Living in a secluded locale can take its toll. One survey participant confirmed this in writing, "Our middle assignment was at a very isolated location (closest road 175 miles away), which created stresses even though we had other co-workers around us."[34] Serving in rural communities can be difficult and sometimes dangerous. If your mission placement is remote, do what you can to keep safe and find companions.

Type. What is the nature of your ministry? Are you working with people or paper? Are most of the tasks you are charged with simple or complex? For whom are you responsible? What does your preparation look like when off the clock? Do you have secondary or tertiary assignments? Try to be aware of how your job(s) can be overwhelming, and work to lessen avoidable pressures: cut back your work hours, ask for extra support, simplify responsibilities, delegate tasks, find ways to manage time more efficiently, and/or simply say no to unreasonable requests asked of you.

Language. Does your job require you to know another language? Can you speak that language? Learning the language of another culture is important because the act of communication is symbolically significant. In its most basic form, "the attempt to speak with people in a foreign country is an acknowledgement of their humanity and individual worth"—a sign that you take them and their concerns seriously.[35] So in case you were hoping to skate through a few years abroad with minimal knowledge of the local language, think about what kind of message that sends, and how that will affect your work and social life. Varying levels of language proficiency between spouses was a frequently mentioned source of tension by survey participants:

- "My husband and I learned the language at very different paces and at different levels. Ultimately, that was frustrating for my husband."[36]
- "My wife's Spanish was always a struggle."[37]
- "My issue was relying on my spouse for language support."[38]

---

34 Ken Wiggers, personal e-mail, March 20, 2015.
35 Storti, *The Art of Crossing Cultures*, 90.
36 Kenny, "Married Missioner/Volunteer Survey," 21.
37 Kenny, "Married Missioner/Volunteer Survey," 23.
38 Kenny, "Married Missioner/Volunteer Survey," 157.

If this is a cause of friction for either you or your partner, discuss possible coping strategies together.

Hours. How many hours a week are you working? If you do not know the answer to this question, calculate it right now to ensure that it is a feasible number. Often, and unfortunately so, prolonged mental, emotional, and spiritual exhaustion/stress is an implicit part of a service experience. Take the necessary breaks from your mission commitment so that you avoid burnout and can properly care for yourself and your marital relationship.

Spouse. Are you working directly with your partner? If so, be mindful that this setup may be a new kind of situation that needs your extra attention. One program staff member shared some counsel concerning this topic:

> Most couples don't work together in the U.S. So if they do in mission this can mean a lot more time together—which they won't necessarily be used to. Individuals in a marriage usually need just as much of their own time and space as individuals who are not married. This can lead to problems if this is not acknowledged and prepared for in advance.[39]

Remember to honor your I–You–We experience of service. Adapting to being with your spouse in a different way may require additional time apart, or additional time together in conversation.

If you and your partner have different ministry placements, it may be beneficial for you both to look at the factors in this section and talk about which ones are unique unto your separate assignments. Contrasts in these variables can influence rates of personal adjustment. As one former missioner related, "My wife had more problems with her boss and that affected her rate of transition."[40] Help one another deal with the hardships present within your respective service sites. Be aware of how your partner's workplace experience may be impacting his/her cultural acclimation.

If one spouse works outside the home while the other does not, you may want to heed this survey participant's advice: "In many cases, the toughest cross-cultural challenges will be for the person who is mostly responsible for running the household; strange food choices, house helpers, open markets and no supermarkets, and raising children in a foreign land."[41] A difference in where you and your significant other spend the majority of your day could create tension in your relationship, which is no one's fault. As mentioned earlier, if one partner loves his/her ministry site and the other spouse barely gets out of the house, then your rates and degrees of ease in becoming culturally immersed could be markedly different.

Community. The two of you may have agreed to live in an intentional community. Due to the complexity and scope of this topic, an entire section has been dedicated to it. To that section we now turn.

---

39 Vic Doucette, personal e-mail, April 11, 2015.
40 Kenny, "Married Missioner/Volunteer Survey," 157.
41 Kenny, "Married Missioner/Volunteer Survey," 36.

Intentional Community

As defined in Chapter 1, an intentional community is a planned, residential living situation where members typically hold similar values and are dedicated to maintaining relationships of cohesion and teamwork. Your volunteer program may have established particular principles or goals for you and your housemates to focus on or meet. A good friend once shared with me a fitting analogy of what living with fellow missioners in such a community is like: someone places several jagged and pointy rocks into a bag, shakes it vigorously for quite some time, and then pulls out the stones, now smooth and polished. Living in community is a painful yet often meaningful and effective experience of personal development. Survey participants shared a wide range of opinions about being part of an intentional community:

- "Community living as a married couple was hard. I wish I had done more reading about community and shared life before going."[42]
- "It was a challenge to share a three-bedroom apartment with three couples, but overall the challenge could only be described as strengthening."[43]
- "The hardest part was the interactions in our house. My husband felt caught in the middle a lot because I had a hard time with people we were living with but no one seemed to have a hard time with him."[44]
- "Living in community was good for my spouse and me. It allowed us to lean on other people, more than on just each other."[45]

If you and your partner are sharing your living space with others, read on to learn about ways in which you can make this lifestyle choice a positive one.

Many of the issues about which you and your spouse are worried as a couple living in community are likely the same concerns your single housemates are harboring. One single missioner shared some of the anxieties she had about being housed with married individuals:

> I was very apprehensive about living with a couple in an intentional community because I feared that they would be so focused on themselves and their marriage that they would not be present or supportive to the rest of the community. Having felt the pain of living with inwardly focused couples in previous communities, I was prepared for loneliness and annoyance.[46]

Similarly, you and your partner may also be nervous about the possibility of neglecting either your marital relationship or the community to which you have committed. If you are housed with other married couples, ideally you will find a collective understanding among yourselves and can help one another navigate such experiences.

While overseas, giving individuals the benefit of the doubt should be exercised beyond the normal boundaries of Westernized prescriptions. People are in reactive mode after having moved to a foreign country. First impressions can easily turn into negative impressions, as

---

42 Kenny, "Married Missioner/Volunteer Survey," 16.
43 Kenny, "Married Missioner/Volunteer Survey," 32.
44 Kenny, "Married Missioner/Volunteer Survey," 21.
45 Kenny, "Married Missioner/Volunteer Survey," 16.
46 Emma Strobel, personal e-mail, April 13, 2015.

you and your new housemate(s) may be uncomfortable for a variety of reasons.[47] You and your partner have a distinct advantage in meeting your community members for the first time, as each of you has the other, and that other is someone who knows and recognizes you for who you are. Your single counterparts do not have these same advantages, at least in the beginning. Be aware of this fact and how that might influence group dynamics. Remember, the path to establishing friendships with your community mates (and others at your ministry site) is a long one. People will come to know who you are over time, so do not feel pressured (or compelled) to disclose your entire life story within hours of meeting someone.

One of the first reactions a husband and wife can have when living in a shared housing situation is to draw inward into their marriage, for it is a safe and familiar place. However, overusing the security found between yourselves can cause you and your partner to disengage from potentially fulfilling friendships. Help motivate one another to create relationships beyond your own, for life outside your marriage needs to be equally as satisfying as life within it. Forming connections with housemates early on in the realization phase is often easier, as your fellow missioners are eager to be understood and valued since they, too, have undergone and are grieving their own losses (e.g., role, material, intrapsychic, etc.). If you or your spouse waits too long to initiate such contact with those whom you share a home, you may find that inserting yourselves into community-mate friendships made months earlier feels forced and may be unreciprocated.

If you are not the kind of person who is quick out of the socializing starting blocks, work to prompt those plodding feet. If the opposite is true, cheer on your partner and keep a steady pace. Each spouse will engage with community members in his or her own way. If you are a couple that is comprised of an extrovert and an introvert, try to ensure that this difference in personality type does not put a strain on your marriage. One survey participant shared her experience of this kind of tension:

> I felt like we were never alone. He [my husband] is very social and liked to be around people more than I did. I would often want to go to our room to be alone with him, but he would want to be in the common space having conversations with those that we lived with. This became very stressful for us.[48]

Such a situation may sound familiar, for it is safe to assume that living in community means that the two of you will not have the same level of privacy you were probably accustomed to in your passport country. One former missioner wrote in agreement, "The walls didn't reach the ceiling, so we felt like we couldn't process things with each other as freely as we would've liked for fear of being overheard."[49] Yet another commented, "We ran a dormitory, and it took a while to set boundaries appropriate for us and our 'couple-ness.'"[50] Living arrangements with a general absence of private space is a reality at most service sites. Do your best to create an environment of solitude and separateness for yourself and your spouse, and work to keep communication lines up and open.

---

47 Pascoe, *Culture Shock! Successful Living Abroad,* 138.
48 Kenny, "Married Missioner/Volunteer Survey," 119.
49 Kenny, "Married Missioner/Volunteer Survey," 119.
50 Kenny, "Married Missioner/Volunteer Survey," 119.

In-Home Help

On a note similar to community living is the topic of in-home help.[51] Some overseas families are able to employ local caregivers. "The introduction of such a new and significant member to a household may enrich ... [or test] the nuclear family in ways that have no precedent in ordinary family life."[52] Making a native caretaker part of your family system is a commitment to contemplate thoughtfully. Like every other matter in this handbook, there are a few variables to consider: Do you want live-in or part-time help? Male or female? Does age matter? English language competency? Is this a trigger situation for a spouse concerning infidelity? How will payment work? What responsibilities do you want this person to assume? Regardless of the specifics of your joint decision, another person in your home will mean less privacy and more emotions to take into account.

Young children build their identities through their relationships with adult caregivers. Because children do not have the cognitive tools to withhold the identification process until their parents are around, they may naturally assume characteristics of their local nanny.[53] You and your partner should talk about your child's personal growth and how it will be impacted by the choice you make in relation to childrearing determinations.

Expatriate counselor Robin Pascoe offers two final pieces of advice on this topic: if you decide to travel without your children and feel a little uneasy about leaving them home alone with your native *au pair*, explore the option of moving your hired caretaker into a friend's house during your trip so that there will be a natural source of supervision.[54] Also, if you have a wonderful individual helping you at home, professional boundaries may start to dissolve. Think about how invested you want to be in this person's life, for issues of money and immigration may be brought up.[55]

Children

Spouses who neglect the health of their marriage while overseas may inadvertently create a stressful family environment. A strained home life has the potential to impede your child's maturation process. "Children who live with unspoken tension in the family may become anxious, depressed, introverted, and withdrawn. Children who live with hostility and contempt become aggressive with their peers."[56] The last thing you and your partner want to do is make your child's transition abroad even harder because of your inability to maintain a healthy marital relationship. "In fact," say Dr. Gottman and colleagues, "the best thing you can do for your child is to take good care of your marriage."[57] This may seem counterintuitive, but when you observe parents who care for each other—who listen and respond to each other's needs—they are in fact providing their kids with great role modeling for how to

---

51 As an author, I want to acknowledge that I have no personal background in this area (or in the following section on *Children*), and thus, am relying on the theoretical and experiential input of others to inform my writing and opinions.
52 Werkman, "Coming Home," 8–9.
53 Kristen Herh, introduction to *Living & Working Abroad: A Parent's Guide*, ed. Robin Pascoe (London: Kuperard, 1994), 19.
54 Pascoe, *Culture Shock! Successful Living Abroad,* 125.
55 Pascoe, *Culture Shock! Successful Living Abroad,* 121.
56 Gottman, Gottman, and DeClaire, *Ten Lessons*, 233.
57 Gottman, Gottman, and DeClaire, *Ten Lessons*, 224.

appropriately form and sustain relationships. Contented spouses make happy parents who are then able to create a relaxed, joyful atmosphere where kids can thrive physically, emotionally, and intellectually.[58] Thus, know that whenever you are working on your marriage, you are also being a more positive and effective mother or father for your child.

Gottman asserts that a common phenomenon that occurs in many marital relationships is the construction of a child-centered marriage. This happens when a couple uses their parenting obligations as an excuse for neglecting their own relationship. In a child-centered marriage, kids become the greatest distraction—a convenient way to ignore one's need for adult conversations or to side-step marital problems that ought to be addressed.[59] Frequent excuses of avoidance include blaming your child's sleeping patterns for your lack of shared intimacy, allowing your child's needs or new activities to trump opportunities for time spent together as a couple, or making the assignment of one spouse an absolute priority because of his/her commitment to your mission organization. Think about the ways in which you may be consciously averting personal responsibilities concerning your partner or your marriage. Give an honest voice to this introspection and, if necessary, dialogue with your significant other about such issues.

How your children transition to international living will directly affect your overseas ministry. One survey participant conceded in writing, "Our youngest daughter was having a difficult time adjusting, and she would cry a lot and loudly in the evenings, which made us feel uncomfortable since we shared a space with another family."[60] Another former missioner shared a similar experience: "The first night we were there one of our daughters came knocking on our door because she had to go to the bathroom. It was pouring rain. With umbrella in hand, we walked to the small room which had only a commode."[61] Be in conversation with your kids about their own experiences of moving abroad and how they feel they are adapting to your host country. Bed-wetting, unprovoked temper tantrums, nightmares, thumb sucking, poor academic performance, and teenage despondency are common symptoms of culture shock seen in children. "Watch for mood changes at holidays, birthdays, or other annual milestones which may make your children long for the way such occasions were marked at home."[62] If you and your partner undergo a shift in parental role orientation, be aware of how your child responds to it. He or she may seek out the parent perceived to be the more competent, which can exacerbate an already tenuous situation. Give your children some autonomy in their adjustment; let them decorate their room, honor reasonable requests to visit new friends, or together re-create a routine your family had in your passport country. You might even consider encouraging your kids to make their own self-care stars by completing part of the exercise *I–You–We Care Stars* in Chapter 2.

Decreased Intimacy

Many married volunteers experience a general decrease in leisure-time companionship, effective communication, and problem-solving skills during the time after their initial move abroad.[63] With such a decline of interpersonal competencies, it is understandable that a

58 Gottman, Gottman, and DeClaire, *Ten Lessons*, 233.
59 Gottman, Gottman, and DeClaire, *Ten Lessons*, 232.
60 Kenny, "Married Missioner/Volunteer Survey," 119.
61 Bridget Studer, personal e-mail, March 28, 2015.
62 Pascoe, *Culture Shock! Successful Living Abroad,* 68.
63 Koteskey, "Missionary Marriage Issues," 31–32.

couple's desire to be intimate is also negatively impacted. Abatement of affection can be compounded if you and your partner live in a shared housing arrangement, as many former missioners attest:

- "Being intimate was difficult. Trying to transition into a new country and new culture would have been easier if we had more privacy."[64]
- "We were timid when being intimate. We knew there were specific times when it would be okay to be intimate, otherwise people could have seen or heard us clearly when walking by."[65]
- "Making room for connection and intimacy at the end of exhausting and challenging days was difficult."[66]

Clearly, the lifestyle of an overseas volunteer is not one conducive of consistent emotional and physical closeness.

Intimacy, as a psychological strength that grounds an individual's capacity to love, is not strictly about sexuality or romance. Being intimate with your spouse means being open to the invitation to understand your partner on a deeply personal level. "Intimacy requires an overlapping of space, a willingness to be influenced, and accepting the possibility of change."[67] Interestingly enough, the Hebrew word used for describing Adam and Eve's intimate and sexual union in the Bible is a noun derived from the verb *yada*, meaning "to know." While the physical piece of intimacy is real and important, the emotional and spiritual "knowing" of the person with whom you are being intimate is a prerequisite of sorts. Without the emotional and spiritual commitment made in the form of marriage, sexual intimacy falls short of its original purpose. Full encounters of intimacy (emotional, spiritual, and physical) have been and continue to be a significant part of married life for Christians.

It can be assumed that couples reading this handbook will have varying opinions about what role lovemaking should have in their marriages. I am not interested in generating value judgments about what anyone decides in that regard. This section exists to call attention to the fact that "no other area of a couple's life offers more potential for embarrassment, hurt, and rejection than sex."[68] Therefore, you and your partner will benefit from being able to talk to each other about lovemaking in a manner that lets you both feel safe. According to Gottman, "That means learning the right way to ask for what you want, and the appropriate way to react to your spouse's requests. Because most people feel vulnerable about whether they are attractive to their spouse and a 'good' lover, the key to talking about sex is to be gentle."[69] Create space for you and your partner to engage in honest and relaxed dialogue about where you both feel you are at in terms of physical closeness. If the two of you decide that you want to strengthen the sexual intimacy of your relationship, then you might consider planning times of shared affection.

"But scheduling sex and romance takes all the spontaneity out of it!" Gottman provides a compelling response to this natural protest. Think about the most romantic times in your

64 Kenny, "Married Missioner/Volunteer Survey," 119.
65 Kenny, "Married Missioner/Volunteer Survey," 119.
66 Kenny, "Married Missioner/Volunteer Survey," 21.
67 Whitehead and Whitehead, *Marrying Well*, 227.
68 Gottman and Silver, *Seven Principles*, 200.
69 Gottman and Silver, *Seven Principles*, 201.

relationship. If you are like most people, you will be remembering those first few dates. Now think back to how you used to get ready for those outings. You may recall preparations that were anything but spontaneous. Those carefully placed spritzes of perfume, packed breath mints, and extra glances in the mirror added fuel to the sense of anticipation and excitement for the evening ahead.[70] Similarly, setting aside time for intimacy not only protects lovemaking from the incessant demands of a married missioner's life abroad, but it can also help focus and give special attention to this act of "knowing."[71] If this kind of scheduling causes performance anxiety, talk about those fears with your partner. Your spouse should be able to offer reassurance and lower his or her own expectations so you both can focus on simply being together. It is OK if sex does not happen during your "dates" of intimacy. You are still fulfilling the commitment to spending time with one another.[72] In order to help you and your partner better manage your time, the following section will address this topic and include a related activity.

Time Management

You are in good company if you find it difficult to juggle taking care of yourself, your marriage and your family, fulfilling your ministerial responsibilities, honoring your intentional community commitments, and so on. Many survey participants admitted it was hard to create a balanced schedule while in mission. In response to the question *"What were some of the greatest challenges you faced as a couple while serving abroad?"* individuals responded:

- "Getting time together, keeping our marriage a priority."[73]
- "It was exhausting to be in constant demand from the community around you to serve, counsel, help, lead, etc. This sometimes left little time and energy to focus on our marriage and family."[74]
- "Figuring out a schedule that included sufficient family time."[75]
- "Finding time for each other while also being present to the kids and other volunteers."[76]
- "Managing our time was difficult, as we were pulled in different directions all of the time."[77]
- "Finding time for each other, communication, balancing service opportunities and community living with our partnership."[78]

As you can see, ensuring that you and your spouse are spending enough quality time together is tough. And yet, making a space in your schedules for time shared is critical in maintaining a healthy marriage. While there are many different ways to spend time together (e.g., trouble-shooting marital problems, discussing conflicts, or actual parenting), leisure time enjoyed as a couple is the first type of activity that gets neglected when lives get busy. However, developing a sense of companionship is what will allow you to get through

---

70 Gottman, Gottman, and DeClaire, *Ten Lessons*, 240.
71 Whitehead and Whitehead, *Marrying Well*, 232.
72 Gottman, Gottman, and DeClaire, *Ten Lessons*, 240-241.
73 Kenny, "Married Missioner/Volunteer Survey," 20.
74 Kenny, "Married Missioner/Volunteer Survey," 33.
75 Kenny, "Married Missioner/Volunteer Survey," 22.
76 Kenny, "Married Missioner/Volunteer Survey," 20.
77 Kenny, "Married Missioner/Volunteer Survey," 33.
78 Kenny, "Married Missioner/Volunteer Survey," 20.

future crises with greater ease. If you consider your partner a friend, facing transitions and changes can be done as a team, with each of you supporting the other.

Synchronized Schedules
Duration: 30–45 minutes

This activity will give each of you an overview of what your weekly schedules look like, help you to prioritize your responsibilities, and grant you the foresight needed in order to plan time meant specifically for nurturing the friendship in your marriage. Please note that this exercise can be unrealistic in certain ministerial settings; as unpredictability and spontaneity are hallmark characteristics of much service work. Engage with this activity at whatever level is appropriate and applicable in your shared context.

STEP 1: Weekly Calendars. Each partner will need a pen or a pencil. Designate a *Spouse #1* and a *Spouse #2*. Take a look at the timetable sheets on the next two pages. Partners are to "shade in" a weekly calendar with his or her own personal schedule. Include ministerial obligations, household responsibilities, individual commitments, etc.

STEP 2: Couple Time. Once you have both finished blocking out your schedules, compare calendars and see where you both have or could create overlapping free time. You should be looking to spend at least <u>two hours</u> of private, leisure time together per week.

STEP 3: Ritualize It. After figuring out what days and times you plan on being together, each of you is to write this information under the "Notes" section. Next, brainstorm relaxing and fun activities attractive to both of you (e.g., watching a movie, walking outside and talking, or reading and discussing a book). Again, write down all your ideas in the same space underneath your respective timetable.

Honor this commitment by making it a top priority in your life abroad. If your mission responsibilities change frequently, you may want to consider designating a day on which the two of you review your schedules for the upcoming week and plan your free time accordingly.

Spouse #1	Sunday	Monday	Tuesday	Wednesday	Thursday	Friday	Saturday
5:00							
6:00							
7:00							
8:00							
9:00							
10:00							
11:00							
12:00							
13:00							
14:00							
15:00							
16:00							
17:00							
18:00							
19:00							
20:00							
21:00							
22:00							

Notes

Spouse #2	Sunday	Monday	Tuesday	Wednesday	Thursday	Friday	Saturday
5:00							
6:00							
7:00							
8:00							
9:00							
10:00							
11:00							
12:00							
13:00							
14:00							
15:00							
16:00							
17:00							
18:00							
19:00							
20:00							
21:00							
22:00							

Notes

Top Ten List

Here is a "Top Ten List" of the things missionary couples did that kept their relationship afloat during their time overseas. This list is in order according to the frequency in which themes were reported by survey participants. It begins with the subject least mentioned (10) and ends with the topic most referenced (1). Introducing this lineup during the realization phase means that you and your partner can implement these practices early on in your service experience.

> 10. Inquire about and ask for help if you are feeling overwhelmed as a spouse (e.g., support groups, marital therapy, spiritual directors, or mentor relationships).
> 9. Make decisions and plans as a couple.
> 8. Get involved in the surrounding community and maintain your individual hobbies.
> 7. Seek out fellowship, receive what sacraments are available to you, and/or read Scripture.
> 6. Encourage, advocate, and support each other through words and actions.
> 5. Create healthy friendships outside of your marriage.
> 4. Take allotted vacation time and/or plan trips to get a break from your ministerial work.
> 3. Make time to be alone as a couple in order to connect and have fun.
> 2. Pray together and for one another.
> 1. Consistently communicate about important and/or difficult issues.

Heed this sound advice, for it comes from those who have been where you and your partner are and have survived to share the counsel.

Miscellaneous

There are so many adjustments to be made during the realization phase. The following points are some other types of dynamics and events you or your spouse may encounter as a couple during the beginning of your time abroad:

Ensure that you and your partner are safe. Many countries in which volunteers serve are developing and lack stable systems of justice and security. If the everyday reality of your host country was misrepresented to you by your sending organization, you may find yourself commuting through hazardous areas, facing threatening situations, and/or working with unpredictable individuals. One survey participant wrote, "When I first started I had zero concerns. Once I saw our actual neighborhood, I thought out loud, 'What did I sign up for?'"[79] Another missioner shared, "The biggest 'shock' for me was the limited/unsuitable housing we were provided. We had been told it would be adequate for a family, but it did not meet my expectations for 'adequate.'"[80] Voice your concerns to authority figures on-site (if there are any), and petition for changes to be made that could better help care for everyone affiliated with the program. Only you and your spouse will be able to decide what kind of tolerance you have for the potential danger/discomfort you may encounter while overseas.

---

79 Kenny, "Married Missioner/Volunteer Survey," 18.
80 Bridget Studer, personal e-mail, March 28, 2015.

Your partner is a source of revelation. You may be aware of the fact that sometimes your significant other sees progress or relapses in your personal development before you do. This is both an exciting and humbling aspect of marriage. Your spouse is a means of self-discovery. Though frustrating at times, having someone around to keep you honest and accountable is a wonderful asset.

Seek out a local mentor. Finding a native guide can be extremely useful in navigating the first few months of your mission experience. While you and your spouse may have done some research on the social mores within your host country, there will always be more to learn. Establishing a relationship with a credible local can deepen your understanding of the conventions that exist in your new home and prevent misconceptions. A former volunteer shared a humorous example of his encounter with a cultural mishap:

> One of our friends from our Papua New Guinea days was living in a remote village with her husband to learn the language for Bible translation. After several months, one of the elderly ladies told her that her name "Judy" was a bad word in their local language that had sexual innuendos! From then on Judy's name became Jaki for all of us. But how long it could have gone on if some trust hadn't been established with this woman, no one knows.[81]

Avoiding these kinds of situations can be easily done if the two of you are able to find same-sex, local confidants (it is easier that way), who can act as advisers and assist each of you in living fully and successfully in (insert host country).

Record your experiences. Adding yet another thing "to do" while you are first adjusting to a new culture may seem like too much at this point, but you and your partner should try to make journaling a part of your daily or weekly routines. Being able to physically hold and read an account of your international experiences will be invaluable when you return home. The following activity can help each of you find a writing exercise that best suits your personal reflection styles.

Write It Down[82]
Duration: 5–20 minutes/ongoing

Several survey participants reported that they wish they had consistently kept a journal of sorts while abroad. The memories you will make (and are currently making) are precious gems of encounters with God, "lived through" wisdom, and occasions of hilarity. Collecting these moments in retrospect is a difficult task, so consider creating a writing regimen now.

STEP 1: Ideas. The following list is comprised of different ways in which you and your partner can record your time in mission. As individuals, review the bullet points and select at least <u>two</u> methods you could imagine turning into a regular form of journaling.

---

81 Ken Wiggers, personal e-mail, March 20, 2015.
82 Adapted from "25 Ways to Fill a Journal Page," *HubPages,* http://createthespark.hubpages.com/hub/25-Ways-to-Fill-a-Journal-Page and Melissa Donovan, "Seven Different Types of Journal Writing," *Writing Forward,* http://www.writingforward.com/news-announcements/journal-writing/journal-writing-styles.

- **Collage.** Take clippings from local magazines or newspapers, assignments completed by your students, artwork made by kids you care for, cards or letters received from individuals, etc., and tape or glue them into a notebook.
- **Continued Blogging.** Post blog entries using one of the free platforms listed in the Appendix.
- **Different Point of View.** Write a journal entry from the perspective of one of your community mates, your spouse, a native you recently met, a person you serve at your ministry site, etc.
- **Dreams.** Upon waking up in the morning (or at night), jot down a synopsis about what you dreamt.
- **Epistle.** Select a special person in your life and write that person a letter of any length.
- **English Haiku.** Compose a seventeen-syllable verse form, comprised of three metrical units. The first line should contain five syllables, the second line seven, and the last five. Haikus often make quirky observations of fleeting experiences using juxtaposition of contrasting concepts or images.
- **Lists.** Create any type of list that comes to mind. Some examples might be: to-do lists, twenty things you are grateful for, names you want to remember, moments that have surprised you, words you need to translate, or favorite new foods.
- **Prayers.** As you come across individuals who may be in need of a prayer or two (yourself included), write down your own petitions for them.
- **Quotes.** Keep a private log of quotes (both funny and profound) you hear others say, shout, or mutter. Children may have especially memorable comments you will want to record.
- **Shared Ledger.** You and your spouse can take turns journaling in a notebook that you will pass between yourselves on whatever timeframe makes sense. Write messages to each other, simple observations of your own experiences, or specific examples of growth you see in one another.
- **Sketches.** Draw an image, or a collection of images, that encapsulates what you have recently seen or encountered.
- **Summarization.** Write a short synopsis of your day consisting of 120 words or less.

STEP 2: Commit. Once you and your partner have identified a few ways of memory recording you would like to try, find a scratch pad and begin journaling at least <u>once a week</u>.

Miscellaneous Continued

Regain equilibrium as an individual and as a couple. During the first few months overseas, it is understandable that you and your spouse may not have the ability to care for your own selves or for your marriage with the same type of dedication you were able to at home. However, do not let this continue for the long term. Gottman warns that things tend to get worse when people adopt crisis-mode behavior beyond the crisis itself—when they turn self-denial into a habit, when marital neglect becomes a lifestyle.[83] Regain balance through creative/relaxing/physical outlets, as they can be the most revitalizing parts of your life. Such outlets

---

83 Gottman, Gottman, and DeClaire, *Ten Lessons*, 86.

can provide you with the energy needed to get through hard times.[84] Refer back to the exercise *I–You–We–Care Stars* in Chapter 2 to update your self and marriage care routines.

Maintain important relationships. This point is for those who organize themselves around connections made with certain people. If you are one of these individuals, the loss of relationships you will experience in international relocation can greatly impact you. One survey participant disclosed that one of their greatest challenges was the "lack of ability to communicate with loved ones and friends back home."[85] This former missioner continued sharing, "E-mail was very new and all dial-up. Not everyone back home had it. That meant communication by 'snail mail.' I still have many of those letters I wrote to people, which are priceless."[86] Like this returned volunteer, make sure that you honor and maintain your most important relationships in some way—letter writing, monthly group emails, phone calls, Skype dates, etc.

Take photos sooner rather than later. Photographers suggest taking most of your pictures within the first six months of arriving to your host country, for this is the time when things will look most fresh to you.[87] That being said, it is important to be aware of any cultural taboos concerning picture taking. Some individuals of indigenous tribes in Australia, Africa, and North America, as well as certain Amish and Mennonite communities, do not like having his/her photo taken for various reasons. Research accordingly, be respectful of such beliefs, and always ask permission before you start snapping your camera.

Be cognizant of cultural favoritism. You and your spouse may experience cultural favoritism. One partner can be given preferential treatment based on physical appearance, language competency, sociable personality, gender, etc. If not communicated about, cultural favoritism can become a problem that breeds resentment, unhealthy relationships, and/or avenues to infidelity. Make time to face these types of issues head-on. After dialoging, you and your significant other may want to outline, for example, what you both expect interactions with the opposite sex to look like.

Find someone outside your marriage with whom to talk. If you consistently debriefed with certain friends or family members in your passport country, do not expect your partner to fill that role while abroad. One former missioner lamented, "We vented quite a bit to one another. If we had others on site, we may have had more people to confide in … instead of wearing down our marriage."[88] If you consider yourself an external processor, try to find a good listener so you can give your spouse's ear a break.

Built-In Support

Husbands and wives are each other's natural advocates. You each hold a central piece of one another's identity and are permanently intimate allies. As one program director put it, "Married couples generally have a built-in support network that helps to carry them through challenging times in mission."[89] As you and your partner begin adjusting to a new

---

84 Gottman, Gottman, and DeClaire, *Ten Lessons*, 87.
85 Bridget Studer, personal e-mail, March 28, 2015.
86 Bridget Studer, personal e-mail, March 28, 2015.
87 Pascoe, *Culture Shock! Successful Living Abroad*, 52.
88 Kenny, "Married Missioner/Volunteer Survey," 21.
89 Kenny, "Program Staff: Married Missioners/Volunteers Survey," 11.

country and culture, both of you are able to provide the other with emotional backing, healthy validation, and general encouragement. More so than their single counterparts, married missioners have the potential to enter into their international ministry in positions of strength and security. Several organizational staff members recognized the advantages of this dynamic:

- "Our program receives the benefit of having two individuals that support one another in their volunteer work. They also provide stability to the house community."[90]
- "Married couples are an instant support system that has 'roots' for other volunteers."[91]
- "They generally have greater life experience before entering the program; different perspectives and levels of maturity."[92]

Being able to start your cross-cultural ministry with such a leg up should motivate you both to share your stability, maturity, and roots with fellow compatriots.

In response to feelings of social isolation, un-attachment, or alienation, single volunteers may "initiate a search—perhaps by trial-and-error or in a frantic or calculating manner— for candidates who might be able and willing to serve as companions, escorts, guides, behavior models, and/or interpreters."[93] If you and/or your partner feel like you can fill this position for someone in your community, know that when you do, a single missioner may be relieved of some internal tensions. According to one interviewee, "As a single volunteer separated from my family and culture, the couples in ministry around me provided me a lifeline of good examples and support."[94] With such encouragement, single missioners can expand the limits of their vision enough to begin to more easily adapt to their new home as well.

Modeling Marriage

Your marriage will be a living example of relationality, and what that represents will be up to you and your spouse. Many survey participants reported that their marital relationship functioned as a model of how to be husband and wife in a way that was different than the norm in their host country. One former volunteer wrote, "In a machismo culture we showed people what equality looks like in a marriage."[95] Another commented, "We modeled love for others and were a good example of a fulfilling marriage."[96] Yet another returned missioner shared:

> Later in our service, as we came to know more neighbors, the young girls and boys who would spend time with us would note the "unusual" responsibilities that my husband would assume, like helping with the laundry, cooking, and dishes. He was an inspiration to many to try something different. At our

---

90 Kenny, "Program Staff: Married Missioners/Volunteers Survey," 11.
91 Kenny, "Program Staff: Married Missioners/Volunteers Survey," 11.
92 Kenny, "Program Staff: Married Missioners/Volunteers Survey," 11.
93 Art Freedman, "A Strategy for Managing 'Cultural' Transitions: Re-Entry from Training," in *Cross-Cultural Reentry*, 22.
94 Christa Hoover, personal e-mail, April 9, 2015.
95 Kenny, "Married Missioner/Volunteer Survey," 167.
96 Kenny, "Married Missioner/Volunteer Survey," 167.

neighborhood going away party, we were pleasantly surprised that the neighbor's sons joined the girls in the kitchen serving food and washing dishes.[97]

Program staff also acknowledged the importance of marriage modeling, "Couples are an example of how men and women relate to each other in the US—a built-in partnership of mutual trust."[98] Sharing with people the healthful habits of your marital relationship is a tremendous experience. Your marriage can positively impact how your housemates, local couples, and/or children in your care view the sacrament and institution of this lifelong commitment.

Similarly, your and your spouse's way of relating to one another can be illustrative of certain principles you both value. One former volunteer stated, "We always respected each other in private and in public. The people commented on how our private and public relationship with each other was an inspiration to them."[99] Another survey participant communicated how their marriage was of service to their overseas community: "We worked at an orphanage, so there were just a few families around for the children to see. It was very important for the kids to have experiences of family, and our marriage served that purpose in some ways."[100] Lastly, your marital relationship can be a testament to what it means to permanently dedicate your life to someone else:

> Because of what was happening for us and because we were living in community, our marriage was "put out on the table" for a lot of people to see. I think that our roommates were able to see the struggles and fights that were happening in a very real way, but they also saw the commitment and love that we have for each other.[101]

Being a real-live demonstration of what marriage entails is a profound kind of ministry, and one in which you and your spouse have the privilege of ministering to and for each other day after day.

Living out your faith together in such a practical and intimate way can bring you and your partner closer together. Sometimes, focusing on something outside of your marriage—serving others, for instance—can bring you a unique kind of fulfillment as husband and wife.[102] You are in a situation where you may be witnessing one another successfully developing new capabilities and utilizing ones already refined. One survey participant asserted, "Getting to work alongside each other and see each other's strengths in action was such an amazing gift!"[103] You and your spouse will likely learn to appreciate engaging in activities you would not have experienced together, such as hand-washing your clothes, cooking new dishes, or learning traditional dances/crafts. You can also help stretch one another in taking on additional projects at your ministry sites, spending more time with a lonely neighbor, or working with an especially trying individual who could use more attention.

---

97 Kenny, "Married Missioner/Volunteer Survey," 167.
98 Kenny, "Program Staff: Married Missioners/Volunteers Survey," 11.
99 Kenny, "Married Missioner/Volunteer Survey," 167.
100 Kenny, "Married Missioner/Volunteer Survey," 168.
101 Kenny, "Married Missioner/Volunteer Survey," 167.
102 Mary Ann Jeffreys, "Divided By the Great Commission" in *Survival Guide: Strengthening the Marriage of Missionary Couples* (Carol Stream, IL: Christianity Today International, 2005), 3.
103 Kenny, "Married Missioner/Volunteer Survey," 31.

Marriage and Sacramentality

On a more theological level, international service experiences precipitates generative love, most particularly for married couples. Husbands and wives possess the impulse to act together in order to create something new from their mutual love, as it is "a natural part of the psychological experience of intimacy."[104] According to the *Catechism of the Catholic Church,* this organic tendency toward generativity is one of the two pieces inherent within a Catholic marriage and stems from its primary purpose—unity. The union of two spouses engenders a love between them that then extends beyond their marriage. According to theologian Karl Rahner, "There is always something free and boundless in a truly personal love which is superior to all the chances and changes of life, so that when a man and a woman truly love each other they grow beyond themselves and enter a stream which flows into infinity."[105] Married missioners have the unique opportunity to concretely witness the Gospel value of generative love in their daily lives as individuals devoted to service.

The sacrament of a Catholic marriage, "expressed in its vow of fidelity and its capability of surviving a variety of weaknesses and failures," is a manifestation of God's enduring love.[106] The Greek word for sacrament, *mysterion,* means "mystery." When applied to marriage, "mystery" can be understood as the pointing toward a reality not easily explained—a reality that has roots so deep and sacred "that they extend into the person of God."[107] Sacraments are symbols and actions created by humans that bring about that for which they stand. They are outward and visible signs of the inward grace instituted by Christ.[108] As theologian Walter Kasper explains, "Marriage, then, in its own way is a form by means of which God's eternal love and faithfulness, revealed in Jesus Christ, are made historically present."[109] Individuals unified in marriage embody God's love, which is supra-cultural, beyond and yet a part of this world. The immensity of this actual reality is a beautiful component of what it means to be a couple in mission.

---

104 Whitehead and Whitehead, *Marrying Well,* 234.
105 Karl Rahner, SJ, *Leading a Christian Life* (Denville, NJ: Dimension Books, 1970), 7.
106 Whitehead and Whitehead, *Marrying Well,* 89.
107 Thomas, *Christian Marriage,* 15.
108 *Catechism of the Catholic Church* (New York: Doubleday, 1995), no. 1131.
109 Kasper, *Theology of Christian Marriage,* 30.

Routinization

Chapter 4
Middle of Abroad Experience

Anyone can slay a dragon, he told me, but try waking up every morning and loving the world all over again. That's what takes a real hero.

—Brian Andreas, *Story People*

Routinization

The fourth phase of an international ministry experience is **routinization**, which occurs during the middle period of one's mission commitment. The term routinization refers to the process of an individual constructing routines—transforming the realities of overseas service into a regular and customary lifestyle. Oftentimes, routinization includes the reduction—the gradual lowering of intensity—of a volunteer's engagement with his or her abroad assignment. Going to the public bus station is no longer a bizarre novelty, certain behaviors of the local people are now understandable, and surprises or new situations occur less frequently. If you and your partner refer to the *Stages of Cross-Cultural Transition* timeline in the Preface, you will see that during this period one or both of you are likely to take a downward turn that concludes with "identity crisis." The identity-crisis low point is often more severe than the initial culture shock dip.

This second plunge occurs during the routinization phase because missioners, whether married or not, have now regained the mental and emotional capabilities needed in order to confront underlying issues associated with their relocation. For couples, this "baggage handling" can include: dealing with lingering insecurities felt in regard to spousal or parental gender role orientations, uncertainty concerning sexual intimacy, or existential exploration pertaining to your marital relationship. Working through these types of tensions can be painful and threatening to one's still-developing cross-cultural identity. But once these kinds of issues have been addressed and resolved in some way, individuals can then begin to more authentically engage with their surrounding environment, as illustrated by the upward movement of the "adaptation" line in the *Stages of Cross-Cultural Transition* timeline. It is at this point that you and your partner are not merely reacting to a culture, but adjusting to it. This chapter will acknowledge and respond to the ups and downs you may undergo as husband and wife during the routinization phase.

Routine and Burnout

During the middle of your overseas ministry, you and your spouse may feel bored, desensitized, homesick, socially isolated, burned out, competent, comfortable, in control, contributive, satisfied, successful, and/or confident. Former volunteers described undergoing mood swings at this point during their time in service—moving from living with a sense of "desert" spirituality to an increased compassion and love for others. It appears as though routinization is a period of marked duality, experiences of both routine and renewal. Let us first start with routine. In Chapter 3, the two of you learned about the importance of routines; they enhance our perceptions of well-being and security and thereby can contribute to higher conceptions of one's self.[1] However, routines, even positive ones, can become confining. Oftentimes, individuals who have grown so accustomed to their uninterrupted habits can lose the ability to think creatively, may forget what values and goals are behind certain systems, and are prone to losing balance among work, relationships, and play.[2] When missioners fail to maintain this equilibrium, burnout occurs that much more quickly.

Burnout can be defined as the "emotional and physical exhaustion resulting from a combination of exposure to environmental and internal stressors, and inadequate coping and adaptive skills. In addition to signs of exhaustion, the person with burnout exhibits an increasingly negative attitude toward his or her job, low self-esteem, and personal devaluation."[3] Many survey participants reported that the roles and responsibilities assumed at their ministry sites caused them to experience symptoms of burnout. One former volunteer admitted:

> I have no doubt that I pushed myself so far that I stopped caring for myself. There were several times I put myself on the back burner to ensure that the children stayed the priority. Our mandatory community nights and retreats were such a blessing. If they had been a choice, I would have felt guilty taking the much needed time for myself.[4]

Yet another survey participant disclosed, "The feelings of exhaustion that I experienced were primarily related to teaching, but these feelings were exacerbated by the intense heat, frequent electricity outages, and having to wash my own clothes on a weekly basis!"[5] Still another returnee conceded:

> Six to eight months into my volunteer year, I started to experience aspects of my well-being simply getting tired. Not only was I physically tired, but mentally and emotionally I was exhausted too. I realized it would take more and more self care for me to feel replenished or ready to give of myself again. Towards the end of my time in service, I truly felt in need of a long rest period, mentally, physically and emotionally.[6]

"Psychologists use the term compassion fatigue to capture this feeling of burnout. Though typically used to describe professional helpers [e.g., physicians, social workers, law enforcement officers, therapists, etc.], it can also occur among people who offer continued informal support to others in need."[7]

---

1   Storti, *The Art of Coming Home*, 22.

2   Meg Selig, "Routines: Comforting or Confining?," *Psychology Today,* September 14, 2010, https://www.psychologytoday.com/blog/changepower/201009/routines-comforting-or-confining.

3   *Miller-Keane Encyclopedia and Dictionary of Medicine, Nursing, and Allied Health*, 7th ed. (Minnesota: Saunders, 2003), quoted in "Burnout," *The Free Dictionary by Farlex,* http://medical-dictionary.thefreedictionary.com/burnout.

4   Laura Rusiecki, personal e-mail, April 20, 2015.

5   Karena Malmgren, personal e-mail, June 28, 2015.

6   Emily Pettinger, personal e-mail, June 25, 2015.

7   Susan Krauss Whitbourne, "The Definitive Guide to Guilt," *Psychology Today*, August 11, 2012, https://www.psychologytoday.com/blog/fulfillment-any-age/201208/the-definitive-guide-guilt.

While burnout is usually induced by what we superficially categorize as job-related stressors, a missioner's particular encounter with burnout can occur because of several, more subliminal determinants. Pope Francis enumerates some of these factors in describing a failure of "missionary dynamism" due to a spiritual fatigue he calls pastoral acedia:

> This pastoral acedia can be caused by a number of things. Some fall into it because they throw themselves into unrealistic projects and are not satisfied simply to do what they reasonably can. Others, because they lack the patience to allow processes to mature; they want everything to fall from heaven. Others, because they are attached to a few projects or vain dreams of success. Others, because they have lost real contact with people and so depersonalize their work that they are more concerned with the road map than with the journey itself. Others fall into acedia because they are unable to wait; they want to dominate the rhythm of life.[8]

If you or your spouse find that your routines are leading to burnout, take a look at how you are balancing your individual and familial needs with your ministerial commitments. You may want to reevaluate how much time you are spending where, *and* how you are actually spending that time. If you have yet to do so, consider revamping your "care stars" using the exercise *I–You–We Care Stars* in Chapter 2.

As touched upon earlier, because you both have settled into your new way of life, deep-seated issues are now able to surface. Your minds are no longer preoccupied with reconstructing culturally appropriate responses to simple tasks; thus, they are free to address underlying tensions that may have been waiting in the wings for the past few months. You have established a sense of normalcy, and along with that comes your ability to experience your worldview with more complexity. Going from "surviving to thriving" can be a tough transition for couples. In the continuation of your service work, you and your partner may still be acclimating to your host country at different rates and degrees of ease. There is nothing unusual about two people adapting to life abroad at varying paces. You and your spouse may not always transition at the same time or in the same ways, so try to be prepared for the impact those differences could still have on your marriage.

Renewal and Engagement

The other defining characteristic of the routinization phase is that of renewal. Now that you feel like *you* in this overseas setting, you can connect with your service work and the people who are a part of it on a more meaningful level. You can relate to people more authentically in part because of your attitude adjustment. Your opinions—what you believe to be factually true—of your host country have been evolving since the day you arrived: *"The caste system exists in India."* However, your attitudes—opinions that include an evaluative and emotional component—toward your host country are just now beginning to change: *"The caste system in India is unjust."*[9] Continued exposure to the realities of your mission location makes your experience of cross-cultural ministry more complicated, yet also more

---

8   Francis, *Evangelii Gaudium* (2013), no. 82, http://w2.vatican.va/content/francesco/en/apost_exhortations/documents/papa-francesco_esortazione-ap_20131124_evangelii-gaudium.html.

9   Elliot Aronson, *The Social Animal*, 10th ed. (New York: Worth, 2008), 113–14.

enriching. One former volunteer wrote about this heightened sense of engagement in her and her spouse's relationships with the local people:

> Throughout the year we struggled to figure out how to relate to our neighbors and their needs effectively and prudently, especially as issues of culture and family muddled clear roles (such as with parents neglecting their kids or beating them, old world gender roles creating struggles, death and disease or ill circumstance and the way they were mediated/navigated).[10]

As you see, you and your partner may naturally start to widen and extend your concern for others. You both are progressing "from being motivated by the chance to demonstrate competency, to being motivated by the chance to find purpose in your lives [abroad].It is the shift from the questions of *how* to the questions of *why*."[11] You may find yourselves brainstorming ways to improve your marriage, what each of you can do to better contribute at your ministerial site(s), or how to more effectively relate to your native colleagues. One survey participant shared such a missed opportunity: "I wish I would have figured out how to embrace my community better and how to be a married couple living in the same house in a healthy way. I took for granted the time we were given."[12] The middle of your experience is the phase during which you and your significant other can work to ensure that neither of you has such regrets.

As spouses, you are able to encourage each other in the pursuit of both your personal and shared goals. There will be invitations for you to explore your individual objectives later in this handbook, but for now, we will be focusing on your mutual ambitions. Take the time to reflect on what joint goals may now be surfacing due to the expansion of your abilities to empathize. The act of creating shared goals can help your marriage to be more open to new joys. "In happy marriages, partners incorporate each other's ambitions into the concept of what their marital relationship is about."[13] These goals can be as concrete as outlining ways of living more simply, or as intangible as viewing life abroad as a grand adventure. Naming and creating goals as a couple is a form of communication about one's dreams and can make your relationship become a place of shared meaning. "When a marriage has this shared sense of meaning, conflict is less intense and perpetual problems are less likely to lead to gridlock."[14]

Goal Creation[15]
Duration: 30–45 minutes

The following activity will guide the two of you in establishing mutual goals—goals prompted by your renewed commitment to living a life overseas well.

---

10 Kenny, "Married Missioner/Volunteer Survey," 163.

11 Bridges, *Transitions*, 76.

12 Kenny, "Married Missioner/Volunteer Survey," 36.

13 John M. Gottman and Julie Schwartz Gottman, "How to Keep Love Going Strong," *YES! Magazine,* January 3, 2011, http://www.yesmagazine.org/issues/what-happy-families-know/how-to-keep-love-going-strong.

14 Gottman and Schwartz Gottman, "How to Keep Love Going Strong."

15 Adapted from Gottman, Gottman, and DeClaire, *Ten Lessons,* 92–94.

STEP 1: Identify a Goal. Each spouse will need a pen or a pencil. As a couple, identify a shared goal that both of you would like to achieve. Think about this objective in a way that is specific and measureable. Go from this: *"We need to pray more"* to this: *"We would like to pray together three times a week for the next two months."*

_____
_____
_____
_____

STEP 2: Benefits and Challenges. Together, make a list of some of the positives outcomes associated with achieving this joint goal. Similarly, write down a few ways in which instituting this goal will be difficult. Use the table below:

BENEFITS	CHALLENGES
Example: *"Consistently praying together will strengthen our spiritual lives."*	Example: *"Adding another thing to our 'to do' list may create additional stress."*

STEP 3: Troubleshooting. For each benefit in the table, close your eyes and imagine receiving this positive outcome. For each challenge, consider how you and your spouse would respond to a friend with the same concern.

STEP 4: Small Steps. Name <u>three</u> small steps you can both take in order to attain your larger goal. A small step to the example goal put forth in STEP 1 may be, *"Every Sunday evening* *we will go over our schedules for the upcoming week and select the three days that will be best for us to pray together."*

•

•

•

STEP 5: Possible Hardships. What obstacles do you foresee? What can each of you do to prevent or overcome these difficulties (e.g., What are you going to do when one of you needs to spend more time at your ministry site for a few weeks?)? Brainstorm back-up plans together (e.g., Will you add those missed days of shared prayer to the next week? Or simply start over?).

_____
_____
_____
_____
_____
_____

STEP 6: Helpers. Designate a *Spouse #1* and a *Spouse #2*. Both of you are to name three people you can count on to support you in this change. Reach out to them when you need encouragement. Make sure to select individuals who are easily accessible, and write their names on the lines below:

Spouse #1   **Spouse #2**

1. _____   1. _____

2. _____   2. _____

3. _____   3. _____

STEP 7: Accountability. How will you and your partner keep track of your progress? A star for each day you achieve your small step goals? Would you find it helpful to have a special calendar or journal related to just this issue? Whatever method you choose, try to:

- Regularly look over your large goal and its small steps, remembering the reasons why you both wanted to make this change in your lives.
- At the beginning of each day, consciously decide on what your intentions are in regard to your goal for the next twenty-four hours.
- Review what happened the day before. Did you successfully complete your small steps? What worked? What did not? What could you do differently today to make more headway?

STEP 8: Rewards. How are you going to celebrate each step achieved in this goal-attaining process? Make a list of things each of you enjoys, and supports the changes you are making. Think of rewards for both short-term and long-term successes.

Rewards for meeting our small steps (e.g., a trip to the grocery store for a specialty food item, an extra phone call home, or back rubs for each other):

-

-

-

-

Rewards for meeting our long-term goal (e.g., a getaway weekend in a new location or taking time off work for a dinner out in the closest town):

-

-

-

-

STEP 9: Review. If you and your spouse are not able to meet the larger goal you have set for yourselves, you may need to reevaluate your objective. Goals should stimulate effort and enthusiasm, but also be realistic. Adjust your long-term goal if it feels unreachable in your current context.

Spousal Dynamics

You and your partner have most likely become co-spouses by this point. That being said, one partner may still be less capable than the other in certain areas, such as language competency or tolerance for unpredictability. Becoming co-spouses does not mean that each partner is equally comfortable in or skilled at his/her ministerial job. Having a co-spousal dynamic is based on the fact that both partners find inherent worth in the work at hand. My own husband considered himself an accompanying spouse at the beginning of our volunteer year. Below is his reflection on how he saw himself become more of a co-spouse after months of living in Honduras:

> Going to work at an orphanage was not a crazy idea to me; it just was not something I had ever thought about doing. It was the kind of decision I would have admired others for making, but not do myself. But, it was too good of a thing to say "no" to. How do you tell your wife that we should not volunteer at an orphanage? I did not like the work, because I was not good at it, but the kids made it the most important thing I ever did. In comparison to the rest of my life, the kids made it the *only* important thing that I had ever done.[16]

While one partner may not enjoy the mission experience to the same extent as the other, ideally both individuals can become equally aware of and dedicated to its intrinsic value.

Part of being mutually committed to international service work is the never-ending swing between feeling contentedly competent and absolutely ineffective. Some days you and your spouse will both have had success in the classroom, church, neighborhood, dormitory, or home. Other days will consist of exchanging similarly themed horror stories of inept supervisors, out-of-control children, lackadaisical colleagues, or nightmare parishioners. For the remaining days, you and your partner will likely be seeking different kinds of emotional support because of the particular situations you faced at your ministry sites. Be aware and in conversation enough with your spouse to know whether he/she needs a person to celebrate with or a shoulder to cry on.

If either of you is still experiencing a low sense of self-esteem, be thoughtful in how you are personally processing this. Instead of accepting his/her own feelings of perceived insecurity, your partner may project these feelings of inadequacy onto you (e.g., if your spouse is struggling with living in community, he/she may scoff at the friendships you have formed in the house). Similarly, "the inability to love certain parts of oneself makes it difficult to love those same parts in another."[17] Like the age-old cliché—we hurt the ones we love the most—our reactions to our own self-doubts can end up injuring our significant other if not properly managed. Take the time to figure out (a) what makes you feel *secure* (e.g., words of

---

16 Patrick Kenny, personal e-mail, April 17, 2015.
17 Stephen Treat and Larry Hoff, *Pastoral Marital Therapy: A Practical Primer for Ministry to Couples* (New York: Integration Books, 1987), 13.

affirmation or meaningful relationships); (b) whether those means of gaining reassurance are appropriate; and if they are, (c) how you can create more situations in which you feel validated and confident in your life abroad. Use the general outline of the exercise *Goal Creation* to formulate individual goals you may have to help facilitate your sense of self.

Trip(s) Home

Many international service programs require missioners to stay in their host country for a certain amount of time before traveling back to their homeland or receiving visitors. There is wisdom in these kinds of policies. While a planned trip to your passport country may be an event that gets you and your spouse through particular rough patches, the return from vacation or furlough can be yet another tough transition to manage. But before we look at post-home difficulties, let us first go over a few pointers in preparing for a short visit home.

As a couple, and even more so as a family, the two of you may find it helpful to stay in a sort of neutral zone when you are on leave. This option depends on the length of your home visit, but if you still have access to your own place of residency, plan on staying there. If not, you may want to consider paying for a hotel room. It is likely that your family and friends will offer to host you, but that kind of living situation can get complicated. If your trip home is a longer one, you and your spouse may have to jump from couch to guest bedroom more than once, which is innately stressful. Furthermore, if you or your partner want to see particular people, you would not have the space to entertain them yourselves.[18] Staying in a neutral zone allows you both the freedom to visit whomever you want, when you want, and gives you the opportunity to process your own temporary bouts of "reverse culture shock."

Reverse culture shock is the set of emotional and psychological reactions a person has in response to returning to his/her passport country from an overseas experience. Often this response includes (1) an individual's initial idealization of their home country, and (2) the expectation of total familiarity. When the euphoria of these two kinds of anticipative assumptions inevitably wear off, feelings of anger, isolation, confusion, guilt, and/or disappointment can set in. *"I cannot wait to take a long, hot shower!"* Fifteen minutes later: *"I just wasted so much water. What would my neighbors in Peru think?"* Or: *"I am so looking forward to this family dinner!"* Thirty minutes later: *"My little sister did not clear her plate. Does she not realize that the kids I work with in Kosovo are constantly hungry?"* Be patient and allow yourself and your spouse to struggle with the implications of such contention. Engage with the conflicting emotions—or even the lack thereof—that you may be feeling. Reconciling the often large gaps in lifestyles between the West and your host country is something that takes time. Think of this short jaunt with reverse culture shock as a practice round—a precursor to what you may feel when you more permanently return from your volunteer site.

In addition to feeling tension within your own self and your family circle, you and your partner may be on opposite pages. Your significant other may want to spend time in different ways than you do while on your home visit. One survey participant wrote, "We find it harder to be on furlough as a couple than working where we both feel God has called us."[19] Respect each other's personal desires and support your partner in doing things he/she truly

---

18 Pascoe, *Culture Shock! Successful Living Abroad,* 156–57.
19 Kenny, "Married Missioner/Volunteer Survey," 32.

enjoys. If you have children, the two of you should work to balance individual free time and childcare responsibilities. But do not forget to spend some quality time together! Plan a date night at your favorite restaurant, visit a park by your house, go bowling with a few friends, etc. If needed, make sure to schedule a doctor appointment or a teeth cleaning ahead of time. Be gentle on your stomach. It is recommended that you ease into eating your favorite foods over the course of a few days.

Returning to your host country after furlough can be bittersweet. Though you are coming back to faith-filled, life-giving work, you are also faced with the realities of simple living once again. One way to help you adjust to this change is to schedule a vacation somewhere in your host country before traveling back to your actual volunteer site.[20] An extended end to your time off can help you and your partner readjust. Several missioners reported that they socially withdrew for a few weeks after returning to their international assignments. Give yourselves the necessary time alone to reflect and recharge, and then look to start getting active in your surrounding community. Try to remember that your experience in mission is limited, so be present and look to enjoy the remainder of it.

Money Management

Increased comfort in your host country can prompt you and your partner to make changes in your lifestyle choices. The more each of you becomes involved with your ministries, the more you may want to give back to the causes for which you are working. For one spouse, this may mean dedicating more time and energy to specific projects, and for the other, it may mean a renewed effort in home-based fundraising. Simply put, you and your partner may have differing ideas of how you want to further support your service program. Personally giving money to locals who utilize your ministry site's assistance is likely not the most appropriate response to your desire to be more contributive. In fact, many mission institutions have set rules against such behavior. Make sure the two of you understand the stance your sending organization has in relation to monetary and material donations, and abide by those guidelines. Discuss with each other the supplementary ways in which you can demonstrate your loyalty to and patronage for your mission program.

Money is one of the main sources of conflict for many couples across the world, whether they have a little or a lot of it. For married volunteers, questions of how much money to spend on in-country vacations, trips back home, hosting visitors, etc., are likely to come up during the routinization phase. Several resources suggest that couples set spending limits on all of the aforementioned items, and then allot each partner a "stipend" every month. This arrangement allows both of you to handle a small amount of money in your own way; savers can save it, spenders can spend it, and givers can give it.[21] Whatever system you and your partner choose to implement in your married life overseas, regular communication about finances is advised.

Continued Conflict

Whether your arguments are about problems that cropped up months ago, or are about new and unexpected matters, conflict between spouses can persist within this phase. Some dis-

---

20 Pascoe, *Culture Shock! Successful Living Abroad,* 164.
21 Koteskey, "Missionary Marriage Issues," 88.

agreements may arise because of homesickness caused by missed family events or holidays spent overseas. Other disputes can occur for less obvious feelings of sadness, resentment, and/or anger (*"I thought we had decided that you would not commute through that neighborhood. Why are you still taking shortcuts to work near that part of town?"*). Whatever the cause, "every long-term relationship has its share of perpetual issues. In fact, our [Gottmans' and DeClaire's] research shows that some 69 percent of all marital conflicts can be categorized as never ending."[22] This statistic attests to the fact that enduring difficulties are a normal part of most marriages. While a particular issue may surface time and time again, what can change is a couple's willingness to accept their differences and to improve their skills at problem solving.[23] Continue to refer to the exercise *Conflict Resolution* in Chapter 3 to ensure that arguments are healthy and productive. Use the tips put forth in the activity to help you soften your startups, prompt further dialogue, implement formal repair attempts, and engage in methods of self-soothing.

Let us say that you and your spouse have been practicing productive conflict handling, and you have managed to talk through major disagreements, but smaller disputes still persist. General and constant disgruntlement can negatively affect how you and your partner perceive each other's actions. Even if the two of you have not been arguing as much as you did in the beginning months of your relocation transitioning, mission settings are usually comprised of a high level of tensions and stressors. Many overseas service sites are confining. You and your spouse do not have access to different kinds of people, activities, food, places, even weather. And who is likely to be the first person with whom you get annoyed when your life begins to feel especially limited? Your significant other, of course.

> **Seven-Week Fondness Plan**[24]
> *Duration: 5–20 minutes/ongoing*

Dr. Gottman's studies show that continually replaying negative thoughts about your partner can contribute to emotional distancing and isolation in your marriage. One solution to this problem "is to train your mind to replace 'distress-maintaining' thoughts about your spouse to 'relationship-enhancing' thoughts. Doing so takes time and practice, but it's worth the effort because it can further create feelings of fondness and admiration in your marriage."[25] If either you or your partner feels like you could use some tender loving care, this activity can help both of you consciously express your affection for one another.

STEP 1: The Plan. Following is a seven-week plan for positively adjusting your perception of your spouse. The tables across the next few pages are divided week by week. Each week has four ready-made thoughts that are meant to get you thinking about your partner from an affirming perspective. As individuals, select four days of the week on which you will designate time to engage with this exercise.

---

22 Gottman, Gottman, and DeClaire, *Ten Lessons*, 24.
23 Gottman, Gottman, and DeClaire, *Ten Lessons*, 24.
24 Adapted from Gottman, Gottman, and DeClaire, *Ten Lessons*, 117–23.
25 Gottman, Gottman, and DeClaire, *Ten Lessons*, 117–18.

STEP 2: Action Steps. There are additional steps listed in the "Do" column that will help make the thought of the day stick. Many of these action steps involve a short writing component, so keep a separate notebook for this activity, or incorporate it into a journal you already have.

STEP 3: Envelopes. Remember the envelope with your partner's name on it that you were supposed to pack? Well, pull it out and keep it handy. Each week you will use one or two of the written statements to verbalize your appreciation of your spouse. Refer to the row under the week number to see how many compliments you are responsible for communicating within that seven-day period. Sharing those positive qualities with your partner can lift his or her confidence and assist him/her in cultivating admiration and fondness for you.

STEP 4: Summary. Four days per week you will review a positive thought and complete the action step associated with it, as presented in the subsequent tables. These two tasks can be done without necessarily interacting with your spouse. Additionally, at the beginning of each week, you are to select one or two statements from the envelope in your possession (the number of which is also noted in the tables) and share those compliments with your partner in the course of a week's time.

Think	Do
Week 1	
One Compliment	
1. I genuinely like my partner.	List one of your spouse's most endearing and lovable characteristics. Write about a time when your partner demonstrated this quality.
2. I can easily remember joyful times in our marriage.	Pick one joyful memory and write a short description of it.
3. I am physically attracted to my partner.	Think of a physical attribute that pleases you. Spend some time thinking about this aspect of your spouse.
4. I get a lot of support in this marriage.	Think of a time when you felt your partner was really there for you.

Think	Do
Week 2	
Two Compliments	
1. We have some of the same general beliefs and values.	Describe one belief or value that you both share. Think about how it feels to know that you and your spouse are united on that front.

2. I am proud of this marriage.	Describe the aspect of your marriage of which you are most proud.
3. My spouse can be cute and spontaneous.	Get dressed up for an evening out or a planned date night at home.
4. There are some things about my partner that I do not like, but I have learned how to live with them.	List one of your spouse's minor faults you have come to accept.

Think	Do
Week 3	
One Compliment	
1. We enjoy each other's sense of humor.	Share jokes that you know with one another or find a funny video to watch together.
2. I am appreciative of my family.	Describe a specific time when you experienced this feeling.
3. I remember many details about deciding to get married.	Describe those details in a few sentences.
4. My partner is an engaging person.	Think of a topic that interests both you and your spouse. Bring it up in a future conversation.

Think	Do
Week 4	
Two Compliments	
1. I was really lucky to meet my spouse.	Write one benefit of being married to your partner.
2. We find each other to be good companions.	Plan an extended activity to do together.
3. We have common goals.	List two such goals. Think about how it will feel to achieve them together.
4. I can recall happy memories about our wedding and honeymoon.	Describe at least one positive memory about those events that you remember vividly.

Think	Do
Week 5	
One Compliment	
1. I believe we are genuinely interested in one another.	Think of something to do with your spouse that you both find enjoyable.
2. There is a lot of affection between us.	Plan a small surprise for your partner tonight.

| 3. We both have a sense of control over our lives. | Think of something important that you planned together that worked out well. |
| 4. I feel relaxed in our private space. | Think about an instance when your spouse helped you to calm down after a stressful situation. |

Think	Do
Week 6	
Two Compliments	
1. My spouse is my best friend.	What fun things do you and your partner do together?
2. My partner has specific qualities that make me feel proud.	Write down at least one characteristic and why it makes you feel admiration for your spouse.
3. I believe we respond well to one another.	Write a love letter to your partner and put it in a place where they will happen upon it.
4. If I had to do it over again, I would marry the same person.	Plan a romantic getaway for your anniversary or another special occasion.

Think	Do
Week 7	
One Compliment	
1. We have come a long way together.	Make a list of several things you have accomplished as a team.
2. There is a lot of mutual respect in our marriage.	Plan to learn a new skill together (cooking a traditional dish, weaving, milking a cow, etc.).
3. My spouse is my confidant.	Think of a time when your partner really listened to you and gave helpful advice.
4. I can easily recall meeting my spouse for the first time.	Write down the details you remember about your initial romantic encounters with your partner.

Infidelity

Couples in mission are not immune to infidelity. Infidelity and the emotional distancing that often leads to it are problems that married volunteers have encountered in the past and continue to encounter. A few survey participants commented on their own experiences of infidelity and emotional distancing:

- "About halfway through our year of service, we came to a place of not knowing how to continue in our marriage. This was by far the greatest challenge we have facedin our relationship. We were both unhappy, but did not know how to navigate through the confusion and hurt."[26]

- "Pornography affected spouse and child (separately)."[27]
- "An emotional affair occurred in the middle of our volunteer year."[28]

Let us take a look at some of the reasons why infidelity can happen from a more general perspective, and then specifically, within a missionary marriage.

Psychological hypotheses behind why spouses do not remain faithful to their partners vary from one mental health professional to the next. Christian psychologist Dr. Willard Harley purports that when conversation and affection are missing from a marriage, one partner tends to seek an illicit association/situation. Other therapists believe that unmanaged or unknown feelings of fear, loneliness, and/or anger induced by past traumas are direct causes of marital infidelity. Dr. Gottman writes that spouses seem to go through four stages of withdrawing from their marriage before infidelity occurs:

(1) One or both partners view their marital problems as severe
(2) Individuals believe that talking things over with their spouse seems useless
(3) Both partners start leading parallel lives
(4) Finally, loneliness sets in

It is during this last stage that either spouse can become vulnerable to infidelity.[29] Categorically speaking, infidelity can be physical, emotional, or a combination of the two. Divorce support expert Cathy Meyer identifies the five most common types of infidelity:

(1) **Opportunistic Infidelity**—occurs when a spouse succumbs to his/her sexual desires for someone other than his/her partner, often while impaired by alcohol or drugs.
(2) **Obligatory Infidelity**—occurs when a spouse is unfaithful because of fear of the disapproval that can come when turning down someone else's sexual advances.
(3) **Romantic Infidelity**—occurs when a spouse is committed to his/her marital relationship but finds it emotionally unfulfilling and satisfies his/her need for an intimate, loving connection with another individual.
(4) **Conflicted Romantic Infidelity**—occurs when a spouse is genuinely emotionally and sexually attracted to both his/her partner and another person.
(5) **Commemorative Infidelity**—occurs when a spouse does not find his/her marriage fulfilling and consciously decides to have an affair with another to meet his/her needs, yet remains with his/her partner for the sake of appearances.[30]

Infidelity is defined not only as a breach of an overt commitment to sexual exclusivity, but also as a breach of emotional exclusivity. While some married volunteers do not have access

26 Kenny, "Married Missioner/Volunteer Survey," 20.
27 Kenny, "Married Missioner/Volunteer Survey," 163.
28 Kenny, "Married Missioner/Volunteer Survey," 209.
29 Gottman and Silver, *Why Marriages Succeed or Fail*, 121–25.
30 Cathy Meyer, "Types of Infidelity," *About Divorce*, http://divorcesupport.about.com/od/infidelity/p/infidelity_type.htm.

to the Internet, those who do need to understand that the Internet and other advancements in technology make the "gray zone" of infidelity broader than before. One can reconnect with a former love interest through Facebook or ignite an old flame through intimate emails. Avatars in online fantasy worlds kiss, date, and even marry. Sexting, direct/instant messaging, cybersex chat rooms, and pornography websites are just a few of the ways people are engaged in "virtual" sexual contact with each other.[31]

In addition to these more general sources of unfaithfulness are the specific circumstances that can negatively affect a missioner's marriage:

- **External Validation.** Because married volunteers (along with volunteers in general) have lost their home-base support systems, they may seek inappropriate sources of validation.
- **Lack of Affection.** There can be cultural customs that limit outward and consistent signs of affection between missionary spouses, which may cause both partners to feel unwanted or unloved.
- **Shared Housing.** Living in an intentional community usually involves married volunteers forming relationships with individuals of the opposite sex. Some spouses may not know how (or choose not) to establish healthy boundaries with those of the opposite sex in general, or in accordance with their partner's requests.
- **Limited Support.** International service sites are not likely to have certified marital therapists on staff. Missioners may know that their marriage is under constant stress and want to seek out extra support, but their locale presumably prevents success in finding a mental health professional.
- **Complexity.** Couples consist of two people going through and reacting to a cross-cultural experience from an I–You–We perspective. This can be complicated, especially as fidelity is notably strained when individuals move at different speeds and in different directions from those to whom they should be faithful.[32]

With so many adverse factors that constitute an international volunteer's reality, married missioners must be aware of the ways in which they can protect themselves against all types of infidelity.

The best thing any married individual can do to prevent infidelity is to work on marital trust. Gottman believes that building trust can be done in any interaction with your spouse, so long as you intentionally choose to connect with your partner instead of turning away from him or her. Here is a modification of one of Dr. Gottman's examples: You are just about to finish a lesson plan for tomorrow's sixth grade English class, when your significant other quickly walks past you, looking quite upset. You have two choices. You could continue working, ignoring your partner's obvious emotional distress, while thinking, *"All I want to do is get this done. I really cannot deal with my spouse's problems right now."* The other option is to turn toward your partner and engage with him or her. Purposefully, you put down your pencil, follow your husband or wife, and ask why he/she seems so troubled. In making this second choice, you have created a moment of trust building. Work to train yourselves to be able to recognize these moments and make them happen time and time again.

---

31 Samantha Smithstein, "(Re)defining Infidelity," *Psychology Today*, June 23, 2011, https://www.psychologyto-day.com/blog/what-the-wild-things-are/201106/redefining-infidelity.

32 Whitehead and Whitehead, *Marrying Well*, 390.

One of Gottman's graduate students, Dan Yoshimoto, created a simple system of building trust using a process called ATTUNE:

- **A**wareness of your partner's emotion
- **T**urning toward that emotion
- **T**olerating two different viewpoints
- **U**nderstanding your partner (or trying to)
- **N**on-defensively responding to your partner
- **E**mpathetically reacting to your partner's needs[33]

This approach can be an effective tool in communicating with your spouse and making your marriage a trustworthy partnership. In avoiding infidelity:

- Share with your partner your personal and intimate needs and desires
- Identify and avoid trigger situations
- Acknowledge the vulnerabilities you may harbor
- Tell your spouse about these vulnerabilities
- Be open to making changes in your behavior, whether they be alterations you recognize yourself or additional requests from your partner

Fidelity is a mobile faithfulness, moving ever toward a never-finished reality.[34] Work to keep progressing forward in loyalty by cultivating a marriage of trust.

Overcoming Infidelity

This section is simply a *starting point* in addressing and overcoming infidelity. Volunteer couples working through spousal betrayal will need support that this handbook cannot provide. Certain sending institutions offer professional and specialized counseling for spouses in such a position; seek out this guidance if it is available. For many under-developed programs, such member care simply does not exist. In either case, it is important for missioners in this kind of situation to decide whether or not they will be able to continue with their ministerial work. No matter who is involved in the infidelity, all individuals associated with the service organization are likely to be negatively impacted. Moreover, the reputation of the program itself may be compromised. Thus, administrators may request that a married couple dealing with infidelity return to their passport country. Whether spouses remain abroad or travel back home, using Dr. Gottman's processes of atonement (described below), ATTUNE-ing, and attachment (also described below) can help to foster feelings of healing and forgiveness.

"Atonement" is a five-step approach to forgiveness that begins with confession. The affair must be terminated and the offender must be willing to be completely honest in answering any questions the hurt partner wants to ask. A recommended boundary here is that details of sexual encounters not be shared. It is important for the offender to be aware of how his/her infidelity has impacted his/her spouse and marriage. The second step in atonement is behavior change. Offenders are to transparently verify that they are no longer engaged in

---

33 John M. Gottman, "John Gottman on Trust and Betrayal," *Greater Good: The Science of a Meaningful Life*, October 29, 2011, http://greatergood.berkeley.edu/article/item/john_gottman_on_trust_and_betrayal.
34 Whitehead and Whitehead, *Marrying Well*, 215.

destructive behavior and have a genuine desire to work on their marital relationship. Offenders must be willing to share information on their cell phones and social media accounts with the hurt partner as to indicate that the illicit relationship is terminated. This sharing gives the hurt spouse evidence that choosing to trust their partner again is a good decision. Next, the offending spouse is to answer the following two questions: *Why did you choose to be unfaithful in dealing with a particular void in your life? Why do you want to stay married?* After these questions have been answered, the hurt partner needs to set clear boundaries and expectations for the spouse in regard to potential areas of future infidelity. The fourth step involves the hurt spouse creating consequences for the offending partner if another betrayal were to occur. Finally, the last step in atonement is forgiveness. Forgiveness cannot begin until the previous steps have been taken. Moving forward in forgiveness is a collective responsibility, although the hurt partner is still called to work through mistakes that the offending spouse will inevitably make. These "mistakes" do not include returning to infidelity; they could be something like the offending partner taking his/her spouse to a restaurant frequented by the offending partner and the person with whom he/she had an affair. Though insensitive, this mistake is pardonable, and the hurt spouse should try to recognize this and forgive the offending partner.[35] For more on this topic, refer to the sections *Forgiveness* in Chapters 3 and 5.

Once the atonement process has been completed, couples are to try to rebuild trust in their relationship. Review the previous section and familiarize yourselves with the ATTUNE method. Practice making that form of communication a habit in your marriage. The third phase of recovering after infidelity is attachment, wherein the ability to ATTUNE reaches intimate reconnection.[36] Intimacy is first achieved through emotional, social, mental, and spiritual attachments. Re-creating these bonds can take a long time, and that is OK. Physical intimacy is the last attachment made, only after the aforementioned bonds have been reestablished. Only when both partners have formed, once again, a mental and emotional relationship with one another, can physical intimacy be healthy and meaningful.

Ministry Extension

If you or your spouse wants to renew your service commitment, this is when you should take the time to enter into a re-discernment period. One program director shared, "We have found that requests to extend mission may include factors that are different from first-time applicants, so we have developed a separate process and application form for this."[37] Investigate what is required by your volunteer organization in order to renew your ministerial commitment. Reviewing activities and topics in Chapter 1 can be helpful as you and your partner begin to more seriously contemplate this opportunity. You may also consider referring to the section *Contributing Factors* in Chapter 6. This section can assist you and your spouse in exploring the variables that make up the individual relationships each of you has with your shared mission experience. Have an honest conversation with your partner about what comes up for you when looking over those factors. While one or both of you may already have anxieties about returning home, choosing to stay at your volunteer site simply because of those worries is neither an effective nor a practical way to handle such apprehensions.

---

35 Chris Cambas, "Overcoming Infidelity," *National Marriage Seminars,* February 10, 2014, http://www.national-marriageseminars.com/about-us/blog/2014/02/11/overcoming-infidelity/

36 Cambas, "Overcoming Infidelity."

37 Vic Doucette, personal e-mail, April 11, 2015.

It is during the middle/middle-end of your overseas experience that you and your spouse can most accurately and effectually take into account the emotions you are feeling about potentially extending your ministry. This calls for emotional intelligence—defined in a *Psychology Today* article as "the ability to identify and manage your own emotions and the emotions of others … [and] to harness emotions and apply them to tasks like thinking and problem solving."[38] Emotionally intelligent individuals interpret and make use of emotion. They do not remove all feeling from their decision-making—only the emotions that have nothing to do with what is being determined. Even if you and your spouse are emotionally disciplined persons, the final months of your time abroad can be sentimentally charged. Your judgment may be clouded by your anticipations and concerns about getting ready to return home. If the two of you have not formally decided to renew your mission commitment before then, you could come to a conclusion that might not be what is best when looking at the long-term well-being of your family. Choosing to extend your stay overseas should be done at least four months (or so) prior to your departure date.

Top Ten List

Try your best to minimize regrets! This next list includes the top ten things survey participants wish they would have done before returning to their passport countries. Introducing this list during the routinization phase can save you from scrambling to "experience it all" in your last few months abroad. (These suggestions are not in any order):

1. Learn more of the local language.
2. Interact more with the native people.
3. See more of your host country.
4. Be more communicative, vulnerable, and patient with your spouse.
5. Spend more time together as a couple.
6. Be more open to the benefits of living in an intentional community.
7. Keep a written journal.
8. Recognize how special the time spent in your host country is.
9. Keep in better contact with family and friends back home.
10. So aptly phrased by one survey participant: "Looking back at 55 years together, what can I say? Love her more."[39] Learn to love your partner more each and every day.

Add a few of your own "bucket list" items to this lineup and start making plans to ensure that your time in mission is all that you want it to be.

Miscellaneous

Though moving on from practical advice offered by seasoned missioners, the following points remain in the same logistical vein:

Share your departure date with others. When asked, openly speak about when you will be leaving your ministry site. Keeping information of that nature a secret is not helpful for

---

38 "What Is Emotional Intelligence?" *Psychology Today,* https://www.psychologytoday.com/basics/emotional-intelligence.

39 Kenny, "Married Missioner/Volunteer Survey," 36.

anyone. According to change management consultant William Bridges, "For every week of upset that you avoid by hiding the truth, you gain a month of bitterness and mistrust."[40] The individuals you are working with have the right to know when you are returning to your home country, as it can directly impact their lives. Allow people to react to this information and start to process what your future absence will mean to them—even if their responses are difficult for you to handle. This topic will be further addressed in Chapter 5.

Laugh a little. Do you remember what it is like to do that? Not the nervous kind, the fake kind, or the kind of chuckle aimed at yourself for making yet another cross-cultural blunder—but real, genuine laughter. If you have access to YouTube videos, sitcom DVDs, or old comedies, schedule a night to watch them. Laughter is good for you! It stimulates many organs, alleviates stress, boosts your immune system, relieves pain, and improves your mood.[41] Seek out an authentic and hearty laugh often.

Should I request a change in ministry? Some missioners move from one placement to another during their service commitment. This seems to happen for a number of reasons: lack of support at current location, greater need elsewhere, failing relationship between parent program and abroad organization, issues of security, etc. Whatever the cause, leaving a mission site can be difficult. As one survey participant wrote, "It was hard having to make the tough decision together as to whether or not we should move to another site or stay with the challenging placement we had."[42] Another volunteer commented, "We were working at the same service site at the beginning of our year. He loved it; I strongly disliked it. This was a stressor for us and, for a few reasons I stopped working there, and started at a new service site. Leaving the original service site was something that I felt helped our marriage."[43] If you feel like your work assignment is unhealthful or inappropriate, advocate for desired changes or a new ministry altogether. Be open to what future opportunities are in store for you if your direction of mission changes.

Making sense of an early return home. Deciding or having to return to your passport country before the end date of your volunteer commitment can be painful. You are not alone. Several survey participants shared the explanations behind their early departures: pregnancies, visa issues, extreme illness, a death in the family, pressure from a new job, starting school date for children, experienced trauma (physical, emotional, sexual), natural disasters, and political unrest. It is crucial to take the time to process the cause(s) behind your unanticipated return home. Reading through topics presented in Chapter 6 and Chapter 7 may help you and your spouse navigate through the stages of re-entry and integration. If either of you feels like you need more assistance, please reach out to a local therapist or marriage counselor. It would do you well to try to find a mental health professional who understands what overseas volunteer work entails.

Visitors and Perspective

Despite any lingering insecurities you may have as individuals, you and your partner have likely created routines at work and at home, and as a result, are more confident in your cross-cultural identities. You may be communicating in a different language and perform-

---

40 Bridges, *Managing Transitions,* 32.
41 Mayo Clinic Staff, "Stress Relief from Laughter? It's No Joke," *Mayo Clinic,* July 23, 2013, http://www.mayoclinic.org/healthy-living/stress-management/in-depth/stress-relief/art-20044456.
42 Kenny, "Married Missioner/Volunteer Survey," 20.
43 Kenny, "Married Missioner/Volunteer Survey," 209.

ing at a high level in a specialized service, and thus are presumably establishing meaningful relationships with others. Witnessing your spouse making the same strides forward can be equally fulfilling. "While experience may not be the best teacher, experiential learning may be the best type of education."[44] And that is exactly the kind of ministerial degree you both are earning! Take the time to reflect on the progress you have made at your volunteer sites as missioners, as well as in your marriage as husband and wife.

Your friends and/or family may visit during the middle of your overseas experience. More often than not, hosting your loved ones can be a positive experience. Before they arrive, kindly request any specialty items you may need or want: school supplies, more special snacks, extra lice treatment, printed photos, etc. Most support people back home want to help you and those you serve, so put those good intentions to use. If you or your spouse is having a hard time recognizing your external and internal development, then allow your visitors' affirming feedback to be an indicator of your growth. Even if you are just asking for directions or conversing with the local baker, family and friends tend to give you the credit both of you have merited. Another benefit of hosting loved ones at your ministry site is their ability to see, touch, taste, hear, and feel what your life abroad is like. This can make your transition home a smoother process for everyone, as those you are close to can better accompany the two of you on your passage through the re-entry and integration phases.

Finally, visitors can help you regain the "right" perspective by reminding you that being a missioner is a privilege, more than it is a sacrifice. When my in-laws came to down to Honduras halfway through our volunteer year, they made me remember just how special the girls I took care of were (and still are). I had become so accustomed to their whining and temper tantrums, I had nearly forgotten that they (a) did not have parents to give them the love and attention they deserved; (b) had experienced severe childhood abuse; and, most importantly, (c) were children of God. Re-framing my world in the orphanage by sharing it with my husband's family was significant for me. Hopefully you and your spouse have similarly enlightening experiences with your visitors, experiences that cause you to realize just how sacred and holy your time in (insert host country) truly is.

Theological Reflection
Duration: 30–45 minutes

Theological reflection is a way of contemplating events that begins with lived experience and then relates that lived experience to the Christian faith, drawing out concrete implications for practical application.[45] Theological reflection places the reflector and his/her interactions with others into conversation with sources of God's past revelation and enduring presence (i.e., Scripture, religious tradition and history, personal encounters of transcendence, etc.).[46] International service is a ministry replete with grace-filled moments, many of which go un-contemplated. This activity will help you and your partner to explore where you see God's divine company and how to best honor that companionship.

---

44 Sam Longsworth, "The Returned Volunteer: A Perspective," in *Cross-Cultural Reentry: A Book of Readings,* ed. Clyde N. Austin (Abilene, TX: Abilene Christian University, 1986), 86.

45 Robert L. Kinast, *What Are They Saying About Theological Reflection?* (New York: Paulist Press, 2000), 1.

46 Kathleen McAlpin, RSM, *Ministry That Transforms: A Contemplative Process of Theological Reflection* (Collegeville, MN: Liturgical Press, 2009), 7.

STEP 1: Roles. Each of you will need a piece of paper and a pen or a pencil. Designate a speaking spouse and a listening spouse.

STEP 2: Recounting. Engaging in theological reflection starts with the naming of a recent experience. This event will probably be linked to your ministerial work or other situations related to living abroad. The speaking spouse is to select such an occasion and recount the experience as though he or she were telling a story with a beginning, middle, and end. Describe out loud to your partner what actions were taken by you or others, what emotions you felt, thoughts that crossed your mind, certain points when you simply observed what was happening, etc.

The speaking spouse should <u>not</u> assign judgment or value to any part of his/her own narrative. This step is merely the communication of what occurred. The listening spouse is not to interrupt the telling of the speaker's story.

STEP 3: General Questions. After reflecting on the speaking spouse's narrative, the listening spouse can now ask clarifying questions about the speaker's account. For example, if your partner tells you about a boy who had a violent outburst in an after-school program, you may ask how the other children reacted or what other adults got involved. The point of these questions is to further explore the experience that was shared.

STEP 4: Themes. Once the listening spouse feels like he/she understands the speaking partner's story, he/she are to brainstorm themes, topics, issues, beliefs, ideas, etc., that are present within the story. Continuing with the example from above; your partner's narrative may make you think more about patience as a virtue, the message in John 2:13–17, appropriate parenting/teaching techniques, etc. The listening spouse can start making a list of ten to twenty themes, to which the speaking spouse can add. Be in conversation with one another as you each write down topics that come to mind.

1. _____
2. _____
3. _____
4. _____
5. _____
6. _____
7. _____
8. _____
9. _____
10. _____
11. _____
12. _____
13. _____
14. _____
15. _____
16. _____
17. _____
18. _____
19. _____
20. _____

STEP 5: Faith Tradition. As the two of you look at the list you have created, think about how these ideas relate to your faith tradition. How do your brainstormed points either challenge or affirm what you have read in the Bible or in your religion's catechism? How are these themes present or not present in what you know of the history of Christianity?

Discuss the tensions you see between your faith heritage/community and the experience you or your partner have recounted. Similarly, share the ways in which this event validates certain beliefs you hold. Your spouse may say, *"Mark 9:36–37 tells me to treat children as I would treat Jesus himself. How can I remember this when my program kids are acting disrespectfully?"*

STEP 6: Surprise. Dialogue with your partner about what element(s) in this shared story surprised you.

STEP 7: Invitations. Take a few moments to reflect on this process and review what you both have gathered. As mentioned, the main purpose of theological reflection is deciding how to live out what you have uncovered from this interactive contemplation. Therefore, you and your spouse are going to create a total of <u>four</u> invitations. On your own pieces of paper, please write and complete the following statements in relation to this exercise:

- I feel called to …
- I believe that my spouse is called to …

Once finished, take turns sharing your personal invitations with one another. Next, take turns sharing your spousal invitations with one another.

STEP 8: Integration. Carry these invitations with you throughout your week. They can serve as reminders of the creative relationship you have with God and your faith tradition. Integrate the insights gleaned from this kind of theology into your daily interactions. This can be an exercise you come back to again and again. (Be sure to switch roles when do you revisit this activity!)

STEP 9: Ink Blot. In closing, both of you are to focus <u>only</u> on the four dots in the center of **Figure 4.1**. As you do so, slowly count to twenty. Upon reaching twenty, close your eyes. In a few seconds you should experience the visual effect of this image with your eyes still closed. What do you see?

Figure 4.1[47]

Maturing Love

Intimacy and separation do not sound as if they are meant to go together. But in married life, they are essentially emotional twins; spouses need both. There is a great parallel between individual growth (separation) and growth within a marriage (intimacy). "Becoming" married is a continual "process of finding a balance between uninterrupted togetherness and exaggerated distance. The aim is a marital bond with clear but permeable boundaries."[48] Serving overseas is an experience that often gives partners the opportunity to consciously establish an equitable balance of separation and intimacy. One former missioner expressed this kind of development in his own partnership: "There came a time when we verbalized to each other that we were 'comfortable together and comfortable apart,' which was not true earlier in our marriage."[49] Another survey participant shared, "We learned to value each other as individuals; having personal hobbies, friends, and outings allowed us to honor our individuality. …Being able to be together, while also being unique was a huge focus for us."[50] Try to take advantage of the ways in which your international mission environment grants you and your spouse this kind of marital maturation.

As you continue to adapt to your host country's culture, you and your partner are able to explore and renegotiate responsibilities, roles, relationships, expectations, and personal identities. Both of you are figuring out how to better support one another, communicate more effectively, and value each other to a greater degree—for you are discovering that your and your spouse's needs and wants change with circumstance. Many former volunteers attest to the fruits of this examination of self and other:

---

47 "Do You See What I See?" Series: The Faith Hall of Fame. Lesson 3. *Three-thirty Ministries,* http://threethirty-ministries.org/2011/01/lesson-3-do-you-see-what-i-see/.

48 Herbert Anderson and Robert Cotton Fite, *Becoming Married* (Louisville, KY: Westminster/John Knox Press, 1993), 33.

49 Kenny, "Married Missioner/Volunteer Survey," 40.

50 Kenny, "Married Missioner/Volunteer Survey," 39.

- "We know each other more deeply and in different ways and have a distinct respect for the other that's different than before the experience."[51]
- "Our service year helped us define each other's needs now that we are living on our own (adult kids live far away). We understand each other much better now that we are nearing the end of life."[52]
- "Our year connected us on another level. It reinforced some of the ideals and principles we both stand for together."[53]

Such comments are representative of the fact that overseas mission work has the ability to help you and your partner continue to "become more married." In becoming more married, you and your spouse ultimately learn to love each other more fully—with the kind of love that is best summarized by C. S. Lewis:

> Love in this second sense—love as distinct from "being in love"—is not merely a feeling. It is a deep unity, maintained by the will and deliberately strengthened by habit; reinforced by the grace which both partners ask, and receive, from God. They can have this love for each other even at those moments when they do not like each other; as you love yourself even when you do not like yourself. They can retain this love even when each would easily, if they allowed themselves, be "in love" with someone else. "Being in love" first moved them to promise fidelity: this quieter love enables them to keep that promise. It is on this love that the engine of marriage is run: being in love was the explosion that started it.[54]

Reflect on and celebrate the ways in which the two of you see this seasoned kind of love in your marriage.

Marital Skill Building

Part of this more complete love is mastering the art of accommodation, a craft greatly beneficial to couples in mission. "Learning to accommodate is an absolute essential ingredient for vital family living."[55] Through accommodation, spouses figure out how to be content when things are not going exactly as they would hope, expect, or plan. One survey participant wrote about growing in this way: "We were able to overcome many different obstacles by relying and finding strength and faith in each other."[56] Another returned missioner shared, "Trials drove us together, as we allowed that to happen."[57] Yet another claimed, "Our experience was the first time that we had to be completely honest with one another. ... I think having to be with my spouse in moments of tension and finding our way through those situations really helped us to get to know each other in a more intimate way."[58] A heightened sense of accommodation can also be realized in concrete actions of kindness. One former volunteer commented on the presence of compliance in her marriage: "In the

51 Kenny, "Married Missioner/Volunteer Survey," 40.
52 Kenny, "Married Missioner/Volunteer Survey," 39.
53 Kenny, "Married Missioner/Volunteer Survey," 38.
54 C. S. Lewis, *Mere Christianity* (New York: HarperOne, 2001), 146.
55 Anderson and Fite, *Becoming Married*, 92.
56 Kenny, "Married Missioner/Volunteer Survey," 30.
57 Kenny, "Married Missioner/Volunteer Survey," 30.
58 Kenny, "Married Missioner/Volunteer Survey," 29.

evenings, I wanted to spend time with our neighbors. My husband would hang out with our kids, giving me the chance to spend time with a single mom or with a child whose father was acting crazy."[59] When spouses come together in compromise, both partners reap the benefits that such mutuality can offer.

You and your significant other may be spending time with each other in new and different ways, both romantically and in friendship. My husband and I had never played as many games of Scrabble or discussed as many books as we did while we were in Honduras. You are likely getting practice at relating to other people as a couple. The two of you may now understand that the kind of adventure you are having is par excellence. For you yourselves are not *taking* the adventure, but rather, God has *taken* you both for a ride—a ride for which you know neither the duration nor the destination. Each of you is probably becoming more physically comfortable with the other; your spouse's sweat stains, frequent trips to the bathroom, and obscene number of mosquito bites simply does not bother you as much anymore. You are in the beautiful process of creating memories that will make you laugh, memories that will humble you, and memories of special people you will hold onto forever. You and your spouse are becoming a better team, or as one survey participant so neatly phrased it, "We have become like salt and pepper."[60] As the most popular table condiments in the world, the two of you are figuring out how to do the hard stuff well.

Personal Reflection

This last section will be the only personal story of considerable length I will share in this handbook—for *Married in Mission* is meant to be about you, your partner, and your time in service. That being said, this particular reflection illustrates just how powerful learning to do the hard stuff well as married volunteers can be.

As you may remember, Pat and I were *Padrinos*, the primary caretakers—the one-year parents—of specific groups of children at an orphanage in Honduras. Pat was on a team of individuals who were responsible for thirty-three boys, ages 5–13. Out of these thirty-three children, Pat often ended up working with one kid in particular. We shall call him José. This boy had been an alcoholic since he was three years old. His father had thought it was "funny" to consistently give his son beer as a toddler. Now age ten, José was struggling with the severe developmental delays he had incurred because of his early alcohol consumption. One minute he would be smiling at you, arms wide open, asking, "*Y mi abrazo?*" The next minute he would be shouting profanities and knocking over benches simply because a *Padrino* had told him that he needed to wash the dishes he had used during a meal. This *Padrino* was almost always Pat. Nearly every day, I would watch Pat tenderly, yet firmly, walk José back into the cafeteria to wash his plate and cup—hoping to instill some kind of accountability within this damaged child.

One evening José was more aggressive than usual. As Pat was making his way toward the cafeteria with José, this young boy was screaming in rage, kicking Pat's legs, wildly throwing punches, and hurling his body into Pat's. I stood about ten yards away, not quite sure what to do, and noticed that more and more people—staff and children—had stopped to observe how this entanglement would unfold. I remember this so clearly, as if it had happened in

59 Kenny, "Married Missioner/Volunteer Survey," 30.
60 Kenny, "Married Missioner/Volunteer Survey," 39.

slow motion. José turned his head, pulled it back, and then spit directly into my husband's face. My whole body lurched. Everyone else waited, with eyes wide open to see what Pat's reaction would be; even little José had paused for that moment. Without a second's hesitation, Pat calmly wiped the spit from his face, and continued to gently lead José back to the cafeteria.

I had never seen Pat so disrespected. I felt helpless and embarrassed. I frantically thought, *"Ali! How could you have done this to him? You dragged your new husband down here to fulfill your own selfish dream, and look what happened. What kind of wife are you?"* It was at that moment my heart understood something that my mind had missed. *"Oh no,"* my heart said to me, *"you did not put Pat in this position Ali. God has allowed him to be here. God has allowed him to be here."* And it was true. God had privileged Pat. It was Pat's *privilege* to be a starkly contrasting male figure to what José had experienced in his life. Pat did not hit, he held; he did not yell, he spoke; he did not become angry, he chose to show love. Pat had learned how to do the hard stuff well; and I really cannot describe how fortunate I felt (and continue to feel) in having been able to walk alongside my husband in that particular moment of his service experience.

Finalization

Chapter 5
End of Abroad Experience

The beginning of the end of the end of the beginning has begun.

—M. Gustave in *The Grand Budapest Hotel*

<u>Finalization</u>

Where have the past _____ months/years gone? The days that have always seemed so long—grouped into weeks that passed by more quickly— are now coming to a close. **Finalization** constitutes the last few months you and your spouse will spend in your host country. Returned married missioners reported feeling a range of emotions during this phase: regret, sadness, panic, anxiousness, conflict, confusion, anticipation, excitement, fulfillment, relief, accomplishment, gratefulness, reflectiveness, and/or preparedness. If you both refer to the *Stages of Cross-Cultural Transition* timeline in the Preface, the upward trajectory of your adaptation will eventually come to a peak at "hope of home" and then will likely take a downward turn of despondency as you and your partner begin to conclude your time abroad. Similar to the phase of preparation, reaching the end of your service experience is both a time of good-byes and a looking ahead toward what is to come. However, instead of equipping yourselves for simple living in a foreign locale, the two of you are now getting ready for the return to your familiar, Westernized lifestyle—an old life to be lived in a new way. Because certain correlations exist between this stage and the second, it may be beneficial for you and your spouse to revisit some of the topics and exercises in Chapter 2.

<u>Spousal Dynamics</u>

Though now assumedly co-spouses, you and your significant other may be approaching your departure date differently. One partner may have had a generally good experience of international service, while the other may be feeling a mixture of both positive and negative emotions concerning his/her time in mission. One survey participant commented on this dynamic in his own marriage: "The nursing position for which my wife was recruited was given to a local person (not a nurse) before we arrived, which created an awkward situation. I ended up having a more meaningful role at the site than she, though we often worked together."[1] When partners have such a diversified ministry experience, it is not surprising if one spouse is more open to extending his/her overseas commitment than the other. The degree of personal engagement (mental, emotional, social, and spiritual) with one's service work plays a large role in how an individual undergoes finalization.

It is important for you and your partner to understand how each other copes with endings. What each of you brings to any transitional situation is a psychological disposition you have developed for dealing with separation. As the product of both early experiences and subsequent influences, your psychological disposition, or coping style, is your own way of navigating through the external circumstances and inner distresses of conclusions. "Your

---

1   Kenny, "Married Missioner/Volunteer Survey," 22.

coping style is likely to reflect your childhood situation, as changes experienced within your family system set different members off on different tasks" in the midst of readjustment.[2] How you adapted to such shifts as a child was impacted by how your parents and siblings handled (or did not handle) events of instability. For example, if your father was not expressive in his display of emotions during times of transition, you may have either followed suit, likely to a greater extreme, or overcompensated by developing strong emotional reactions to change. In normal human development, individuals continue to construct their coping styles by picking up certain characteristics of significant others' psychological tendencies, and making them a part of their own approach to processing endings.[3] Simply put, how you and your spouse will each respond to this upcoming transition in your lives is complex, yet it can be explored through guided reflection.

Coping Styles[4]
Duration: 45–60 minutes

Learning how your partner reacts to separation can help you to better support him/her during these final months abroad. The following exercise will direct both of you in exploring the defining features of each other's coping styles.

STEP 1: Individual Reflection. Each spouse will need a sheet of paper and a pen or a pencil. As individuals, read through the next few paragraphs and respond to the questions below on your respective pieces of paper.

Looking back at your past experiences of endings, what can you say about your own style in handling occasions that are coming to a close? Is your style abrupt or gradual? Active or passive? Internal or external? Emotion-filled or emotionless? Privately or communally managed? Think about how you tend to act at the end of an evening at a friend's house or a night downtown. Do you try to drag things out by starting new conversations and activities as others seem ready to leave, or do you suddenly say that you had a nice time and dash out with spouse in tow?

Write down a few adjectives describing your coping style, and several concrete examples of how you have said good-bye in the past. Once you are both finished, share what you have uncovered with each other.

STEP 2: Life Changes. With your own coping styles in mind, look over the points on the next page as individuals. When you come across a loss or a change you have experienced in the past few years (excluding this point of your time overseas), follow the prompts and write about the details of that event:

---

2 Bridges, *Transitions*, 15.
3 Bridges, *Transitions*, 15.
4 Adapted from Bridges, *Transitions*, 15, 22–23 and B. Razak, *Peace Corps Close of Service Workshop: Trainer Guidelines and Workshop Materials* (Washington, DC: Peace Corps Office of Programming and Training Co-ordination, 1981), 163–65, quoted in Clyde N. Austin, "Appendix E: Moving On," in *Cross-Cultural Reentry*, 269–70.

- **Loss of Relationship.** List the relationships in your life that have recently come to an end. Include the death of a loved one, a friend or family member moving away, marital separation, children leaving home, or the alienation of a former colleague. Consider the death of a pet, the loss of some admired hero, or anything else that has narrowed your field of relationships.

- **Personal Change.** List the personal changes you have undergone in the last few years. Include getting married, having a child, becoming a grandparent, returning to school, getting sick or recovering from an illness, experiencing notable success or failure, changing your eating habits, sleeping patterns, or expressions of intimacy, or making other marked alterations to your lifestyle or appearance.

- **Work and Financial Change.** List the employment and economic changes that have recently impacted you and your family. Include an increase or decrease in income, getting laid off, starting a different job, retiring or having a spouse retire, undergoing adjustments made within your work organization, taking on new loans or mortgages, or realizing that career advancements have been either blocked or revealed.

- **Inner Change.** List the internal changes you have experienced in the past several years. Include spiritual awakenings, a deepened social/political awareness, psychological insights, shifts in self-image or primary values, the discovery of a new dream or the abandonment of an old one, or simply one of those nameless turns that caused you to say, *"I am not the person I was before."*

STEP 3: Discussion. Once the two of you have finished writing, share with each other some of the major life changes you have identified from above, how those changes impacted you, and what coping styles you utilized for each situation.

STEP 4: Coping and Emotions. Designate a *Spouse #1* and a *Spouse #2*. Each partner is to answer the following two questions in the appropriate columns:

1. List <u>five</u> emotions you remember feeling during the endings you named in STEP 2.
2. List <u>three</u> things you did that helped you navigate through those times of change.

Spouse #1	*Spouse #2*
Emotions	**Emotions**

-

-

-

      •

Spouse #1	*Spouse #2*
Self-Help Actions	**Self-Help Actions**

-
-
-

   •

   •

   •

STEP 5: Dialogue. *Spouse #1* can start the conversation by discussing the answers he/she wrote in response to the questions in STEP 4. Continue this discussion in talking through the following prompts:

- Did any of the emotions you identified above affect your ability to manage past transitions?
- Are you beginning to experience similar emotions during the finalization phase?
- Do any of the self-help actions you listed reflect your coping style?
- Will you be able to employ any of those self-help actions during the conclusion of your international ministry?

Once *Spouse #1* has finished sharing, *Spouse #2* is to repeat this step. If you and your partner have the time and energy to continue with this exercise, please move on to the following step. If either of you needs a break, take it here. Come back to STEP 6 within the next few days.

STEP 6: Finish That Sentence. The last part of this activity is a sentence completion assignment. Completing the statements in this step can help you and your significant other verbally process some of the thoughts you may have about your forthcoming departure and re-entry experience.

Designate a *Spouse #1* and a *Spouse #2* (or keep continue with the same labels as had in the first part of this exercise). *Spouse #1* will begin by reading the written portion of the first sentence aloud, and then completing the statement with whatever thought comes to mind as quickly and honestly as possible. (Think free association.) *Spouse #2* is to jot down a few notes about what *Spouse #1* shares. Next, partners are to switch roles and *Spouse #2* is to repeat and complete the same sentence. Continue alternating until you both have made it through the entire list.

- When I think of leaving, I feel ...
- My experience here has been ...
- (Insert host country) has taught me about ...
- The things that I will miss are ...
- The things I will be happy to leave behind are ...
- God is present here in ...

- Before we return home, I want to …
- The most stressful part of leaving will be …
- Through this experience, God has shown me …
- I will be going back to …
- I expect the process of returning will be …
- When I think of seeing our families again I …
- I think my family will expect me to …
- In terms of a career, I hope to …
- I assume that my friends will …
- I think the hardest part about going back to our passport country will be …
- I think the easiest thing for me to handle will be …
- To me, being Christian/Catholic means …

STEP 7: *Discussion*. Both spouses are to take turns verbally summarizing the notes he/she wrote down. If a certain part of your partner's summary is incorrect, say so, and clarify what you initially shared. Talk about what common themes you see in each other's answers, what surprised you, and offer any pieces of advice or words of encouragement you may have.

Grief

As your departure draws nearer and nearer, both you and your significant other may start to experience symptoms of grief. Because most missioners know the circumstances in which they are leaving their service site(s), their grieving process is unique in that it can be categorized as an *anticipated loss*. According to pastoral theologians Mitchell and Anderson, "Loss that occurs over a period of time may be particularly painful exactly because it is prolonged. … This gradual process often feels so threatening that people avoid acknowledging it. Such avoidance works to the detriment of managing the final loss when it occurs."[5] Recognizing that your time overseas is limited and finite is important. To mentally, emotionally, and spiritually ready yourselves for this change is one of the best things the two of you can do to honor the volunteer work of which you were a part. One way you and your spouse can prepare for this transition is to let go of the roles you have taken on in your ministries. Because we identify ourselves within the circumstances of our lives, moving from one context to another requires us to release the identities we have constructed for ourselves in particular roles and their supporting frameworks. The starting point in psychologically dealing with your transitional situations is not the outcome, but the ending you and your partner will have to make in order to leave the old condition behind.[6] As William Bridges explains, "Unmanaged transition makes change unmanageable."[7] Thus, international missioners are encouraged to hand over or let go of the roles and responsibilities they had at their service sites.

If you and/or your spouse has a volunteer successor, it will do you well to gradually entrust the duties associated with your job to him/her. Be aware of the dynamics between yourself and this person. Your perspectives, attitudes, and motivations as a seasoned missioner may clash with your successor's perspectives, attitudes, and motivations as a newcomer (or a local). Moreover, your personal styles of working and relating to others might contrast. Try

---

5   Mitchell and Anderson, *All Our Losses,* 58–59.
6   Bridges, *Managing Transitions,* 7.
7   Bridges, *Managing Transitions,* 7.

to make this handing over of responsibilities a conversation, not a one-sided instruction. First, ask what information your successor needs or wants, and *then* supply him/her with the information you have prepared (e.g., individual biographies, lesson plans, or project summaries). The person taking over your job will do it differently, and that is OK. You fulfilled your ministerial position differently than the missioner (or local) who came before you. Those with whom you worked have benefited from your particular approach to service, and they will also benefit from the approach of the next volunteer. Acknowledging this can be comforting in and of itself. As you and your spouse reflect on your past efforts, recognize the invaluable impact you both have made and wish your successors the same kind of positive outcome.

Moving on from your mission assignment also entails saying good-bye to people whom you have grown to love. Natives in the community with whom you have served—though most likely having experienced the transitory presence of expatriates before—might feel that you and your partner are leaving them behind. They may express, openly or covertly, their pain, anger, and/or resentment. This is especially true of children. "The underlying thought is that the leaving person has chosen to do so … and is deliberately abandoning the one left. Whether the 'leaver' actually has a choice is irrelevant; the feeling of being abandoned is present."[8] Handling the conflicting emotions you may experience in response to local people's reactions to your pending departure can be confusing and difficult. The following section will help you and your partner construct meaningful good-byes, so that each of you is able to part with others on good terms.

Constructing Goodbyes

Minister and counselor Victor L. Hunter poetically conceptualizes departing as he writes:

> The language of farewells has its own set of nouns and verbs. The nouns are persons, places, and events. The verbs are intransitive and belong to the category of being—for to say goodbye or to grieve always touches the verb "to be." That is, they are related to who we are as persons, to our existence, to those realities and relationships that at the deepest level make us who we are.[9]

In short, saying goodbye is important. Ensuring that you and your spouse leave behind the friendships you have formed during your service experience in a meaningful way can give you both the closure most people need in transitions as substantial as these. Not only are the two of you leave-taking relationships as they currently exist, but, as mentioned earlier, you and your partner are moving away from the particular self-images that accompanied the roles you filled in establishing those connections. My own departure centered around creating a sense of release for myself and the sixteen little girls for whom I had cared during my volunteer year. I was called to let go of the motherly role to which I had grown accustomed. From whoever and whatever you are parting, the way in which you do so is paramount. "Without a meaningful goodbye, an effective release, there cannot be a creative hello, a hopeful commencement."[10]

---

8   Mitchell and Anderson, *All Our Losses*, 50.
9   Victor L. Hunter, "Closure and Commencement: The Stress of Finding Home," in *Cross-Cultural Reentry*, 182.
10 Storti, *The Art of Coming Home*, 43.

Each person's approach to closing a chapter in his/her life will vary. Some might need the recognition that comes with a formal departure, while others prefer the unrestrictedness found in a less-acknowledged sendoff. If you are an individual who likes to slip away unnoticed during times of change, keep in mind that good-byes involve other people. Even though you feel comfortable leaving on open-ended terms, your favorite colleague, fellow missioner, child, or neighbor may need a more confirmatory farewell from you for their own well-being. In other cases, the opposite may be true. Natives of your host country might not approach transitions in the ways you and your spouse might hope or assume. One former volunteer wrote about such an experience:

> We tried to prepare our kids for leaving. Our oldest, at age 17, was ready to move on and go to college. Her younger brother was nine, I think. He was born overseas. His first two languages were not English. He had a village grandfather he was very close to. We told our son we were leaving. We told his grandfather we were leaving. The older man's way to handle this was to disappear into the bush. Our son did not get to say goodbye to him. We tried to prepare them, but other folks can behave in different ways and things may not work out as expected.[11]

If you are able to, create a celebratory and ritualized kind of conclusion that honors the local people you love. This kind of acceptance and appreciation can be positively constructive, for an observed ending is a healthy form of boundary-making.

An intentional act of closure acknowledges what has been gained, as well as what will be lost. It affirms the blessedness—the sacramentality—of the bond that exists and will continue to exist between you and your special companions. Plan final meals to be shared, write letters to individuals, take pictures with friends or groups of people with whom you worked, host a going-away party, schedule time for final conversations, and/or give small mementos to significant persons. One former volunteer commented on how he and his spouse prepared for their departure during the finalization phase:

> Finding new homes for our "possessions" acquired during our time in community was a way for us to give back—we did have different opinions about what we should do (give away versus sell to those who could not afford it). It took several conversations to resolve, but we did reach an agreement.[12]

Be thoughtful in your gift-giving. One program director cautioned, "Most organizations are very clear about missioners giving money or materials to the local people—it can create unrealistic expectations, a sense of favoritism and even issues of security."[13] As touched upon in Chapter 4, ensure that any kind of memento-sharing is done in accordance with your institution's stance on the matter. Gratefully accept cards or trinkets people may pass on to you. If you or your partner does not yet have one, find an object you can take home with you as a physical representation of your host country. "Endings occur more easily if individuals can take a bit of the past with them."[14]

---

11 Colin Murphy, personal e-mail, May 15, 2015.
12 Kenny, "Married Missioner/Volunteer Survey," 210.
13 Vic Doucette, personal e-mail, April 8, 2015.
14 Bridges, *Managing Transitions*, 35.

Anxieties

There are many questions to be answered before returning to your passport country: In what city/town are you going to live? Will you be moving into your old house? Renting or purchasing a new place? Are you trying to find a different job or are you going back to the one you had before? Starting a graduate degree? Adjusting to a life of retirement? Do you need to re-enroll your kids into their previous school or start the process all over again at another one? What other familial obligations do you foresee needing to address? Negotiating all these considerations as two different people with two different experiences of a shared service commitment must be done with an accommodating attitude. One survey participant attested to the flexibility necessary in managing such logistics: "We needed to make the decision about where we would be living when our time was up. We were on very different pages and both had to make a compromise before we finally decided on a location."[15] Each of you will be preoccupied with figuring out what personal preparations need to be made in regard to your return home (I–You), which means you both must consciously try to stay in conversation with each other concerning joint arrangements (We). It can be a lot to think about now, but approaching your departure from an I–You–We perspective is a critical step in maintaining the overall balance you and your spouse seek in your marriage.

In terms of readying yourselves as individuals for life back home, there are a few things you and your partner may want to think about pertaining to your future professions. If you have access to the Internet, you can subscribe to electronic journals to stay informed on whatever topic or field of study is most applicable. You may also want to sign up for online classes to review specific material. Some mission organizations have information on universities or companies specifically seeking to enroll or hire individuals with cross-cultural volunteer experience. In whatever way you can, educate yourself so that you remain competent as a potential graduate student or employee. Remember to update your résumé by adding the ministerial work responsibilities with which you were charged and the skills you have acquired. (See the exercise *Elevator Speech* in this chapter for brainstorming ideas.) Catching up on what is happening more generally in your home culture is also a good thing to do during your last few months abroad. Integrating small tastes of what your lives will be like when you and your partner return to your passport country can give you modest boosts of confidence and assist with your pending transition.

But let us get back to the bigger picture. You and your spouse may be making some major changes to the life plans originally in place at the start of your time overseas. The people you have met, the situations you have encountered, and the reality in which you have lived for a considerable period has presumably transformed you both. Thus, you and your partner may be rewriting parts of your "five-year-plus" plan. Taking what you respect about your host country's culture with you to your home country is a complex yet potentially fulfilling task. Integrating your life abroad with your more permanent lifestyle is something that can only be done once you and your spouse have actually returned home. However, it may prove to be helpful if the two of you start to dialogue about how you would like to incorporate elements of this experience into your future goals or dreams. In order to begin this conversation, you and your partner will need to consciously reflect on your overseas ministries, and this next exercise will have you do just that.

---

15 Kenny, "Married Missioner/Volunteer Survey," 210.

Shared Ministry Timeline[16]
Duration: 30–45 minutes

It has been said that a picture is worth a thousand words. If so, then capturing your shared service experience on paper may be worth millions. In this timeline exercise, you and your spouse are going to create a grid that will give you both a bird's eye view of this particular period in you lives. Partners who make their overseas ministry into a timeline are able to identify and connect themes that cut across each other's life events.

STEP 1: Reflection. Each spouse will need a piece of paper, a pen or a pencil, and a larger sheet of paper to share. Take about ten to fifteen minutes to personally reflect on the course of your own experience abroad—its highs and lows, as well as the stable moments. Write down all of the important events, special people, personal conversions, etc., that come to mind. Try to name between ten and twenty items.

STEP 2: Rank. As individuals, put these items in chronological order. Next, place a plus sign in front of the items that were generally positive, and a minus sign in front of the ones that were generally negative. Rank the intensity of each event on a scale of 1 to 10, with "1" being completely negative and "10" being completely positive.

STEP 3: Combined Chronology. Once you both have finished rating the items on your own lists, combine them while maintaining the correct chronology. Now that you have each completed the preparatory steps, you are ready to construct your shared ministry timeline. If you have difficulties with any of the following steps, refer to **Figure 5.1** on the next page for an abbreviated example.

STEP 4: Axis. Together, take your larger sheet of paper and fold it in half along the horizontal axis. Draw a line along this crease.

STEP 5: Top and Bottom. Place a plus sign on the top-right corner above the horizontal axis, by which to classify the positive items. Place a minus sign on the bottom-left corner below the horizontal axis, by which to classify the negative items.

STEP 6: Adding Items. Draw a dot on the horizontal axis of your shared timeline for each of the key items recorded on your combined list, with the left side of the paper being past-oriented and the right side being more present-oriented. Be sure to maintain the correct chronological order. Allow ample space between items so that they are evenly spread across the paper.

STEP 7: Line Intensity. From these dots, the two of you are to draw a line for each of your events (either above or below the horizontal axis). Make the line as tall or short as its indicated intensity, based on the numeric value that you have assigned it. As you and your

---

16 Adapted from Athena Staik, "How to Create a Timeline: The Power of Re-working Your Life's Story, 1 of 2," *PsychCentral,* last modified January 5, 2013, http://blogs.psychcentral.com/relationships/2012/04/the-power-of-creating-a-timeline-of-your-lifes-story/.

spouse create your shared ministry timeline, be open to adding additional items. It is natural for one event to trigger the memory of another.

+

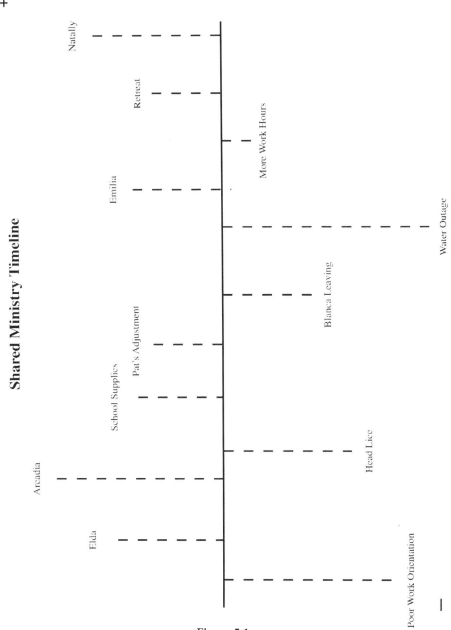

Figure 5.1

STEP 8: Remembrance. Once you both have completed your timeline, put it in a place where you will see it every day. This image will serve as a gentle reminder of your departure, while also calling to mind the entirety of your overseas experience. This exercise can provide you and your partner an opportunity to examine how you each relate to your time spent in ministry.

Anxieties Continued

As reported by several former missioners, the issue of finances can be a source of enduring stress. One survey participant wrote, "Preparing for what was next was a hardship for us. We also realized that we lost significant amounts of money by volunteering."[17] Returning to your passport country can be expensive. The cost of getting new cell phones with updated plans; obtaining or renewing auto, life, and health insurance; stocking your home with food and household supplies; and possibly having to rent vehicles and pay for travel costs because of a homeland relocation can really add up. One thing you can do to help ease the anxiety that this initial excess spending can cause is to create an anticipated budget for your and your partner's re-entry expenses. Try to be as detailed and accurate as possible. This may mean you will have to research your home country's price trends. A few service programs give their volunteers a grace period during which the organization continues to provide them with health insurance. Some institutions pay missioners a return stipend. Still others cover the cost for an individual's re-entry retreat. Inquire about what kinds of monetary compensations your sending program offers.

Children also need to be actively engaged in preparation during the finalization phase. One survey participant wrote, "Returning to the USA with children raised overseas and their adjustment was difficult for them and us."[18] Current age and length of time abroad are two principal factors in estimating the degree of difficulty your children may have when relocating to their passport country. Teens have the hardest time adjusting to a new lifestyle, even if it is a lifestyle to which they were accustomed before. If your adolescent has started to cement peer relationships and develop an adult identity overseas, uprooting him/her from that environment can be a painful experience.[19] No matter what their age, encourage your children to prepare to leave (insert host country) in their own ways. Listen to your kids. Expatriate counselor Pascoe advises, "Take your children to lunch before your departure and hear out what they have to say about going home. Listen carefully to their expectations and apprehensions."[20] Communicating with your children about their experience of the finalization stage allows them to process externally, which in turn tunes you into their needs. Before you officially resettle, traveling within your own country for a week or two after your initial return is a good way to bring your family up-to-date, culturally speaking.[21]

Forgiveness

Lastly is forgiveness. In Chapter 3, you and your spouse learned about how forgiveness is the ultimate "Christian relational skill."[22] While it will be hard to leave certain relationships

---

17 Kenny, "Married Missioner/Volunteer Survey," 210.
18 Kenny, "Married Missioner/Volunteer Survey," 210.
19 Fontaine, "International Relocation," 46.
20 Pascoe, *Culture Shock! Successful Living Abroad,* 202.
21 Pascoe, *Culture Shock! Successful Living Abroad,* 203.
22 Thomas, *Christian Marriage,* 11.

behind, there will be some from which you will move on with relief and gratitude. There may be particular people who want to seek out your forgiveness. Similarly, you may be in pursuit of forgiveness from others. Beyond these more disagreeable kinds of tensions is the unfortunate reality that some missioners experience trauma during their service abroad. If you are one of those volunteers, you may consider seeking help from a mental health professional upon your return home. As mentioned before, it would be best to find a counselor with whom to work that has a specialty or concentration in both trauma and cross-cultural relations. In learning to cope with past abuse and managing troublesome relationships, understanding what it means to forgive may be helpful.

Forgiveness is not a capacity we earn; it is something that God has unreservedly given us. Forgiving another person is "a transformation of human relationships that requires more than we ourselves can achieve," says reconciliation specialist Fr. Robert Schreiter. "In forgiving we recognize the work of God within us—restoring our humanity."[23] Schretier asserts that forgiveness is not so much about the deed that has caused someone pain, as it is about the relationship that the pained individual has with the deed's ongoing effects. When you forgive someone, whether they are present or not, you give yourself the freedom to have a different future.[24] Forgiving is not forgetting or ignoring the past; forgiving is remembering the past in a different way. Forgiveness is a central and powerful piece of the Christian tradition. Be generous in your pardoning and humble in your asking of it. "God … calls us to a ministry, a praxis of forgiveness. This is the intent of Jesus' breathing the Holy Spirit upon the disciples after the resurrection, and giving them the power to forgive sins (Jn 20:22–23)."[25] As Christians enjoined to a praxis of forgiveness, we recommit ourselves to it every time we say *"and forgive us our trespasses as we forgive those who trespass against us."* As you are able to, work to actualize this commitment during your last few months abroad.

Miscellaneous

Here are a few more things for you and your spouse to consider during the finalization phase:

Second thoughts about your departure date. One former volunteer shared, "At the end of our commitment, I began to wish we had a little more time. I was really missing my family and friends back home, but I also wanted to stay longer."[26] As stated in Chapter 4, the choice to renew your overseas commitment should already have been made. Try to navigate through the conflicting emotions you or your partner may feel without second thoughts. Stick to the emotionally intelligent decision you both made during the routinization stage as you near the end of your stay, despite some of the sadness and regret you may encounter.

Say goodbye to special places. A particular classroom, church, restaurant, or hidden spot on the bank of a nearby river could hold a certain significance for you or your spouse. Make a point to visit these places before you leave so you can take a mental picture of where some special memories were created.

---

23 Robert Schreiter, CPPS, "The Ministry of Forgiveness in a Praxis of Reconciliation" (presentation, International Seminar on Reconciliation, Lima, Peru, August 21, 2006), 9, http://preciousbloodspirituality.org/spirituality-and-theology/ministry-forgiveness-praxis-reconciliation.

24 Robert Schreiter, CPPS, *The Ministry of Reconciliation: Spirituality & Strategies* (New York: Orbis, 1998), 58–59.

25 Schreiter, "The Ministry of Forgiveness," 9–10.

26 Bridget Studer, personal e-mail, March 28, 2015.

Be hopeful about your return home. While most of this chapter is dedicated to your pending losses, you have so much about which to be excited. Amenities of your home culture will be yours once more: clean and running water, a variety of food, privacy, temperature-moderated buildings, safety and security, and an ant-less kitchen. Beyond these more superficial thrills are the people to whom you will be returning: grateful mothers, sentimental fathers, relieved adult children, dear friends, and so on. In other words, look forward to your homecoming!

But do not be too expectant. There always seems to be a "but." It would do you well to lower the expectations you may have of yourself and/or your loved ones back home. As Shakespeare was once thought to pen, "Expectation is the root of all heartache." You have changed. Your friends and family have changed. Life at home has gone on without you there. Do not assume that you will simply fall into who you were and what you did before your time abroad. The re-entry phase can be the hardest stage through which to maneuver for many volunteers. Hope—do not assume, suppose, or expect—for hoping is an act in the present that leaves the future in God's hands.

Be ready for changes in gender roles. It may be beneficial for you and your partner to revisit the section *Role Orientation* in Chapter 3. Once again, spousal and parental gender role orientations can shift when moving back to your passport country. You and your significant other should look to have conversations about what employment and childcare responsibilities will work best for the both of you upon your return home.

Individual Skills

As your time overseas comes to a close, you may be instinctively reflecting on all the positive memories you have created during your service experience. Before exploring the more profound ways in which your international ministries have impacted the two of you, let us start with the more cursory benefits. These are the kinds of things you would share with acquaintances asking about your life abroad. The reality is that the majority of conversations you will end up having back home about (insert host country)—even those with close friends and family will be fairly superficial. The ever-well-intentioned *"So how was South America?"* is usually an inquiry that desires no more than a few lighthearted sentences about your experience in mission.

Elevator Speech
Duration: 30–45 minutes

The following exercise is meant to take those more perfunctory conversations and infuse them with the potential to become meaningful exchanges. You and your partner can honor your ministerial experience by speaking about it in a thoughtful and open manner.

STEP 1: Ministries. Both spouses will need a piece of paper and a pen or a pencil. To start the brainstorming process, each of you is to write down all of the jobs and responsibilities you had while overseas. Do not overthink this. Simply write out statements about what you did for each position you held ("*I was a nurse at a local clinic in Yemen.*" Or, "*I was the logis-tics coordinator for retreat groups that came to visit a particular neighborhood in Ecuador.*").

STEP 2: Transferable Skills. Designate a *Spouse #1* and a *Spouse #2*. Below is a list of skills most commonly associated with a successful international volunteer. Both of you are to place checkmarks next to the competencies that you developed in the ministries you wrote down in the previous step under the appropriate columns:

Spouse #1		Spouse #2
_____	Adaptability/flexibility	_____
_____	Leadership	_____
_____	Independence	_____
_____	Problem solving	_____
_____	Non-judgmental perspective	_____
_____	Intercultural awareness	_____
_____	Cross-cultural competency	_____
_____	Self-direction	_____
_____	Patience	_____
_____	Resourcefulness	_____
_____	Ability to be with the marginalized	_____
_____	Conflict resolving	_____
_____	Dedication/commitment	_____
_____	Intentionality	_____
_____	Curiosity	_____
_____	Simple living	_____
_____	Project management	_____
_____	Resiliency/perseverance	_____
_____	Advocacy	_____
_____	Open-mindedness	_____
_____	Knowledge of self-care	_____
_____	Self-reliance	_____
_____	Communicativeness	_____
_____	Creativity/innovativeness	_____
_____	Project supervision	_____
_____	Troubleshooting	_____
_____	Trauma-informed care	_____
_____	Staff coordination	_____
_____	Empathy	_____
_____	Dependability/responsibility	_____

Spouse #1		**Spouse #2**
_____	Time management	_____
_____	Introspection	_____
_____	Mission driven	_____
_____	Self-motivation	_____
_____	Discipline	_____
_____	Self-initiative	_____
_____	Confidence	_____
_____	Perceptiveness	_____
_____	Tolerance for differences	_____
_____	Active learner	_____
_____	Compassion	_____
_____	Acquisition of new language	_____
_____	Ability to accept failure	_____
_____	Self/other-awareness	_____
_____	Objective envisioning	_____
_____	Critical thinking	_____
_____	Growth as a global citizen	_____
_____	Sense of humor	_____
_____	Other: _____	_____
_____	Other: _____	_____
_____	Other: _____	_____
_____	Other: _____	_____
_____	Other: _____	_____

STEP 3: Prompts. Please answer the following questions as individuals, being in conversation as it naturally occurs:

What five words come to mind when you think about your international service experience?

Spouse #1

1. _____
2. _____
3. _____
4. _____
5. _____

Spouse #2

1. _____
2. _____

3. _____
4. _____
5. _____

What do you think most people will misunderstand about your time overseas?

Spouse #1: _____
_____
_____
_____
_____

Spouse #2: _____
_____
_____
_____
_____

How do you see this experience impacting your life in your home country?

Spouse #1: _____
_____
_____
_____
_____

Spouse #2: _____
_____
_____
_____
_____

What are three of your favorite ministerial stories?

Spouse #1: _____
_____
_____
_____
_____

Spouse #2: _____
_____
_____
_____
_____

What kind of career now interests you? Describe your dream job.

Spouse #1: _____

_____

_____

_____

_____

Spouse #2: _____

_____

_____

_____

_____

For what has your service experience made you most grateful?

Spouse #1: _____

_____

_____

_____

_____

Spouse #2: _____

_____

_____

_____

_____

What were two of your greatest successes or accomplishments?

Spouse #1: _____

_____

_____

_____

_____

Spouse #2: _____

_____

_____

_____

_____

STEP 4: Combine Reflections. Review what you have written down for each of the previous steps and start to make connections between similar themes. Using your reflections, begin to fill in the mock elevator speech (on the following page) on your respective pieces of paper. If either of you feels constrained by the template, feel free to start writing on your own.

"Hey, you were in (insert host country) for a while, right? How was that? What did you do there?"

"It was both _____ *and* _____*! I spent most of my time there* _____
_____.

I was fortunate enough to learn how to/about _____
_____.

But the most interesting/meaningful part of the whole experience was _____
_____
_____.

I will never look at _____*the same way.*
Now I am trying to/doing _____.
I really want to remember/do _____
_____.

Did you have any specific questions about my work?"

STEP 5. Discussion. Once you and your spouse have finished, share your elevator speeches with one another. Practice saying it aloud, and give each other feedback. This is an exercise you can tailor to other types of conversations you may have about your overseas ministry as well, such as job interviews or shorter speaking engagements.

If you feel like STEP 4 unfairly reduced this activity into one short paragraph, try to re-member that day-to-day conversations about your time abroad will likely be abbreviated. If you would find it helpful, continue the process of reflecting on your experiences in a more detailed way. This can assist you in mentally organizing your thoughts, so that you are able to share different kinds of insights and stories with individuals who want to have a more in-depth discussion about your mission work.

Strengthened Partnership

Now that you and your partner have more actively contemplated the benefits of your inter-national ministry in the context of re-entry, let us return to the present and address some of the benefits specific to the finalization stage. With your departure date in sight, you and your spouse may feel a renewed sense of energy. You are no longer susceptible to the de-sensitization that can occur in the middle of your abroad experience. As you both prepare for this conclusion, you will likely be inspired to finish it well. As partners, you are able to encouragingly push each other to complete one last ministerial project or host a date night for a couple with whom you have grown close. Adopt a perspective of gratitude in these last few months abroad, and use that appreciativeness to motivate yourselves for the betterment of others.

On a final note, the two of you should make a point to look back at the special roles you have occupied in your particular communities. Fulfilling those roles has allowed you to grow in effectively and faithfully living out the I–You–We reality of your marriage. Few couples are able to develop together so intimately. You both have mastered a uniquely challeng-ing opportunity. One sure sign of a strong marriage is a couple's tendency to "elevate" the struggles they have been through as a team. Contented married individuals often "describe their marriage in terms of a worthwhile journey"—a saga in which they faced adversity and became closer because of it.[27] Many survey participants wrote about their marriage in such terms:

- "Safety was a real and constant concern. Not having space and money for restful or marital activities was also hard. However, getting through that in that environment helped us learn that it was possible to love each other and our neighbors well in that setting."[28]
- "Going into unfamiliar and uncertain situations strengthened our feelings of unity, the sense of 'it's us against the world,' which perhaps all healthy couples have."[29]
- "We felt like if we could make it through some of the difficult decisions we had to make in our mission, then we could make it through any others."[30]
- "Because we were able to get through this experience together, it seems like 'we can do anything.'"[31]

Do not be afraid to grant you and your spouse the chance to be proud of what you have done with God's help.

The next two chapters will allow you and your partner to further explore how this experience has enriched your lives. But for now, be present. Enjoy these last few months in your host country. For what you and your significant other are doing is a virtuous thing, with an inevitably melancholy end. As A.A. Milne's Winnie the Pooh once was thought to so charmingly say, "How lucky I am to have something that makes saying goodbye so hard."

---

27 Gottman and Silver, *Why Marriages Succeed or Fail*, 224.
28 Kenny, "Married Missioner/Volunteer Survey," 29.
29 Kenny, "Married Missioner/Volunteer Survey," 30.
30 Kenny, "Married Missioner/Volunteer Survey," 29.
31 Kenny, "Married Missioner/Volunteer Survey," 29.

Re-entry
Chapter 6
Post-Abroad Experience—Pre-Integration[1]

I have this strange feeling that I'm not myself anymore. It's hard to put into words, but I guess it's like I was fast asleep, and someone came, disassembled me, and hurriedly put me back together again. That sort of feeling.

—Haruki Murakami, *Sputnik Sweetheart*

Re-entry

"Re-entry is the process that occurs when an individual attempts to return to a social system of which he was once a part."[2] This sixth phase of one's service experience is often the most difficult. **Re-entry** is the time immediately following the departure from your volunteer site, up until the point of the consciously, actualized integration of your past ministry. This phase can last anywhere from six months to two-plus years after your homecoming date. Most individuals will go through reverse culture shock during re-entry. As has been defined, reverse culture shock consists of the emotional and psychological reactions a person has in response to returning to his/her passport country from an overseas experience. If you and your spouse refer to the *Stages of Cross-Cultural Transition* timeline in the Preface you will see the majority of the re-entry phase is spent in a downward pitch of "emotional processing" toward "reverse culture shock." While certain similarities exist between the culture shock you both went through in adjusting to your host country and the reverse culture shock each of you is now undergoing in readjusting to your passport country, variations between the two are notable. This chapter will address the individual symptoms felt during this post-service period and how such symptoms can potentially impact your marriage.

Reverse Culture Shock

Volunteers coming back from their international mission assignments often experience initial emotions of excitement, euphoria, intimacy, gratitude, relief, and/or freedom. In the first few weeks after returning, re-entrants tend to focus only on the positive aspects of becoming part of their past social system(s) once more, often denying the potential problems of re-acclimation. This is the time during which former missioners may try to prove to themselves that nothing has changed in their absence; or if something is different, that such contrariety is not all that significant.[3] As the weeks pass by, however, you and your partner will come to realize that things have changed and those changes *feel* significant. One or both of you might perceive a certain distance from family members with whom you were close before, may not be excited about the new buildings and businesses that have invaded your once quiet neighborhood, and could find yourself missing a certain friend who has moved to a faraway city. "As you are busy discovering that your former home no longer fits the

---

1 This chapter is informed by the service that **From Mission to Mission** has provided the missioner community for the past 35 years.

2 Diane P. Jansson, "Return to Society: Problematic Features of the Re-entry Process," in *Cross-Cultural Reentry*, 49.

3 Jansson, "Return to Society," 51.

bill, your overseas home is already receding into memory. To reenter, it turns out, is to be temporarily homeless."[4] It is not so much that things are different in and of themselves; in fact, they are most likely quite similar to what they were before you left. The problem is that you and your spouse are viewing your homeland from a new perspective, while also holding onto expectations of returning to the familiar. Experiencing your surroundings in this way can be more shocking than actual differentiation.

Moreover, it may feel that no one outside of your significant other seems to truly understand (or even want to understand) how your overseas ministry has impacted you. The inadequate check-in of *"How was it?"* can feel constricting, forcing you to construct a trite description of the immensity of your time in service. As you haphazardly string together stories about important people and events, your questioner's eyes glaze over in an attitude of unknowing. (This can happen even if you did use the meaningful and succinct elevator speech you wrote in Chapter 5.) Most people simply do not know how to react to your responses to their posed queries. Such a disconnect is no one's fault, so it is best to keep that pointing finger at your side. It is at this point that the more negative emotions associated with re-entry can arise: irritability, hostility, disjointedness, fear, anxiety, discontinuity, helplessness, lethargy, grief, guilt, sadness, imbalance, anger, self-doubt, isolation, disappointment, unfulfillment, and/or numbness. From these kinds of feelings come the symptoms that constitute one's experience of reverse culture shock:

- Somatization (headaches, fatigue, colds, muscle pain, etc.)
- Frequent mood swings
- Judgment of others
- Inability to concentrate or relax
- Trouble sleeping
- Social withdrawal
- Internal bargaining
- Physical/emotional exhaustion
- Depression
- Selective memory
- Intimacy issues
- Unwarranted suspicion
- Panic attacks
- Various forms of resistance[5]

Managing emotions associated with reverse culture shock, and the manifestations of those feelings as a couple, must be done from the I–You–We perspective.

Certain kinds of questions can surface during this phase: questions of relevancy (*"How do I apply what I learned in Slovakia to my life here?"*); questions in regard to the social psychology behind your homecoming (*"How are my thoughts, feelings, and behaviors influenced by the actual, imagined, or implied presence of others?"*);[6] and questions about the interactional

---

4   Storti, *The Art of Coming Home*, 29.

5   Adapted from Jo Ann McCaffrey, *At Home in the Journey: Theological Reflection for Missioners in Transition* (Chicago: CCGM Publications, 2005), 70.

6   Kendra Cherry, "What Is Social Psychology?," *About Education*, http://psychology.about.com/od/socialpsychology/f/socialpsych.htm.

processing of your re-entry (*"How do I, as a changed person, want to relate to others?"*). The answers to these kinds of inquiries can only be arrived at in good time, in good company, and in good reflective action. Living in this in-between time is symbolized by how many returned missioners self-identify with prefixes such as "ex-," "post-," or "re-." *"I am an ex-volunteer ... I am in a post-service transition ... I am re-adjusting to life here."* The current images you and your spouse may have of yourselves exist only in relation to who you were or where you were just a month (or so) ago. This kind of self-perception is OK to employ for now. But as you and your partner move through the re-entry phase, toward the stage of integration, both of you will presumably begin to experience feelings of congruency, creativity, and peacefulness. It is at this time that each of you will be able to name yourself, not as a deviation of your overseas ministry, but as a transformed synthesis of the past and present you.

Individual Adjustment

A significant piece of working through the re-entry process is the addressing and handling of unmet expectations. Whether consciously held or not, you and your spouse have certain hopes of what you want your initial arrival to your passport country to look like, as well as assumptions of how the continuation of your coming home should unfold. More often than not, many of your expectations will be disaffirmed: the job to which you have returned is not as fulfilling as it once was, time spent with your partner surrounded by Westernized comforts feels empty and boring, and the death of your grandmother is a reality now more acutely felt. Even your more superficial suppositions are being invalidated—your dog barely remembers you and the McFlurry you have been craving for months tastes too sweet. Hopefully the promptings in Chapter 5 helped you and your significant other to lower your return-home expectations. If not, your new reality has likely adjusted your presumptions. Try to acknowledge and work through the discomfort or anger either one of you may feel from your idealized pedestals being fractured. Living in a developed nation is an unwarranted privilege, a flawed and complicated opportunity.

Many former missioners experience reactions of aversion to particular realities within more developed societies. Wastefulness in your passport country can be especially troubling if your ministry site was located in an impoverished community. The pace of life can run at a much faster clip than the culture from which you have just returned. Coming back to an environment of constant commercialism and materialistic consumption was a hardship expressed by several survey participants: "Reverse culture shock was very real. I could not go to a big grocery store, for example, and had to shop at a very small one in our town. Even then it was hard because of the number of choices."[7] Another returned volunteer wrote, "I hated shopping in the big box stores and supermarkets, while my husband seemed not to mind. He accepted returning to the United States while I questioned the excessive ways we consume things here."[8] (Figuring out how to handle differing reactions to such matters will be addressed in the section *Spousal Dynamics* in this chapter.) Lastly, re-entrants can feel frustrated by the general ignorance of international affairs, narrow worldviews, and/or racial prejudices held by fellow compatriots. In meeting these challenges, you and your partner have the opportunity to practice the patience and tolerance you have both developed during your time overseas. You simply cannot hold other people accountable for the

---

7   Bridget Studer, personal e-mail, March 28, 2015.
8   Kenny, "Married Missioner/Volunteer Survey," 217.

experiences each of you has had. Instead, focus on incorporating mission-inspired princi-ples (e.g., conservation, peace, open-mindedness, global citizenship, spirituality, etc.) you now hold in higher esteem within your own family system.

Contributing Factors

It is likely that you and your spouse are responding to returning home in different ways. One survey participant agreed with this sentiment in writing, "It is normal for all persons to have differing rates and intensities of re-entry experiences. It is always potentially frus-trating within a couple when the two are not experiencing the same thing at the same time. However, because we knew this would happen, we were gentle with one another."[9] Beyond having distinct personalities, you and your partner each have a unique relationship with your overseas service, even though it was a shared ministry. Below is a list of the primary factors that contributed to your individual experience abroad:

- Difference between host and home countries
- Length of commitment
- Degree of immersion
- Type of work
- Age(s) while volunteering
- Amount of interaction with home culture (via communication with loved ones or through technology) while in host country
- Decision to extend service
- Intensity/complexity of attachment to experience (positive, negative, or mixed)
- Reason for leaving (voluntary or involuntary)
- Previous re-entry experience(s) had
- Type and amount of change in home culture while away
- Presence (or lack) of support systems upon return to home country
- Type of lifestyle in place upon return to home country[10]

Some variables will be the same for you both (length of commitment or difference between host and home countries), while others will be exclusive unto each of you (degree of cul-tural immersion or type of work). While these elements will impact the experience of your re-entry process, they do not necessarily define it. That being said, I have developed an equation based on several of these factors that can give you and your partner an estimate of how long it may take the two of you to move from the re-entry stage to the final integration phase. Approach this formula as simply a food-for-thought proposition:

The Transition Equation[11]

$$[(A \times B) + (Y + Z)]/2.5 = M$$

A = Degree of cultural immersion, with "1" being not at all immersed and "10" being com-pletely immersed.

---

9   Kenny, "Married Missioner/Volunteer Survey," 215.

10 Adapted from Storti, *The Art of Coming Home*, 70.

11 Adapted from Samantha Limberger, "The Break-Up Equation," *Let's Ask Violet,* April 19, 2013, http://www.letsaskviolet.com/2013/04/19/the-break-up-equation/.

B = "1" if you left on the expected end date. If you returned home early, place a "2" in the equation.

Y = Intensity/complexity of attachment to experience, with "1" being purely negative and "10" being purely positive.

Z = Type of lifestyle in place upon return to home country, with "1" being mentally, socially, emotionally, and spiritually fulfilling and "10" being mentally, socially, emotionally, and spiritually unfulfilling.

M = Number of months before you will move from the processing of re-entry to the period of integration.

Here is my own mathematical process as an example:

$$[(7 \times 1) + (8 + 2)]/2.5 = M$$
$$[(7) + (10)]/2.5 = M$$
$$[17]/2.5 = M$$
$$6.8 = M$$

One re-entrant shared his opinion of the equation:

> $[(7 \times 1) + (6 + 6)]/2.5 = 7.6$. This actually feels quite accurate to my experience. The first few months were pretty awful, and that period lasted longer than I thought it would. I sort of assumed that my readjustment would be quicker/easier this time, given that this was my fourth time moving back to the States after living abroad. But it ended up still being difficult, in different ways.[12]

Yet another former volunteer wrote:

> Here's how my formula worked out—$[(8 \times 1) + (7+3)]/2.5 = 7.2$. I think rounding this out at seven months is pretty spot on for me. My reentry retreat at the six-month mark gave me the tools for integration and another month later I was pretty much out of the reentry phase. Of course it's always going to be a little blurred, and the event of retreat played a big role, but this is pretty close I would say, if you're going to stick a number on it. This is such a cool exercise.[13]

Several other returned missioners plugged in their own service variables into this equation and generated numbers that yielded a similar accuracy. If you and your spouse believe that this formula would be interesting and possibly helpful, try it out!

---

12 Benjamin Umhoefer, personal e-mail, May 1, 2015.
13 Joanna Gardner, personal e-mail, April 26, 2015.

Loss

"There are three sources for the feelings associated with grief. The first is contemplation of the loss itself; the second is contemplation of a future without the lost object; and the third is contemplation of the unexpected experience of grief itself, i.e., feelings about grieving."[14] You and your partner have contemplated the first two feelings associated with grief during your final months abroad. This section is about confronting "the unexpected experience of grief itself." Both of you have left particular realities and people behind in your host country. Engaging with the emotions felt in response to these losses is one of the first steps in the bereavement process. Once again, here are the six major types of losses, as defined by Mitchell and Anderson:

(1) **Material**—loss of object or familiar surrounding
(2) **Relationship**—loss of ability to relate to a particular person or persons
(3) **Intrapsychic**—loss of an emotionally important image of oneself
(4) **Functional**—loss of muscular or neurological operation of the body
(5) **Role**—loss of accustomed place in a social network
(6) **Systemic**—loss of belonging to some interactional structure[15]

Let us take a closer look at several of these losses and how you and your partner may be experiencing them in your return to your passport country.

Material Loss. Some former volunteers may miss the rural setting of their ministry site if they have returned to city living or vice versa. The dilapidated playground, the small corner store, or your old classroom could be places that you find yourself yearning for at this time. Paradoxically, my husband felt a loss in the material wealth we came back to after our service year. He is a minimalist in every sense of the word, and truly enjoyed having less "stuff" while we were abroad. Moving into our new apartment was a tenuous experience; I clung to many of my possessions while he tossed most of what he owned into our donation boxes. Pat still jokingly threatens to throw out our bedframe, so we could sleep like we did at the orphanage—on the floor atop a mattress. Though I am quick to veto such a suggestion, we still share one pillow, which was something we started doing while in Honduras. (Pillows are rare commodities down there.) In either case, missing the presence of a certain object or place may be a loss that you or your spouse is currently experiencing.

Role Loss. It could have taken you months upon months to finally feel capable and contributive at your ministerial site. Several returned missioners reported that their departure date came too soon after reaching such a state of competency. One survey participant commented:

> We were in Ghana, Africa for just short of two years. Looking back I can see that it took the better part of the first year to really settle in and have it become home for us. Early into the second year, we had to start planning and thinking about returning. It seems we only enjoyed a few months of "belonging" between the coming and going. I wish we could have spent another

---

14 Mitchell and Anderson, *All Our Losses*, 61.
15 Mitchell and Anderson, *All Our Losses*, 36–44.

year for a total of three years. That way we could have really and more deeply developed an in-culture life there.[16]

The loss of a role established at your service placement can be difficult to manage, as it was likely a role that took much time and energy to construct.

For many, a symptom of leaving behind the role had at a volunteer assignment is the seeming decrease of intensity in one's home life. Multicultural communications expert and author Craig Storti asserts that it may have felt like there was always something striking or unusual happening while you were serving abroad. Your international experience could have had a depth, now seemingly absent. Overseas mission work often demands strength and qualities you did not know you had, or had to that degree, or which you were obliged to develop on the spot. You likely felt yourself actively growing.[17] Living in an environment where much is expected of you, where you work directly with people, and where the services you provide may be visibly impactful or transformative is a hard lifestyle to sustain, but it is also one that is difficult to replace. When you and your partner come back to your passport country, you could feel ordinary and anonymous again. Your current jobs may not be positions in which either of you can utilize the new set of skills you mastered while abroad.

Intrapsychic Loss. It is here that identity precariousness can present itself—teetering between who you became in your host country and who you are figuring yourself out to be at home. Creating a new self-image in your passport country can be more frustrating than originally anticipated. "You may find yourself a marginal person on the edge of groups, observing more than participating."[18] Because your move back to your homeland is, in most cases, a permanent one, the actuality of having lost your abroad self-concept will be more sharply felt. During my first months back from Honduras, I remember feeling like I had nothing against which to struggle, the daily weight I had carried as a volunteer had been lifted. I felt a sense of nakedness without my identity as a *Madrina*—almost too free and too clean. I went from helping traumatized and abused girls with their psychosocial development to figuring out how to put money on a bus pass. Initially, my life in the US seemed trivial and hollow.

Relationship Loss. For now, we will focus on the loss of the friendships you formed while overseas. (The loss or changing of relationships with those at home is a topic that will be taken up in the section *Grief* in this chapter.) Your identity and role abroad existed because of the connections you made with individuals at your ministry site and within your missioner community. "Relationship loss is the ending of opportunities to relate oneself to, talk with, share experiences with, touch, settle issues with, and otherwise be in emotional and/or physical presence of a particular other human … ."[19] Not being able to live out the relationships had with people you loved and respected in your host country can be a hard situation with which to come to terms. Because such losses are painful, any kind of practical advice given on how to cope with the absence of certain friendships may sound banal and obvious. (Pause of hesitation.) But the following suggestions come from the hearts and experiences

---

16 John Studer, personal e-mail, March 24, 2015.
17 Storti, *The Art of Coming Home*, 37.
18 Ronald L. Koteskey, *Before You Get "Home": Preparing for Reentry*, (Wilmore, KY: Ronald L. Koteskey, 2008), 47, http://www.missionarycare.com/ebooks/Preparing_for_Reentry_Book.pdf.
19 Mitchell and Anderson, *All Our Losses*, 38.

of many. If any of your housemates decided to extend their ministry term, or if you developed a healthy relationship with your on-site supervisor, keep in touch with those people. Continued communication with in-country volunteers and staff members can keep you up-to-date on the well-being of those with whom you were close, as well as on the changes occurring within the organization. If you do not have any readily accessible connections at your ministry assignment, find ways to maintain direct contact with local friends via Facebook, international cell phone applications or plans, e-mails, packages and letters sent down with visitors, etc.

No matter how you or your spouse is able to keep in touch with those whom you served, you may find it peace-giving to hold them in your thoughts and prayers. Prayer has two dimensions: (1) the internal form of self-reflection and self-awareness; and (2) external contact with something bigger than the self.[20] Prayer can create a deeper sense of communion with oneself, others, and God. Work to carve out time in your daily routine to cultivate this feeling of community. Pray for the safety, health, happiness, and growth of those you love overseas. The action of prayer has been known to benefit those who engage with it in improving self-control, increasing the ability to trust and willingness to forgive, and offsetting negative health effects caused by stress.[21]

Hand in Hand[22]
Duration: 20–35 minutes

The following exercise is a prayerful reflection that will guide you and your partner in honoring the relationships the two of you made in your host country.

STEP 1: Hands. Each spouse will need two sheets of paper and a pen or a pencil. As individuals, place your hand on one of your sheets of paper and trace it—making the fingers slightly larger than their actual size.

STEP 2: Free Association. Take turns reading aloud to one another the bulleted questions below. In your traced hands, both of you are to write down the names of the people that come to mind when you personally reflect on the question that is being asked. You may write the same name as many times as it presents itself or—to save space—put tally marks next to it. See **Figure 6.1** on the next page as a reference.

- Who inspired you to pursue international service work?
- Who helped you to better understand mission?
- Who were some of your cultural guides?
- Who were mentors in your ministries?
- Who were some of your favorite co-workers or collaborators?
- With whom did you feel a true sense of community?

20 Michelle Roya Rad, "The Positive Psychological Effects of Prayer," *The Huffington Post: Healthy Living*, April 11, 2013, http://www.huffingtonpost.com/roya-r-rad-ma-psyd/prayer_b_3055127.html?.
21 Clay Routledge, "5 Scientifically-Supported Benefits of Prayer," *Psychology Today*, June 23, 2014, https://www.psychologytoday.com/blog/more-mortal/201406/5-scientifically-supported-benefits-prayer.
22 Adapted from Julie Lupien, "Hand Prayer" (presentation, From Mission to Mission Workshop, Chicago, IL, October 24–26, 2014).

- Who were leaders who inspired you?
- Who was an example of hospitality? Humility? Sacrifice? Faith? Resiliency?
- Who showed you how to celebrate?
- Who challenged you in a good way?
- Who made you laugh?
- With whom did you have good conversations?
- With whom did you love to be around?
- Who touched your heart?
- Who had the greatest impact on you?

Figure 6.1

STEP 3: Recognition. When the two of you have finished reading all the bullet points, look at the names you have written inside the outlines of your hands. Take a few moments for your eyes and hearts to acknowledge each name. Breathe.

STEP 4: Further Reflection. On your remaining sheets of paper, individually answer the questions below in reference to the names written in your traced hands:

- What did you learn from these people?
- What did you learn about <u>yourself</u> from these individuals?
- What would these people be saying to you right now?
- Many missioners say, "*I received more than I gave.*" What did you receive from these individuals?
- What do you want people "here" to know about people "there"?
- What does "mission" mean to you now?

STEP 5: Dialogue. Once you and your spouse are done writing, take turns sharing your responses with one another.

STEP 6: Prayer. Read the following quotes. Each of you is to select the statement that most resonates with what you are currently feeling. Take a few minutes to reflect on its message. For the remainder of this exercise, use your quote to pray in gratitude for the individuals written in your traced hands.

"Now join your hands, and with your hands your hearts."
—*William Shakespeare*

"I'm a little pencil in the hand of a writing God, who is sending a love letter to the world."
—*Mother Teresa*

"Friendship is a knot tied by angels' hands."
—*Unknown*

"God has given us two hands, one to receive with and the other to give with."
—*Billy Graham*

"What does love look like? It has the hands to help others. It has the feet to hasten to the poor and needy. It has eyes to see misery and want. It has the ears to hear the sighs and sorrows of men. That is what love looks like."
—*St. Augustine*

"You hem me in, behind and before,
and lay your hand upon me."
—*Psalms 139:5*

"The fragrance always remains on the hand that gives the rose."
—*Mahatma Ghandi*

"Children are the hands by which we take hold of heaven."
—*Henry Ward Beecher*

"He who works with his hands is a laborer. He who works with his hands and his head is a craftsman. He who works with his hands and his head and his heart is an artist."
—*St. Francis of Assisi*

"The final forming of a person's character lies in their own hands."
—*Anne Frank*

"In joined hands there is still some token of hope, in the clinched fist none."
—*Victor Hugo*

"But when you give alms, do not let your left hand know what your right hand is doing … ."
—*Matthew 6:3*

Grief

Many of the emotions felt in response to reverse culture shock stem from grief: emptiness, loneliness, isolation, fear, anxiety, guilt, shame, anger, sadness, disorientation, and despair. As a reverse culture shock symptom, somatization (headaches, fatigue, colds, muscle pain, etc.) can also arise from grief. Undergoing bereavement is inescapable, for "the genesis of grief lies in the inevitability of both attachment and separation for the sustenance and development of human life."[23] Living will always involve loving and leaving. Because of the inherent presence of grief in our lives as human beings, understanding grief and its effects is important.

You and your partner may be familiar with Elisabeth Kübler-Ross' model of the five stages of grief—denial, anger, bargaining, depression, and acceptance. Consciously recognizing where you see yourself in this model can be helpful during the stage of re-entry. More generally speaking:

> The experience of loss at any time in life triggers a momentary preoccupation with the self that is necessary for psychological survival … at times of significant loss, needs for nourishment and protection mount sharply and are often left unsatisfied; at such a point, the grief-stricken person may recapitulate an early infant selfishness.[24]

As a couple returning from international mission work, this response to grief may make it challenging to maintain a marriage of mutuality. Be patient with yourself and your partner if either of you experiences such a turn inward during the re-entry phase. Work together to make your marriage what it once was—a relationship based on the simultaneous exchange of love and support.

Because returning to one's home country after a mission experience often "involves separation, loss, and an inability to adequately communicate what one has experienced,"[25] re-entrants call for specific kinds of care:

---

23 Mitchell and Anderson, *All Our Losses*, 20.
24 Mitchell and Anderson, *All Our Losses*, 22.
25 Clyde N. Austin, "Overview of Reentry," in *Cross-Cultural Reentry*, 3.

Reprieve. Returned volunteers need relief from the expectations of others and require time, space, and assistance with ordinary tasks. After their arrival home, single young-adult missioners are likely to receive extra resources and/or support from their parents. This kind of help may be hard to come by as a married couple. Accept what assistance your families offer, and then communicate with your spouse about how you can best take care of one another. This is a time when adaptability should be at the forefront of your marriage. Try to be flexible with temporary unemployment, an uncomfortable living situation, gender role reversals, and/or extra household responsibilities.

Expression. Re-entrants need to be able to express their feelings and have those emotions be validated. Although spouses cannot eliminate the lonely work of each other's grieving, they are able to at least mitigate the isolation that can intensify grief.[26] Listening to your partner's reaction to having left your host country should be done empathetically, and with an openness and willingness to being attentively silent. Husbands and wives should not focus on trying to resolve questions of confusion, cries of sadness, or outbursts of frustration. Your presence is what is needed at this time, not premature answers or interpretations.

Recollections. Returnees may need encouragement in creating cherishable memories of their time overseas. "One gains emotional release from what is lost by actively making it a memory."[27] With that being said, try to form your memories in balanced remembrance. It is important to keep a realistic view of the past and its current unfeasibility. While a preoccupation with nostalgia succeeds in making individuals forget current difficulties, it also succeeds in reducing efforts necessary for them to engage in their new life.[28] Do not let the romanticization of your past international service keep you from living in the present moment. Yes, the time spent in your host country was life-giving, fulfilling, and powerful, but it was also exhausting, potentially unsafe, and, most likely, unsustainable for the long-term. Allow the positive and negative aspects of your ministry to be held together in creative tension.

Connections. Lastly, returned missioners need to reestablish relationships in their home country and consciously return to significant communities. Sometimes, however, becoming part of a former community may not make sense. One survey participant wrote about facing this kind of situation, "We shared a powerful experience together, but it left us less able to relate to a parish with no sense of our third world experience. Reintegrating into a far less dynamic Catholic community was and has remained difficult."[29] Similarly, you and your partner may want to take time to reflect on your friendships. Some of your past relationships may have run their course, while others can and should be re-created. One former volunteer shared her experience in reconnecting with old friends during the re-entry phase:

> When I first got back home I couldn't relate to anyone. Everything I had to share was from my past experience and no one could understand it. Things that my friends had to share seemed unimportant to me. ... I found I became less upset and frustrated when I just accepted the situation. Going abroad was my choice. You find the people and time to share little memories with

---

26 Mitchell and Anderson, *All Our Losses*, 117.
27 Mitchell and Anderson, *All Our Losses*, 126.
28 Werkmen, "Coming Home," 13.
29 Kenny, "Married Missioner/Volunteer Survey," 31.

eventually. But you won't share all of what you want or maybe in the way you want. I realized that even though my friends didn't talk about things that were important to me, they still loved me. I didn't want to throw away those friendships just because we had different interests. After I accepted them for who they were it became easier to be back with them. And now I'm finding new friends and other ways to share and express my cross-cultural interests.[30]

As you and your spouse rebuild important relationships, the two of you should also be open to seeking out new friendships to develop and new communities of which to become a part. Find an Arabic-speaking social group, volunteer at a local refugee or immigrant center, or meet up with other former missioners. Making connections with people and organizations that share your values is a good way to maintain continuity from your time abroad.

Some days you and your spouse will feel satisfied with your home life, and other days you may still experience the pain and senselessness of continued grief. "For in grief nothing 'stays put.' One keeps on emerging from a phase, but it always recurs. Round and round. Everything repeats. Am I going in circles, or dare I hope I am on a spiral? But if a spiral, am I going up or down it?"[31] You are not alone in this corkscrewed journey. Here are a few comments from several survey participants about their own grieving processes as had in the re-entry phase:

- "My wife experienced significant discouragement and almost depression when we returned to the United States. It affected many parts of her life."[32]
- "I was glad that our return period was in winter. It was OK for us to be quiet, read, stay indoors, and not interact with too many other people in our neighborhood and lives, which worked well for me because I found the re-entry period quite stressful."[33]
- "I started grad school in a new city. This compounded our inability to process our year and transition into a new life."[34]

Allow your faith, stable relationships, and actualized methods of self-care to help get you through this sixth stage.

Guilt

Guilt seems to be a prevailing emotion many missioners experience when returning to their passport countries (*"I feel guilty about all the clothes I own ... opportunities I have ... money I am spending ..."*). Dr. Susan Krauss Whitbourne, a professor of psychology at the University of Massachusetts Amherst, asserts that guilt is an emotion, an internal and negative state.[35] Whitbourne has identified five types of guilt, two of which are commonly experienced by returnees during the re-entry phase. The first of these two kinds of guilt manifests itself when a former volunteer believes he/she did not do enough to help a person during his/her time in service. While this belief may be true of a particular instance (we do fall short every

30 Emilia Pettinger, personal e-mail, April 14, 2015.
31 C. S. Lewis, *A Grief Observed* (New York: HarperCollins, 1961), 1.
32 Kenny, "Married Missioner/Volunteer Survey," 255.
33 Kenny, "Married Missioner/Volunteer Survey," 255.
34 Kenny, "Married Missioner/Volunteer Survey," 255.
35 Whitbourne, "The Definitive Guide to Guilt."

now and then), in most cases, this feeling of guilt does not accurately represent the entirety of an individual's mission experience. The majority of missioners not only do enough at their ministry sites, they go above and beyond what is required of them. Even though a re-entrant may have had an overall meaningful and successful volunteer career abroad, the guilt of failing in certain situations may overshadow that greater truth. If you or your spouse find yourselves struggling with this type of guilt, try to remember this: the desire to help others was likely a major motivator in your choosing to serve overseas and you did that—you both helped people. In the same breath, you and your significant other are humans, meaning that there were probably times where one or both of you were not patient enough, loving enough, caring enough, etc. Though these moments may invoke feelings of disappointment, those same moments were the times when your absence left a place that could, in that instant, only be filled by God. As Christians we are called to help bring about the Kingdom of God here on earth, but we are not charged in bringing about its complete fulfillment. That actualization can only be instituted by God himself. The serenity prayer says it all: "God, grant me the serenity to accept the things I cannot change, the courage to change the things I can, and the wisdom to know the difference."

The second kind of guilt some former volunteers may experience during the re-entry phase comes from the privilege of living in a developed country. This type of guilt is a strain of survivor's guilt—*"How come I am able to return to this kind of reality and (insert name) cannot?"* Such a feeling of culpability can be particularly burdensome. It may make you feel obligatorily responsible in some way.[36] Which raises the question—*"But responsible to whom and for what?"* The answer to this inquiry is often unclear. From a practical perspective, the differences between your host country and passport country are due to hundreds of years of history. You and your spouse may find it helpful to educate yourselves on why some international communities have the economic struggles they do, and why many Westernized societies live in relative prosperity. Being actively grateful and good stewards of the advantages you have are other ways of assuaging and overcoming survivor's guilt. Work to more deeply explore the roots of your feelings of guilt, and brainstorm action steps that you can take in order to ease such inner conflictions. As time passes, you and your partner will be able to make more concrete and permanent commitments that will pay tribute to your past mission experience. (*Honoring Your Experience* in Chapter 7 will put forth some ideas on how to do this.)

Spousal Dynamics

Before reading this section, you and your spouse may want to refer back to *Contributing Factors* in this chapter. It might be beneficial for you both to talk through the variables listed in that section and see how they apply to you as individuals. Communicating about the differences between your service experiences can help the two of you identify why and how those dissimilarities may be influencing each of your current attitudes and behaviors. Additionally, examining particular aspects of your mission work can assist you and your significant other in figuring out what parts of your life abroad generated the most meaning. Your partner may have really enjoyed living in an intentional community, while you thought that that was the most stressful part of your time overseas. Thus, during this sixth phase, your spouse may find value in maintaining contact with your former housemates, while you have chosen to not keep in touch with the same group of people. Allow your

---

36 Whitbourne, "The Definitive Guide to Guilt."

partner to honor the significant parts of his/her ministerial experience in his/her own way so long as it reasonable.

You and your spouse may consider specifically addressing the factor "type of lifestyle in place upon return to home country." This is one of the most influential variables in the success of an individual's management of re-entry. When married returnees spend the majority of their time in different environments after an international service experience, the consequent variation in each person's re-entry process can create unpleasant conflicts. One survey participant wrote, "I had school lined up, but my spouse was following me to a new geographic location with no job interviews in place."[37] Yet another shared, "In our transition back to our home country, it was difficult finding a job, especially with a pregnant spouse. This was a very frustrating time for me."[38] Partners returning to either a previously held employment routine or a position aligned with their abroad experience tend to have an easier time working through the re-entry phase. If this seems to be the case in your marriage, the spouse with more structure and continuity in his/her daily life should try to take on a more supportive role.

Psychological research has produced mixed results in regard to the differences in emotional processing between the sexes. "Strong evidence has been found that there are significant variations in the way males and females detect, absorb, and express emotion. Other studies show that men and women share more emotional similarities than not."[39] Thus, whether husband or wife, you may be more emotionally expressive when reflecting on your overseas ministry than your spouse. As a personal example, I would randomly burst into tears when looking at a photo of a particular child from the orphanage, sniffling as I asked Pat if he thought the kids in Honduras still remembered us. He, on the other hand, communicated little about his experience of transitioning home. One survey participant related a similar experience: "Communication as male and female was challenging. We did not always communicate in the same way, even though we had the same values and goals."[40] Differences in emotional exchanges and displays can be an obstacle for couples during such a period of significant change.

Remember the exercise *Coping Styles* in Chapter 5? We learned that each individual has his or her own style of coping, informed by childhood experiences and exposure to other coping mechanisms.[41] Your partner is wired a certain way and reacts to loss in accordance with that wiring. If Jack thinks that Jill is "overreacting" during the re-entry phase (or vice versa), he is overlooking two things: (1) that changes cause transitions, which cause losses, and it is the loss, not the changes, that Jill is reacting to; and (2) Jill is responding to a piece of her world that is now gone, not necessarily a piece of Jack's, and he himself may react similarly if a part of his own world had been lost in the same way.[42] One survey participant shared, "We process things very differently. I am at a place now where this no longer frustrates me and I can appreciate the process that my husband goes through."[43] Try to be as accommodating as

---

37 Kenny, "Married Missioner/Volunteer Survey," 215.

38 Kenny, "Married Missioner/Volunteer Survey," 215.

39 Dennis Thompson Jr., "Gender Differences in Emotional Health," *Everyday Health,* last modified July 14, 2010, http://www.everydayhealth.com/emotional-health/gender-differences-in-emotional-health.aspx.

40 Kenny, "Married Missioner/Volunteer Survey," 21.

41 Bridges, *Transitions,* 15.

42 Bridges, *Managing Transitions,* 26–27.

43 Kenny, "Married Missioner/Volunteer Survey," 215.

this returned missioner's comment illustrates. As long as grieving is handled in a reasonable manner, let your significant other work through his/her bereavement in whatever way is best for him/her.

In Chapter 4, you and your partner read that "becoming married is a delicate process of finding harmony between uninterrupted closeness and exaggerated distance."[44] In transitioning home, the two of you must re-create a balanced marriage of solitude and togetherness. "Without knowing why, people in the middle of change tend to find ways of being alone and away from all the familiar distractions."[45] Make time to be by yourself, and let your partner do the same. Go on long walks or jogs outside. Listen or play music indoors. Journal or read anywhere in between. Do things that are therapeutic and give you joy. Take a break from *reacting* to your life. Remember space and pace—the privacy to find your transformed self, and the self-conducted tempo at which you make that journey.[46] Likewise, make time to be together and have fun with your partner. Engage with your surroundings by going on dates or family outings. Get reacquainted with your marital relationship in this old-but-new context.

As a last point, be aware of any accompanying spouse issues that may surface during this phase. Even if the two of you developed a co-spousal dynamic abroad, going through yet another life-changing event can stir up past resentments held by former accompanying spouses. Past accompanying spouse concerns—previously addressed or compensated for by the service experience itself—can reemerge in full flower at this time (*"I told you that volunteering was too big a financial commitment to make."* Or, *"Look at our children. They are not readjusting well."*). If negative accompanying spouse sentiments arise, try to make time for a conflict-handling conversation in order to attend to such apprehensions. As a former leading spouse, demonstrating that you genuinely care and want to make this transition easier for your partner may be exactly what your significant other is seeking in his/her seemingly unfair comments or complaints.

External Factors

Now that we have covered some of the more internal dynamics present in re-entry, let us consider several of the external variables also at play. When you and your spouse move back home, there are many things to get done, and it seems as though every task needs to be completed as quickly as possible. Hopefully you and your partner created to-do/budget lists while reading Chapter 5, so that the bombardment of all these responsibilities is not wholly unforeseen. If you have not, please go back and read the sections *Anxieties* and *Anxieties Continued* to figure out what chores and expenditures you may need to take into account. "People can deal with a lot of change if it is coherent and part of a larger whole. But unrelated and unexpected changes, even small ones, can be the proverbial straw that breaks the camel's back."[47] Thus, as the two of you read through (or make) your to-do/budget lists, try to view the logistics of it all as a necessary step in processing your overall transition home. (See the link in this footnote for a simple way to prioritize the items on your checklists.)[48]

---

44 Anderson and Fite, *Becoming Married*, 33.
45 Bridges, *Transitions*, 113.
46 Hunter, "Closure and Commencement," 186.
47 Bridges, *Managing Transitions*, 45.
48 "How to Organize Your Thoughts on Paper," *wikiHow*, June 13, 2015, http://www.wikihow.com/Organize-Your-Thoughts-on-Paper.

Related to the initial and overwhelming amount of things that need to be managed upon your return is the project of finding a job. Faced with the necessity of making money, couples may find themselves in the same situation as this former volunteer: "The pressures of generating income meant that one of us had to find employment quickly, which had little to do with our missionary work."[49] Another survey participant shared a similar story: "While I knew that I was returning to the same employer, I would have wished to have had more time to transition. I could not delay the employment, however, since my husband was interviewing and searching for a position. We knew that several weeks or months would pass before he would begin to earn income."[50] If you have any flexibility in your financial situation, take your job hunt at a slower pace. You and your partner are at a point in your lives that demands contemplation and emotional processing. Not giving yourselves the time and space to reflect on your mission work and how the loss of it has impacted each of you can be detrimental. Quickly committing to permanent positions unrelated to your new values and goals can cause a lack of fulfillment in your lives. Several resources suggest that former volunteers try to find a temporary and somewhat "mindless" job for the first few months after their return if they need to make money. This kind of employment can provide a source of income, while also leaving individuals the head-space to contemplate their service experience. Practically speaking, a provisional job can give you some financial security as you look for more meaningful work. You and your spouse should approach this issue as a team in order to figure out how each of you can (a) process your overseas ministry, (b) make some money, and (c) find a long-term career that is in line with your current beliefs and dreams. The lesson here is that you and your partner should try not to curtail your re-entry experiences of reflection and bereavement because of financial issues.

The last significant external factor to account for is family—both the children who may have been abroad with you and the relatives who were not directly involved with your mission work. Many former volunteers feel that their loved ones simply do not understand how their time spent in international service has impacted them. You have been transformed by your experiences, and if you are not able to adequately share the story of your transformation with those close to you, how can they know this new person who has come back to them? And if they do not know who you have become, then what kind of relationship do you have?[51] These kinds of thoughts can be unnerving. A crisis such as this can cause any missioner to retreat internally and withdraw from others. A single re-entrant's social retraction from family members is usually brief, as he/she naturally needs and begins to seek out human interaction after such a reprieve. When a couple withdraws from others—they do so together. They create their own exclusive and confined community, often for a longer period of time than their single counterparts. As married individuals, be especially open to the hard work it may take to reestablish bonds with your family and/or close friends. Give them the opportunity to get to know the transformed you. Meet each of your loved ones where they are at, which is most likely not where you are. Try to be just as empathetic, patient, and nonjudgmental toward your parents, children, and grandchildren as you were with the locals with whom you worked in your host country.

---

49 Kenny, "Married Missioner/Volunteer Survey," 257.
50 Kenny, "Married Missioner/Volunteer Survey," 215.
51 Storti, *The Art of Coming Home*, 30.

Practical Advice

The first piece of practical advice here is about reference groups. A reference group is a community with which an individual identifies—and whose values, experiences, goals, opinions, attitudes, behaviors, beliefs, or preferences are used by group members as guiding principles.[52] "The reference group can serve as a forum of exchange of information, expression of feeling, and support from those who have had a similar experience."[53] This "exchange of information" in reference groups can meet your and your spouse's more interpersonal aspects of your bereavement needs:

> Grieving is a process in which the deep feelings aroused by the loss are acknowledged and relatively fully expressed. It should be possible for the grieving person to discover and to express the pain, anger, guilt, and other feelings that are common consequences of loss. To express these feelings also requires that they be heard and responded to by others.[54]

A reference group can provide an outlet for both verbalization and validation. Some service programs provide structured retreats for returning volunteers. These kinds of workshops often give re-entrants the space and audience they need to "tell their story." If your sending organization does not arrange for such guided processing, you may find the upcoming exercise more than helpful.

As the two of you know, international ministry involves a certain degree of emotional intensity. You and your spouse developed unique and important relationships, your work likely required heightened physical and/or mental engagement, and moments of spiritual significance may have occurred more frequently or noticeably. After several months back in your home country, the two of you may feel the need to share both the positive and negative elements of your individual cross-cultural experiences:

> What happens in the telling of a story is the healing of memory. So much of our identity is tied up with memory. ... The memory of persons and events important to us are stored in narratives. As our circumstances change, our sense of those narratives changes: we recall elements that we thought we had forgotten, or find a different perspective from which to view the narrative.[55]

For many former missioners, it is difficult to find someone (or a group of people) who will (a) take the time to listen to their ministerial narratives, (b) understand them on some level, and (c) be empathetic to the meaning their stories hold. Fortunately, you and your partner have each other to fulfill all three of these needs.

---

52 "Reference Group," *Dictionary.com*, http://dictionary.reference.com/browse/reference%20group.
53 Jansson, "Return to Society," 56.
54 Mitchell and Anderson, *All Our Losses*, 95–96.
55 Schreiter, *The Ministry of Reconciliation*, 44–45.

Unabridged Stories[56]
Duration: 1–2 hours

The desire to debrief after a significant event is a natural, psychological response. Self-disclosure helps individuals become aware of unfinished business that they have put out of awareness, but which continues to take an emotional and physical toll. Through processes of self-disclosure, such as storytelling, people are able to assimilate, come to terms with, and reconcile past experiences in their lives.[57] Storytelling has also been known to relieve emotional stress, help cognitive ordering, and provide therapeutic benefits.[58] This exercise will give each spouse the opportunity to tell the unabridged version of his/her time in mission.

STEP 1: Roles. Each partner will need two pieces of paper and a pen or a pencil. Designate one of you to be the listening spouse and the other to be the speaking spouse.

STEP 2: Brainstorming. As individuals, take time by yourselves to reflect on your mission journey, and as much as possible, prepare your story. Below are several prompts that can help you to construct your narrative. Write down your responses to these questions on one of your pieces of paper. (If either of you still has it, you can refer to the timeline you created in the exercise *Shared Ministry Timeline* in Chapter 5.)

- What were your expectations, hopes, and fears before embarking on your cross-cultural mission experience?
- Review and write down the major themes and motifs that best describe your time overseas.
- Identify the highs, lows, transformational moments, and points of change while you were abroad.
- Which names surfaced the most in the exercise *Hand In Hand* in this chapter? Why are those particular individuals so important to you?
- As you read through these questions, note the significant feelings, issues, questions, or unresolved conflicts you may have.
- What colors, textures, sounds, shapes, symbols, or images best express your narrative?

STEP 3: Storytelling. The speaking spouse will start by telling the unabridged version of his/her service experience. Do not be too conscious about time. Be aware of the physical reactions you may have during this exercise. You are likely to feel spurts of energy throughout your storytelling, and even a natural feeling of release at the end, as though you have run out of gas. Share honestly and speak about what feels right. Refer to the notes you made in response to the aforementioned prompts, and ad lib accordingly.

---

56 Adapted from Julie Lupien, "Storytelling" (presentation, From Mission to Mission Workshop, Chicago, IL, October 24–26, 2014), 5.

57 Chris L. Kleinke, *Common Principles of Psychotherapy* (Pacific Grove, CA: Brooks/Cole Publishing Company, 1994), 96.

58 Pamela B. Rutledge, "The Psychological Power of Storytelling," *Psychology Today,* January 16, 2011, https://www.psychologytoday.com/blog/positively-media/201101/the-psychological-power-storytelling.

As the listening spouse, be attentive. Listen with reverence and respect. Write down general impressions on your second sheet of paper. When does your partner get the most emotionally expressive? What topics, people, or situations come up frequently? How is his/her narrative organized as a whole? Try not to interrupt or change the flow of your spouse's story. Some parts of what he/she reveals may seem unfair or hurtful to you. Internally acknowledge this discomfort, and either let it go or make a note to yourself to bring it up in later conversation. Only pause your partner's recounting if something is unclear.

STEP 4: Questions. After the speaking spouse has finished telling his/her story, the listening spouse can ask clarifying questions. Once these queries have been resolved, the listening partner is to share any comments he/she has. Talk to your partner about what elements of his/her story surprised you. This may also be the time to disclose what parts of his/her narrative made you feel uncomfortable or upset.

You may have noticed that your spouse did not speak about a certain child, a particular trip, or a specific incident. Call his/her attention to your observation and listen to your partner's response. The purpose of these questions is to help facilitate deeper contemplation on the part of the speaking spouse.

STEP 5: Role Reversal. Switch roles and repeat STEPS 3 and 4.

STEP 6: Repetition. Once both of you have told the unabridged versions of your mission experiences—relax! Close with a prayer if you feel like it. Be sure to keep the notes you made of each other's stories in a safe place.

Several months later, complete this activity again and compare your records. Dialogue about what has changed and why those changes may have occurred. Identifying and discussing differences in each other's narratives can lead to some interesting and informative insights.

Practical Advice Continued

If you or your partner is asked to speak about your overseas ministry, be open to accepting that request. One survey participant wrote, "Our faith sharing group invited us to 'just talk' about our experience for one of our faith sharing evenings. This was wonderful for us."[59] Another former volunteer commented, "We have received numerous speaking engagements from service organizations to talk about our story. Many of these service organizations provided the financial support to improve the public schools we worked at in El Salvador."[60] Speaking events, no matter how big or small, allow you and your spouse to continue your mission work in a different kind of way. Informing others of the reality of which you were once a part is a means of honoring your commitment to the international community of which you continue to be a part. Additionally, the two of you are helping others become more globalized citizens. You and your partner may be the only contact someone in your home country has to issues concerning water sanitation in Africa, religious suppression in China, or social justice movements in Latin America. Thus, ensure that the connection you are making between these two worlds is both honest and memorable. You can modify the exercise *Elevator Speech* in Chapter 5 in preparing for a particular speaking engagement.

59 Kenny, "Married Missioner/Volunteer Survey," 262.
60 Kenny, "Married Missioner/Volunteer Survey," 255.

See the Appendix for supplementary online resources that can guide you in the organization of your thoughts.

While leading a retreat, Julie Lupien, executive director of *From Mission to Mission*, shared
an insight that was particularly striking: "Re-entry is the time during which a person's soul
tries to catch up to their body."[61] William Bridges puts it this way: "The outer forms of our
lives can change in an instant, but the inner reorientation that brings us back into a vital
relation to people and activity takes time."[62] Allow your soul to find its way across the miles
between your host country and where you stand today. In conclusion, here are a few more
pieces of practical advice: use the exercise *I–You–We–Care Stars* in Chapter 2 to create updated routines of self and marriage care; only make interim and short-term commitments
during your first few months back home; put concrete reminders of your service experience
(photos, souvenirs, artwork, etc.) in places where you will be able to see them every day;
stay connected to your host country through the news; and do not intellectualize your feelings—just feel them.

Miscellaneous

This section contains more counsel in regard to the re-entry process as reported by former
missioners in the handbook survey and within existing literature on the topic:

Establish updated family routines. Try to be as communicative as possible with your children at this time by observing their behaviors and adjusting family system structures as
needed. Your home life will be a sort of "psychological huddle"—a place where you can
consistently touch base with one another and regroup.[63] You and your spouse may need to
renegotiate parenting procedures in regard to policies for Internet/cell phone use, curfews,
driving privileges, etc. As for shopping, do not buy in bulk just yet. Figure out how much
your family is eating before you load up on Costco-sized supplies.

Help your children get re-acclimated. As you and your family readjust to life in your passport
country, you and your partner should listen to your children, rather than impose upon them
how they "ought to" feel during this period of transition.[64] Like the two of you, your kids
have a particular relationship and understanding of their time abroad, so let them process
this life change in their own way. If you are parents to a teenager, keep in mind that children
raised overseas oftentimes have a late entrance into adolescence, as they have been especially protected in their past social interactions.[65] "According to the experts, many TCKs [Third
Culture Kids] take the experience of what would have been adolescent rebellion well into
their twenties, while their non-mobile friends have already worked it out of their systems."[66]
Be aware of this dynamic as your teens reaccustom themselves to life back home.

Stay the course. Have faith in the transitional process (see the Preface). Religiously speaking,
this progression can be framed within the Paschal Mystery: the conclusion of Jesus' minis-

---

61 Julie Lupien, "Storytelling" (presentation, From Mission to Mission Workshop, Chicago, IL, October 24–26,
    2014).
62 Bridges, *Transitions*, 78.
63 Hunter, "Closure and Commencement," 186.
64 Hunter, "Closure and Commencement," 188.
65 Clyde N. Austin, "Reentry Stress: The Pain of Coming Home," in *Cross-Cultural Reentry*, 124.
66 Robin Pascoe, *Living & Working Abroad: A Parent's Guide* (London: Kuperard, 1994), 174.

try = ending, his crucifixion = neutral zone, and subsequent resurrection = new beginning. When you have confidence in the way change begets transformation, you will "not need to make distress comfortable."[67] You will be able to allow distress to be exactly what it is—distressing.

Set some shared and individual goals. Now is a time when people can get easily discouraged. It often seems as if nothing important is happening during the re-entry phase. Therefore it can be helpful to give you and your partner a sense of achievement and movement.[68] Let us say you both want to maintain the new language you learned while overseas. Refer to the exercise *Goal Creation* in Chapter 4 to start brainstorming ways in which you can best do that together (e.g., designating Swahili-speaking days or going to Mass/church service in Spanish), and as individuals (e.g., taking advanced online Mandarin courses or reading books in Russian). Constructing personal and shared goals can aid in countering the sixth stage feelings of meaninglessness, self-doubt, and being lost.[69]

Creative Expression

As touched upon in the beginning of this chapter, the first few weeks back home can be euphorically exciting. However, this high wears off fairly quickly. Materialism, commercialism, and wastefulness present in many Westernized communities can seem remarkably ugly. Furthermore, setting up shop again may be a lot harder than you and your partner had anticipated. Your dreams of a seamless transition slip away with each new stressor that emerges. When re-entrants realize that their hopes and assumptions cannot be fully met, they need to be assisted in establishing more realistic expectations. A "helping person can convey acceptance of the re-entrant's anger by allowing him to ventilate it and can encourage its expression through acceptable forms, such as the arts and media."[70] You and your spouse are the other's "helping persons." The two of you can guide each other through experimenting with healthy forms of inventive self-articulation during re-entry. "Things look different in the neutral zone, for one of the things you let go of in the ending process is the need to see the past in a particular way."[71] Exploring this in-between time—an existence with one foot in the yesterdays of overseas living and the other in the tomorrows of home life—can be a spiritually fruitful undertaking. In lacking clear systems and signals, the neutral zone is a period of tumultuousness. However, this absence of predictability is also the reason why the neutral zone is more hospitable to new ideas.[72] If you allow it to be, your re-entry experience can bring about imagination and ingenuity.

---

67 Bridges, *Managing Transitions*, 103.
68 Bridges, *Managing Transitions*, 46.
69 Bridges, *Managing Transitions*, 46.
70 Jansson, "Return to Society," 53.
71 Bridges, *Transitions*, 124.
72 Bridges, *Managing Transitions*, 42.

Neutral Zone Log[73]
Duration: 5–20 minutes/ongoing

"Any attempt to place order on chaos is a creative act."[74] This exercise is meant to help you and your spouse more innovatively understand your past service experience. Furthermore, this activity can facilitate your individual searches for unlived potentialities and ways in which you want to enrich your shared future.

STEP 1: *Log Dedication.* You and your partner are to make a notebook into a "neutral zone log." This log should be put in a place where you both have regular access to it.

STEP 2: *Entries.* The approach you take in recording experiences is important, or else you run the risk of turning this log into a trivial kind of diary-keeping. What each of you wants to write down are the "peculiar" events had within a single day—situations that cause you to pause, cause you to feel something, cause you to think more deeply. These daily events will then become pieces of a larger theme, all of which point toward the transcendent—toward God. Here are three examples of entries I wrote in my own neutral zone log:

"I had a dream about Nelly last night. I came and visited the orphanage and she was so happy to see me. She started to repeat the nickname I had given her, and then giggled uncontrollably. I woke up with a feeling of hope."

"I walked for six miles today. I did not really think about anything in particular. But it felt good for me to be alone and outside."

"I was waiting by the bus stop today and I randomly looked at a flier taped onto a light pole. It was an advertisement for a play coming to the neighborhood. The title of the production was 'Arcadia.' This just so happens to be the name of my favorite child at the orphanage where I worked. My heart caught in my chest and tears started forming in my eyes. I took a picture of the flier."

Photo Credit: Alexis C. Kenny 2014

Following are several questions that may assist you and your partner in identifying what types of experiences to record in your log:

---

73 Adapted from Bridges, *Transitions*, 122.
74 Hunter, "Closure and Commencement," 182.

- What was *really* going on during your day?
- What was your mood?
- What were you thinking about, perhaps without realizing it, at a certain time?
- What puzzling or unusual things happened?
- What dreams do you remember having?
- What particular phrases stood out to you?
- What surprising things occurred today?

STEP 3: Photo Sharing. Images symbolize experiences. They capture the totality of an individual's emotional response to any given situation. Images encourage multiple aspects of meaning in events, crises, celebrations, adventures, etc.[75] Thus, image exploration can be a powerful form of introspection and communication.

Each week, both of you are to find a photo you can share with your partner. The photo should be an image that resonates with you on some level. Below are a few websites with unique pictures that are free and downloadable:

- StockSnap.io: stocksnap.io
- Unspalsh: unsplash.com
- Little Visuals: littlevisuals.co
- Snapwire Snaps: snapwiresnaps.tumblr.com
- Jay Mantri: jaymantri.com
- Picjumbo: picjumbo.com
- Superfamous Studios: superfamous.com
- Life of Pix: lifeofpix.com
- Gratisography: gratisography.com

STEP 4: Dialogue. Schedule a time each week when you and your spouse can sit quietly together to go over your neutral zone log and selected photos. Talk about the entries you wrote and why they were significant to you. Each partner should take turns sharing the photo chosen for the week and what it symbolizes to him/her. If you have printed your picture, place it in your neutral zone log. Continue this exercise for as long as you both find it stimulating.

Source of Continuity

The main task with which you and your spouse have been charged during the re-entry phase is to *reflect* on how you want to situate your service experience within your greater life narratives. Beginning this kind of process can be easier to start when you have a partner. You are each other's sources of continuity—a constancy that fuses together your lives before (insert host country), your lives in (insert host country), and now, your lives after (insert host country). This is invaluable. One of the three social system elements necessary for a successful re-entry is a strong significant other—someone who can reassure the "re-entrant that he/she is able to resume active family and community life and is capable of being a whole and adequate person once more."[76] While single volunteers have to seek out this kind of individual, you have a ready-made significant other at your side, forever! Your

---

75 Patricia O'Connell Killen and John de Beer, *The Art of Theological Reflection* (New York: Crossroad, 1994), 37.
76 Jansson, "Return to Society," 51.

spouse was a part of nearly every single moment had abroad—laughing, playing, yelling, crying, walking, waiting, and smelling—just as much as you were. Many survey participants commented on the significance of viewing their partner as such an interminable variable:

- "Serving together gave us shared, unique experiences that we still discuss with enjoyment."[77]
- "We've been married 46 years and still have fond memories of our time spent in Uganda in the early 1970s."[78]
- "We have a shared experience that is a continuous source of conversation."[79]
- "The experience of living in a radically different culture and enduring the physical hardships was a truly bonding experience. It was a touchstone in our lives and we reflect back on it frequently, even after almost 20 years."[80]

It is obvious that these married individuals have realized what a blessing and benefit it is to have their partners' presence throughout all the growth and change they have undergone. The period of re-entry can be trying because of its stresses, pressures, and grief. But do not let such pieces of this phase define its entirety, for transition is intrinsically developmental and can be a genuine source of renewal.[81] Continue to support one another in what is to come, for "there are far, far better things ahead than any we leave behind."[82]

---

77 Kenny, "Married Missioner/Volunteer Survey," 38.
78 Kenny, "Married Missioner/Volunteer Survey," 39.
79 Kenny, "Married Missioner/Volunteer Survey," 29.
80 John Studer, personal e-mail, March 24, 2015.
81 Bridges, *Transitions*, 3.
82 C. S. Lewis, *Letters to an American Lady* (Grand Rapids: Eerdmans, 1967), 22.

Integration

Chapter 7

Post-Re-entry—[1]

Ahh home, let me come home.
Home is wherever I'm with you.
Ahh home, let me come home.
Home is wherever I'm with you.

—Edward Sharpe and the Magnetic Zeros, "Home," *Up From Below*

Integration

Simply put, **integration** is the period following the re-entry stage. Integration is an interesting word to dissect, as its Latin root, *integrō*, means "to renew" or "to restore." If broken down further, you find that *integrō* is comprised of *in-* and *tangō* ("touch"). *Tangō*, in turn, translates as "reach," "arrive at," "move," or … "come home to."[2] "Coming home" is the point and purpose of the integration phase. It is a road homebound—with many twists and turns, ascents and descents, and an occasional swampy marsh through which to wade. The West seems to be especially preoccupied with the idea of home. Think about all the compound English words that include the term: homemade, homecoming, homesick, homework, homebody, homeland, homestead, homestretch, etc. Look at some of our "home"-driven maxims: home is where the heart is, home away from home, there is no place like home, home sweet home, etc. It appears as though we are in search of a residency of sorts, a dwelling place that is not a purely physical location. For Christians, this path homeward leads to God. As St. Augustine so aptly phrased it, "Our hearts are restless until they rest in Thee." We are called to walk the path that God has cleared for us—a byway headed from whence we came—a pilgrimage that ends in God himself. Making a particular life filled with particular people and particular circumstances more *homey* is a lifelong pursuit. At this point in time, your and your spouse's home-making will be focused on the integration of what you learned from your shared service experience with where you are today. To that process we now turn.

Value Integration

Experience is to be reflected upon, and thereafter seeks application. Just as the re-entry phase was devoted to processing your time overseas, so is the integration stage dedicated to putting that processed experience into action. Integration comes after re-entry and goes on … well … indefinitely (as illustrated in this chapter's subtitle, "Post-Re-entry–"). If you and your partner refer back to the *Stages of Cross-Cultural Transition* timeline in the Preface, you will see an upward climb of "implementation" from the low point of "reverse culture shock," which then begins to taper off into the plateau of your assimilated, everyday life. As the two of you lean into this seventh and final period, the distressing emotions more acutely felt during re-entry (e.g., disconnection, guilt, incongruence, loneliness, social discomfort,

---

1 This chapter is informed by the services that **From Mission to Mission** has provided the missioner community for the past thirty-five years.

2 "Tango (English)," *WordSense.eu: Dictionary*, http://www.wordsense.eu/tango/#Latin.

doubtfulness, etc.) will presumably fade in intensity and frequency. As time passes, such feelings should blend into the normal ups and downs of day-to-day living. As the months continue to go by, you and your partner can expect to experience the emotions and behaviors more commonly associated with actualized integration: spiritual fulfillment, conscientiousness, gratitude, solidarity, groundedness, joy, self/other-awareness, compassion, peace, etc.

In a sense, integration is the genuine starting point of your lives back in your home country. The two of you have made your way through the neutral zone, emerging with new understandings, values, attitudes, and, most significantly, new identities.[3] Beginnings establish, once and for all, that endings are final. This may be why some former volunteers have a hard time leaving the re-entry phase behind. A new beginning "ratifies" an ending, which can be both exciting and unnerving.[4] Gone are the re-entry provisions—temporary jobs, supplementary support, and generous allowances or leeway. You and your partner are back on your feet again. You have both picked yourselves up from the confusing whirlwind that returning from a service experience often is and are now ready to answer the question: *Where exactly are we headed?* Your and your spouse's journeys proceed when the timing of the transition process allows it, just as flowers and fruit appear on a schedule that is natural and not subject to anyone's will but God's.[5]

That being said, the unfolding of your shared beginning can be encouraged, nurtured, and reinforced in the following four ways:

(1) **Dialogue.** Discuss with your partner the basic purpose(s) behind the lifestyle you seek.
(2) **Vision.** Paint a picture of how this philosophy of/approach to life will look and feel. Share this depiction with your significant other.
(3) **Blueprint.** Lay out a flexible plan for phasing into this hoped-for and conceptualized way of living.
(4) **Communication.** Give people and personal values a part to play in both the plan and its outcome.[6]

As laid out in the last step, movement forward during the integration phase revolves around values (e.g., who you value, what you value, and why you value such people, ideas, structures, etc.). Thus, someone with a value-integrated life consciously prioritizes what he/she deems worthy. Examples of such principles include: a healthy family system, positive external relationships, faith in God, constructive personal habits, meaningful work, membership in a specific community, the pursuit of particular goals, etc. What integration looks like for each person is unique. However, there are two common denominators that must be in place in order for you and your spouse to achieve value-integrated lives—balance and generativity.

If you are spending the majority of your time and energy on only one or two of your principle values, you cannot reach integration. Similarly, a significant change, a milestone event,

---

3 Bridges, *Managing Transitions*, 58.
4 Bridges, *Managing Transitions*, 59.
5 Bridges, *Managing Transitions*, 59.
6 Bridges, *Managing Transitions*, 59.

or a notable loss can negatively impact a person's ability to live a balanced and integrated life. Generativity, as the other underlying component of genuine value integration, is the ability to actively create. What is behind this drive to beget? The answer—human growth and maturation. In the sixth stage of psychoanalyst Erik Erikson's theory of psychological development, young adults test out their social skills in the exploration of personal relationships. The successful resolution of this stage is the virtue of love, which, for many, is traditionally marked by marriage—*unity*. The following stage is a period during which adults seek to conceive and nurture things that will outlast them, such as children or work that benefits others—*generativity*.[7] (If you are Catholic, see this interesting footnote.[8]) In bringing this back to your specific pilgrimages of integration, the service in which you and your partner partook as former missioners is inherently generative. You dedicated yourselves to the cultivation of something that will remain long after the two of you have gone. Conclusively, your overseas ministry has given each of you one of integration's two common denominators. The task at hand is deciding how you want to appropriately add this experience into the balancing act of the rest of your life's personal priorities (I), the priorities of your spouse (You), and those of your marriage (We).

Integration Questionnaire[9]
Duration: 30–45 minutes

The following exercise is a set of questions meant to guide you and your partner in reflecting on the various components of integration. This activity highlights some of the major steps in the process of transition and implementation and will invite the two of you to find yourselves within that spectrum of progression.

STEP 1: Questionnaire. Each of you will need a pen or a pencil. Designate a *Spouse #1* and a *Spouse #2*. *Spouse #1* is to individually read through each question and then circle "Yes," "Unsure," or "No" under the appropriate heading in response to the prompt. Jot down any notes that come to mind in the space provided as you make your way through the next few pages. If you and your partner do not have time to complete the entire list of questions in one sitting, break up the prompts into smaller groups. Approach each section over the course of several weeks.

STEP 2: Repeat. Once *Spouse #1* has finished, cover up the questions to which he/she has responded. *Spouse #2* is to repeat STEP 1. Wait to share your comments with each other until both of you have gone through the prompts that you have decided to address at this time.

---

7   Kendra Cherry, "Erikson's Stages of Psychosocial Development: Psychosocial Development in Young Adulthood, Middle Age, and Old Age," *About Education*, http://psychology.about.com/od/psychosocialtheories/a/psychosocial_3.htm.

8   This specific part of Erikson's psychology might sound familiar to you. Similar to the sixth and seventh stages of adult psychosocial development are the two purposes for which a Catholic marriage is instituted—unity and generativity. (This was touched upon in Chapter 3.) The unitive piece of this sacrament is the mutual love had between a husband and wife, and from this love, the generative quality of marriage emerges, most typically manifested in the conception of children. Union inspires generation.

9   Adapted from Julie Lupien, "How To Manage the Transition Experience" (presentation, From Mission to Mission Workshop, Chicago, IL, October 24–26, 2014) and Bridges, *Managing Transitions*, 37, 54–55, 73–74, 116–17.

Have you worked to unpack all of your emotional baggage, heal old wounds, and bring to a close all unfinished business?

Spouse #1				*Spouse #2*		
Yes	Unsure	No		Yes	Unsure	No
	Notes				Notes	

Have you decided what in your life is over and what is not—what to let go of and what to hold on to?

Spouse #1				*Spouse #2*		
Yes	Unsure	No		Yes	Unsure	No
	Notes				Notes	

Are you comfortable with the idea that change is an inevitable reality?

Spouse #1				*Spouse #2*		
Yes	Unsure	No		Yes	Unsure	No
	Notes				Notes	

Have you taken the now-passing phase of the neutral zone to think about your career?

Spouse #1   *Spouse #2*

Yes   **Unsure**   **No**   **Yes**   **Unsure**   **No**

<u>Notes</u>   <u>Notes</u>

Have you sorted your losses into those you can *reverse*, those you can *replace*, those you can *rebuild*, and those you must simply *relinquish*?

Spouse #1   *Spouse #2*

Yes   **Unsure**   **No**   **Yes**   **Unsure**   **No**

<u>Notes</u>   <u>Notes</u>

Have you accepted and dealt with the mourning that accompanies working through your losses?

Spouse #1   *Spouse #2*

Yes   **Unsure**   **No**   **Yes**   **Unsure**   **No**

<u>Notes</u>   <u>Notes</u>

Are you adequately protecting yourself from inessential changes?

	Spouse #1			*Spouse #2*	
Yes	**Unsure**	**No**	**Yes**	**Unsure**	**No**
	Notes			Notes	

Have you found a way to go beyond *coping* with change to making change *work for* you?

	Spouse #1			*Spouse #2*	
Yes	**Unsure**	**No**	**Yes**	**Unsure**	**No**
	Notes			Notes	

Have you gathered all the information you need in order to effectively manage your process of integration?

	Spouse #1			*Spouse #2*	
Yes	**Unsure**	**No**	**Yes**	**Unsure**	**No**
	Notes			Notes	

Have you taken some time alone to just *be*, preferably away from the regular routines of home and work?

Spouse #1				*Spouse #2*		
Yes	**Unsure**	**No**		**Yes**	**Unsure**	**No**
	Notes				Notes	

Have you revisited the question of your personal purpose? (I.e., "*Why has God put me in this particular place at this particular time?*")

Spouse #1				*Spouse #2*		
Yes	**Unsure**	**No**		**Yes**	**Unsure**	**No**
	Notes				Notes	

Have you gained an understanding of the style of how you make decisions and the timeline along which your resolutions occur?

Spouse #1				*Spouse #2*		
Yes	**Unsure**	**No**		**Yes**	**Unsure**	**No**
	Notes				Notes	

Have you studied your own recent work and life experiences for clues that indicate what kinds of new possibilities you should explore?

	Spouse #1			*Spouse #2*	
Yes	Unsure	No	Yes	Unsure	No

Notes   Notes

Are you making sure that you do not stake too much claim on a particular future you or someone you love is forecasting?

	Spouse #1			*Spouse #2*	
Yes	Unsure	No	Yes	Unsure	No

Notes   Notes

Have you cultivated a habit of experimentation?

	Spouse #1			*Spouse #2*	
Yes	Unsure	No	Yes	Unsure	No

Notes   Notes

Have you found some low-risk settings in which to test and practice what you have learned and continue to learn?

Spouse #1

Yes   Unsure   No

Notes

Spouse #2

Yes   Unsure   No

Notes

Are you regularly checking to see that you are not pushing for certainty and closure, when it would be more conducive to living creatively and ambiguously for a little while longer?

Spouse #1

Yes   Unsure   No

Notes

Spouse #2

Yes   Unsure   No

Notes

Have you identified the continuities in your life and work situations and made a point to strengthen them?

Spouse #1

Yes   Unsure   No

Notes

Spouse #2

Yes   Unsure   No

Notes

Have you moved beyond a community of which you have become a part in pursuing individual interests?

Spouse #1				*Spouse #2*		
Yes	**Unsure**	**No**		**Yes**	**Unsure**	**No**
	Notes				Notes	

Have you converted the possibilities you discovered in the re-entry phase into clear objectives?

Spouse #1				*Spouse #2*		
Yes	**Unsure**	**No**		**Yes**	**Unsure**	**No**
	Notes				Notes	

Have you helped your spouse to discover the new part you want him/her to play in your transformation?

Spouse #1				*Spouse #2*		
Yes	**Unsure**	**No**		**Yes**	**Unsure**	**No**
	Notes				Notes	

Do your actions model the attitudes and behaviors you are asking your children and/or partner to develop?

Spouse #1				*Spouse #2*		
Yes	**Unsure**	**No**		**Yes**	**Unsure**	**No**
	Notes				Notes	

STEP 3: Dialogue. Together, go back through each prompt and discuss your responses and corresponding notes. Spend extra time dialoging about the questions that you and your partner answered differently. If you are the spouse who responded to the prompt positively, share with your significant other what actions/steps you have taken in order to be at the place where you are.

Continued Grief

No matter how many times either of you circled "Yes" in the previous activity, mourning the relationships you left behind in your host country can, and often does, continue in this seventh phase. One former volunteer reflected on her prolonged bereavement:

> The biggest challenge I faced with reintegration was discovering ways to express the love I had for the children I worked with. Everyday I was able to give hugs, play games and care for the children I loved. It was all so tangible. I pray with all my heart that the kids are well: that they're happy. It's been challenging to accept that that's maybe all you can do for the day: wish them well. I hope to continue to find ways in my everyday life to express my love for them.[10]

Another survey participant wrote, "The initial experience of 'reverse culture shock' was a real and profound event. It took a couple of years for me to feel anyway normal in the U.S."[11] "When old losses haven't been adequately dealt with, a sort of transition deficit is created—a readiness to grieve that only needs a new ending to set it off."[12] The importance of properly working through your enduring grief is crucial. If you or your spouse has not acknowledged and managed the losses that accompanied your return home (e.g., relationship, role, intrapsychic, etc.), then future change in your lives may be particularly difficult. Continue to engage with your individual approaches to grieving, for the integration stage

---

10 Emilia Pettinger, personal e-mail, April 10, 2014.
11 John Studer, personal e-mail, March 24, 2015.
12 Bridges, *Managing Transitions*, 27.

can include the continued fading of relationships created at your ministry site. It is hard to keep a friendship alive when so many limiting factors exist: distance, language, disparate lifestyles, differing opportunities, and so on. Life in (insert host country) goes on, and it goes on without the two of you there.

Some days you will experience definitive satisfaction; other days will feel more stagnant, and the remaining few will pull you back into a yearning for what used to be. "I thought I could describe a state: make a map of sorrow. Sorrow, however, turns out not to be a state, but a process."[13] Like all processes, there are no quick answers and often no sense of clear direction. There can be, however, a purpose to your grief. "The goals of grieving include these: to enable a person to live a life relatively unencumbered by attachments to the person or thing lost; to remake emotional attachments; to recognize and live with the reality of the loss and the feelings occasioned by it."[14] In working through your mourning, you and your spouse are able to exercise important life skills that both of you will undoubtedly need in the future. Consciously dedicate the emotional energy and time needed in order to meet some of these goals in your movement through the integration phase.

Honoring Your Experience

The ways in which you live with the reality of your losses can greatly impact the management of your grief. How you honor and continue to recognize the significance of your overseas experience is important, and yet potentially difficult. One survey participant shared, "I remember one thing I struggled with for a while was trying to discern what God's will was for my life, now that I was back. ... I started volunteering for a program at one of the elementary schools, and then a part-time job came up in speech therapy, my profession, so I started doing that. But for some reason I kept thinking I needed to be doing more."[15] As indicated, working in a position formerly held may not be as fulfilling as it once was. The integration phase provides you and your partner with the opportunity to take the now explored, creative chaos of re-entry and transform it into revitalized plans of potential. One former missioner commented on such exploration and transformation:

> Planning for my future felt like too big of an undertaking, but I knew I needed to start somewhere. I knew that I wanted to continue working in a field similar to what I was doing abroad, but I didn't know exactly what that meant. It wasn't until I spoke with several people in various lines of work that I gained some direction. I really benefited from sitting down with my journal and reflecting on what I most enjoyed from my volunteer experience. It has been a major challenge but I feel at peace with my decision to pursue a master's in public health.[16]

Such reflective action embodies the point and purpose of the seventh stage and reveals how such contemplated commitments can eventually lead to actualizing integration.

One of the most obvious ways in which you and your spouse can pay tribute to your life abroad is through the career each of you chooses to pursue. Career is defined here as simply

---

13 Lewis, *A Grief Observed*, 32.
14 Mitchell and Anderson, *All Our Losses*, 86.
15 Bridget Studer, personal e-mail, April 3, 2015.
16 Laura Rusiecki, personal e-mail, April 20, 2015.

the work a person spends the majority of his/her time doing. For some, a career is a professional occupation; for others it means raising a family; for many, it is a combination of the two. The integration phase is a period during which you take the exchange of information had within the reference group(s) you joined in the re-entry phase and allow it to unfold as a step forward within your current context. Here is an example of this process: Jack has become an active member in a new faith community. He genuinely enjoys being involved with this particular parish. In going to Mass and attending social outreach events hosted by the congregation, he has noticed how divided the Anglo-Saxon and Hispanic populations are. Jack decides to get in contact with a ministerial leader to see if there is a way he can help with this issue, as his years of service in Mexico exposed him to similar kinds of dynamics. Oddly enough, he finds out that the church's Spanish-speaking contact person is taking a job elsewhere in a month's time. The pastor asks Jack if would be interested in filling out an application for the position.

Here is another example: Jill moved to a new city because her husband was offered a teaching position at a university. In meeting some of her spouse's fellow colleagues at a social event, she strikes up a conversation with an interesting woman named Mary. Mary is a therapist and has a job at a nearby refugee center where she provides counseling for children. After Jill meets up with her a few times over coffee, Mary invites her to visit the center, as Jill has told her about her own experience working with families as a community organizer in Cameroon. It was a wonderful visit. Jill begins thinking about pursuing some kind of graduate degree in mental health. She does a little research and discovers that the university where her husband teaches has a master's program in school psychology. After much personal reflection and ongoing discussion with her spouse, Jill decides to apply to the program. Several weeks after going through the interview process, she receives a packet in the mail, and it feels pretty full.

Figuring out your career path may not unfold as smoothly as the above illustrations, but these are actual experiences of two former volunteers! In both cases, their reference groups and the provisional commitments they made gave them the connections to pursue more permanent opportunities. These returned missioners crafted integrated careers for themselves. That is what you and your partner are able to do if you so choose. Take part of what you loved from your service experience, combine it with the realities of your present circumstances, and you will find yourselves on the way to something new and invigorating. The aforementioned examples demonstrate how helpful becoming part of new communities and establishing new relationships can end up being. But careers are just one way of incorporating your past into the here and now.

For married couples with children or with the hope of having children, perhaps the most meaningful way of blending your overseas experience with life in your passport country is through your family. Many survey participants commented on the significance of this kind of integration:

- "Our service was so early on in our marriage that we had a lot of time to frame our future family and marriage priorities in the context of our experience."[17]

---

17 Kenny, "Married Missioner/Volunteer Survey," 264.

- "I think our experience gave us a perspective on life that we wouldn't have otherwise. We now have a clearer picture of what sort of teachings around social justice that we want to impress upon our children."[18]
- "Our work at an orphanage made us more aware of the special opportunity that adoption is, and as a result, it has become a piece of our plan as we look to start a family."[19]

Other survey participants wrote about how their shared ministry has directly influenced the development and interests of their children:

- "It was a tremendously rich experience for the entire family. Our children have a worldview that they wouldn't have had if we remained in our home country."[20]
- "Two of our children have enjoyed powerful experiences in Latin America and our mutual understanding and closeness has been strengthened by that."[21]
- "My daughter was the most homesick when we started our mission, but now she is the one I can't keep in the U.S.! She's lived in Spain, France, and Argentina, has travelled to Nigeria on a mission trip, and is now in France improving her French. She speaks two languages besides English."[22]

While single missioners can certainly incorporate their service abroad within their future families, couples who have shared such an experience have the potential to make that kind of integration into their home life with greater ease and to a greater extent.

In conclusion, here is a Top 25 List (not in any order) of other practical ways you and your spouse can make what you appreciated in your host country a part of your home life:

1. Be an ecologically sound shopper
2. Keep in touch with those with whom you shared this experience
3. Walk, bike, or take public transportation more often
4. Advocate for those in need
5. Eat simple meals like you did while overseas
6. Be a lifelong learner
7. Conserve water, electricity, and other such resources
8. Donate to your service program or a similar institution
9. Reduce the amount of possessions you own
10. Volunteer on a consistent basis
11. Compost
12. Spend less money
13. Sponsor a child or a family you worked with in your host country
14. Commit to a common prayer time
15. Stay informed as a global citizen
16. Recycle
17. Formally pursue training in line with your new values

---

18 Kenny, "Married Missioner/Volunteer Survey," 264.
19 Kenny, "Married Missioner/Volunteer Survey," 40.
20 Kenny, "Married Missioner/Volunteer Survey," 42.
21 Kenny, "Married Missioner/Volunteer Survey," 39.
22 Bridget Studer, personal e-mail, March 28, 2015.

18. Continue a hobby or craft you picked up while abroad
19. Be a bridge builder between different communities
20. Incorporate your host culture's gestures, phrases, or rituals into your daily routines
21. Limit your use of technology
22. Maintain the language you learned
23. Keep your faith a priority
24. Continue to support your sending organization using your time and talents
25. Celebrate holidays, feast days, or special events in ways that you did while in mission

If you and your partner have more ideas to add to this list, please do so! Honoring your overseas ministry is a personal and creative experience, so tailor the means of paying tribute to your time in service in ways that fit you and your marriage.

Spousal Dynamics

What happens when you and your spouse are in conflict with how each of you wants to integrate? *"Let's only speak in Farsi when we are in the house together ... I want us to become vegetarians ... Honey, I think we should use cloth diapers ..."* Your partner's responses may sound something like this: *"No thanks ... Nope ... Heck no!"* Because you both have different relationships with your abroad experience, you will likely have differing opinions on what were the most important pieces of your host culture. Even if both of you want to incorporate the same ministry-inspired values into your current lives, you may have different ideas of how you would like to go about doing that. If you and your spouse are missing each other on some level in regard to integration, it may be beneficial for the two of you to refer to the exercise *Finding Common Ground* in Chapter 1. But this time, instead of writing out what variables each of you wants in a service experience, you will be naming which aspects of life in (insert host country) you want to make a part of your lifestyle at home. Remember, practice compromise and accommodation.

If one or both of you is continuing to go through more life changes—new jobs, another relocation, retirement, pregnancy, becoming grandparents—then you are likely still adapting to fluctuations in marital and/or parental gender roles. Communicate with your spouse about how you are adjusting (or not) to those shifts. Seek out guidance if you find yourselves struggling to transition into new roles on your own. Working with a psychologist, preferably as a couple, can help you to process the baggage that comes along with serving abroad and then returning home. One survey participant commented on the benefits of such assistance: "Some years later while on home assignment for a couple years, (after another four years of foreign assignment), we sought marriage counseling, which was a great help and stabilized our relationship."[23] Long-term, cross-cultural experiences involve a lot of psychological adjusting, some of which can be difficult to navigate by oneself. Do not be afraid to reach out externally for a little direction.

When transitioning home as husband and wife is not healthily managed, international service work can negatively impact your marital partnership. One former missioner admitted,

---

23 Kenny, "Married Missioner/Volunteer Survey," 33.

"It would have been helpful to have a therapist work with us earlier in our marriage."[24] A program director reported, "We had one couple early on that was new to marriage and ended up separating after their year."[25] Yet another staff member shared, "As a personnel administrator in bygone days I've worked with couples who needed professional help. In some cases they both recognized the need, in some, only one of them wanted help. Then there were those who could have really benefited but neither was willing to make the commitment."[26] Protect your marriage by strengthening it. Do some research and find out if there are marriage counselors in your area, couple seminars or relationship-enhancing workshops you can attend, or other married volunteers who have successfully managed their own integration with whom you can communicate. As mentioned earlier, if you decide to seek out a psychologist, it would do you well to try to find a mental health professional who understands the realities of cross-cultural mission work.

As the turbulence of the re-entry phase subsides, you may find—as you resituate your own self—that all those bumps and jostles have put you in a completely different place. You have changed, and the changes that you have undergone are neither superficial nor temporary. Similarly, you look over at the spot where your spouse once was and see it vacant. Upon looking around, you finally spy him/her and think, *"By gosh, they have moved clear across the way!"* While getting reacquainted with this new version of your partner can be refreshing and intriguing, it can also be daunting. One survey participant wrote, "I think the greatest challenge was trying to get to know the people we had become (this is still a great challenge for us). We realized that we are not the same people that we were when we married four years ago."[27] Another former volunteer added, "Our year has had a great impact on our marriage. I don't know the extent of that impact, but we are very different people now versus the people we were when we first started."[28] It sounds like these couples might benefit from updating their "love maps."

Update Your Love Maps[29]
Duration: 20–35 minutes

According to Dr. Gottman, a love map refers to the part of the brain where you store important information about your partner and his/her life experiences. "These maps hold details about your spouse's personal history, daily routines, likes, and dislikes. Research shows that couples who maintain accurate and extensive love maps have happier marriages. These pairs are also better prepared to weather difficult life passages."[30] Important events, like serving abroad, have the ability to change an individual's whole view of him/herself and his/her place in the world. That is why it is especially important for the two of you to keep your love maps up-to-date during this time of transition.[31] Engaging in the following exer-

24 Kenny, "Married Missioner/Volunteer Survey," 36.
25 Kenny, "Program Staff: Married Missioners/Volunteers Survey," 13.
26 Ken Wiggers, personal e-mail, April 7, 2015.
27 Kenny, "Married Missioner/Volunteer Survey," 32.
28 Kenny, "Married Missioner/Volunteer Survey," 38.
29 Adapted from Gottman, Gottman, and DeClaire, *Ten Lessons*, 94–96.
30 Gottman, Gottman, and DeClaire, *Ten Lessons*, 94–95.
31 Gottman, Gottman, and DeClaire, *Ten Lessons*, 95.

cise can help you and your partner grow closer together, rather than drifting apart, during the integration phase.

STEP 1: Find Time. This activity is most beneficial when completed over the course of a month or so. Schedule some uninterrupted time each week so that the two of you can engage with this exercise at a relaxed pace.

STEP 2: Roles. Designate one partner as the speaking spouse and the other as the listening spouse.

STEP 3: Questions. Following is a list of questions that will guide you both in revising your love maps. The listening spouse should ask his/her partner the first question of the two to three that that you have mutually decided to address. As the speaking spouse searches for honest answers, the listening partner should do his/her best to attend and respond to his/her significant other in an open and supportive manner.

- How has serving cross-culturally altered how you feel about your life?
- How has it changed the way you feel about your role in our immediate family? Extended family?
- How has it changed the way you feel about your job?
- Have your priorities changed since working and living overseas?
- How has it changed your views regarding religion, spirituality, and/or God?
- How has it changed the way you think about the future?
- How has it changed the way you think about serious illness or death?
- Name the top three moments in <u>our marriage</u> when you felt closest to God while serving abroad.
- How has your service changed your experience of time? Relationships?
- What are your current stresses? Concerns? Hopes?
- Who are the new and significant people in your life?
- How has being in mission changed what you need for yourself?
- How has it changed your sense of security in the world?
- How has it affected your daily mood?
- What kind of support do you need from me as you enter this new period of life?

STEP 4: Role Reversal. Once the speaking spouse feels like he/she has shared all that he/she wants, switch roles so that the speaker becomes the listener. Repeat STEP 3, and complete this process until each of you has addressed the questions you selected.

STEP 5: Marriage Mission Statement. After you have finished this exercise at whatever pace you were able to, consider revisiting the exercise *Marriage Mission Statement* in Chapter 1. With new experiences and reflections, the two of you may want to make amendments to the mission statement you created during the discernment phase. Once you have completed the activity for the second time, write your revised marriage mission statement in the second blank heart.

Return Visit

Taking a trip back to your ministry site can be both affirming and slightly unsettling. In preparing to travel to their host countries, several former missioners reported feeling excited yet anxious, hopeful but with doubts. Before a visit, you and/or your spouse may be wondering: *"Will those whom I loved remember me? Can I still communicate in a different language? What will our interactions with new members from this community look like? With what attitude will I re-engage in this environment? Should I bring gifts? Will I be able to work/ serve in a similar capacity as before or will my time be spent differently?"* While entertaining such thoughts is not necessarily an issue, placing too much weight on such matters can be. Most life events are comprised of both positive and negative elements, so allow for such synchronicity to exist. A trip to your former service placement(s) will likely be a mix of heartwarming and heartbreaking moments. For example, the colleague with whom you were closest may have found another meaningful friendship, demonstrating the growth in his/her ability to form relationships, while also calling attention to the distance that is now present between the two of you. The following four paragraphs are responses from volunteers who have visited their ministry sites since their initial departure. These quotes illustrate both the complexity and the joyful opportunity a temporary return to (insert host country) can provide you and your partner as individuals:

> Going back to Gambia after a year away was unknowingly one of the more difficult things I have done. During my year as a volunteer in Gambia, I made many meaningful relationships; however, after being stateside for a year, I let myself drift away from my strong connections. Upon return, I was awakened to what I had forgotten, or even had become numb to during my year as a volunteer: the pressures families had to put food on the table every day, the constant struggle of having enough water, and the substandard housing conditions, to name a few. Returning was a blow to the chest; I had forgotten how my loved ones abroad suffered daily. Although challenging, the visit was necessary to help me move forward with my life in the United States. It helped me to be grateful for the lessons Gambia taught me, the unconditional love given, and to realize the importance of making myself present to the people I am with, wherever that may be.[32]

> Going back was powerful because it showed me that even though I had left and no longer lived there, I could always go back and I will always be in the lives of the kids I worked with. … Long-term service trips are difficult because it becomes your normal, day-to-day life for a whole year or more, but then you have to leave. It feels like your world is turned upside down and adjusting to your old culture is a long and tough journey. Going back to visit helped me realize that it's okay for both worlds, for both cultures, to exist at the same time, and for both to influence me and be a part of me.[33]

> At the point of my first return trip, I felt burdened by guilt for leaving Ecuador when my year came to close. I felt like I abandoned my Ecuadorians and that my heart was ripped out when it was time to go home. When I made my

---

32 Allison Clayton, personal e-mail, August 24, 2015.
33 Rachel Severino, personal e-mail, April 15, 2015.

return, I wanted to "have" Ecuador, like it was a possession. I was desperate to validate my year and my friendships by proving to myself they existed if I could see myself in pictures we'd take together or see my Ecuas enjoying the *regalitos* I brought for them. It was a nice trip back, I had a lot of fun, but my second trip back proved to be much more life-giving and free. By this time, I had grown and developed more of a life for myself stateside, I was no longer grieving my time as a volunteer. I went back empty-handed and was completely fulfilled and overwhelmed by the love and acceptance I was welcomed with. I barely used my camera and was able to be present to the people and moments before me. I was free and without all the baggage. The second time around, God reminded me the relationship I have with Ecuador is something bigger than me and that I don't need to give jars of peanut butter away to earn, receive, give or share God's love with the Ecuadorian people.[34]

Returning for a visit was like coming home. I was so surprised by the overwhelming feeling that I had never left, that time had stood still at my volunteer site while my life in the states went on, and the amazement that it seemed I could return to my life in Honduras without missing a beat. ... The hardest part was leaving a second time, but it wasn't as hard as the first time. Even though there was still a lot of guilt, the visit showed me beyond a doubt that the kids really were okay without me. All of the children I had worked with had improved in leaps and bounds in the eight months I was away and that was amazing to see. I knew that in some small way I had contributed to that, but I also could see that this community was continuing to move forward. So yes, visiting opened a few old wounds afresh when it was time to say goodbye, or when I saw again, even in just a few days, the ways the kids and the system were still broken, but mostly it healed old wounds. I was forced to let go of some of the guilt by seeing the way they had thrived.[35]

Clearly, return trips to your ministry assignment(s) can be emotionally laden. Such visits can offer further confirmation of and/or a healthy challenge to how you and your spouse are integrating your past experience with your current reality. Try not to be afraid of the beautiful messiness that can occur when re-entering this former world for a second, third, or fourth time, as you will be inevitably encountering a distinct context carrying a different set of accompanying perspectives with every visit.

Miscellaneous

Here are a few more topics worth mentioning as you and your partner move onward in your journey of integrated and holistic living:

Continue to talk about your financial situation. Unfortunately, economic insecurity can be a lingering stressor during this stage. One survey participant wrote, "The financial transition is still difficult. To return to a traditional job/family situation and provide for our family needs is still extremely challenging."[36] Yet another former missioner claimed, "I left a thriv-

---

34 Elizabeth Castellano, personal e-mail, August 19, 2015.
35 Joanna Gardner, personal e-mail, August 15, 2015.
36 Kenny, "Married Missioner/Volunteer Survey," 164.

ing dental practice the year before to disengage and prepare for our mission, along with one year after we returned to reengage and recover. I lost at least four years of income and used a good bit of savings to carry on. It was a major sacrifice."[37] Hopefully you and your spouse feel that the economic hardships you may still be facing are worth what you have been given by your international service. Read and reread the last few sections in each chapter to help you both realize that what you have acquired because of your mission experience, money cannot buy.

Your developed skill set. Here are the most well-respected traits that returned volunteers are believe to have developed while in cross-cultural mission: resourcefulness, low goal/task orientation, adaptability, a sense of humor, and the ability to accept failure.[38] Hopefully you and your partner see one or more of these characteristics in yourselves and can put them to good use wherever you are.

Tell your incredible tales. Chapters 5 and 6 prompted you and your significant other to develop stories you could share in everyday conversations or at speaking events. Crafting such wholesome, meaningful, and spiritually animated anecdotes is important. But do not forget about those I-cannot-believe-this-is-actually-happening narratives. Like the time your supervisor was the only person qualified to give you a shot in the bum to cure whatever tropical malady you had recently contracted. Or that night when you and your spouse were on the back porch in your skivvies, frantically trying to finish your outdoor bucket showers, in fear that the visiting nuns were going to round the corner at any moment. Or the minor surgery you had to perform in removing a botfly maggot from the armpit of a student in your class. (Sorry.) Take a look at the last sentence of the section *Physical Realities*. ... I told you so! Enjoy the incredulous looks and uncontrollable laughs you will trigger when you unveil these kinds of adventures at the appropriate times and places.

Remember that you are a disciple. It would seem that you and your partner have kept your faith in the transitional process. Your combined pilgrimage through the phases of separation, liminality, and incorporation shall proceed in renewal. "A couple grows in holiness by journeying with Christ through the mystery of His life, death and Resurrection. This movement through life to death to new life is called the Paschal Mystery."[39] Press on in your mission as married persons, returned volunteers, and whatever other lifework God calls you to next. "And remember, I am always with you, to the end of the age" (Mt 28:20b).

You have got a friend in me. You likely created unique friendships with those whom you worked abroad in your host country. If you want them to, these kinds of relationships have the potential to last a lifetime. One former missioner shared:

> It's often said that our co-workers in ministry become family. My wife and I met another couple during our pre-field training. We were then assigned to the same country and became neighbors. In recent years our assignments have most often been in different parts of the world, but our friendship re-

---

37 John Studer, personal e-mail, March 24, 2015.
38 Kohls, *Survival Kit,* 72; Pascoe, *Culture Shock! Successful Living Abroad,* 47.
39 Committee on Laity, Marriage, Family Life, and Youth, United States Conference of Catholic Bishops, *Marriage: Love and Life in the Divine Plan* (Washington, DC: United States Conference of Catholic Bishops, 2010), 33.

mains. We stay in touch, and when our travels give us the opportunity, we manage a visit, which is 'just like old times,' only 55 years worth.[40]

As noted, connections made while serving overseas can be relationships you find joy in maintaining for the rest of your lives.

Celebrate your evolving and synthesized lifestyle. If you have yet to do so, take the time to commemorate moments of integration. Celebratory mile-markers can be as small as a date night listening to music you acquired while abroad or as big as a getaway weekend for you and your spouse to decompress together. Breaking from the routines that you have recently established to acknowledge the goodness of their presence can be a rewarding kind of activity.

Marital Skill Building

As you and your spouse near the end of this seven-stage, cross-cultural experience, you are now able to survey all of the skills you have personally acquired and/or refined throughout the entire process. As a result of this individual development, your conjoined skill set as a couple has grown, a fact that was attested to by many returned volunteers:

- "We know how to better approach and deal with conflict together."[41]
- "I think we trust each other and communicate better."[42]
- "Our service year pushed us to be open, work on our communication skills, and share our relationship with others."[43]
- "We figured out how to truly be with one another, not being distracted, and placing value in honoring each other as partners."[44]
- "We learned the importance of boundaries, 'saying no,' and communication."[45]
- "We improved our communication skills and really learned to value and appreciate the amount of time we spent together as a couple and with our son."[46]

The improvement of many essential and interpersonal life skills appears to be a principal benefit of serving together as husband and wife. Continually utilizing proficiencies like the ones mentioned above—during your abroad experience, throughout the re-entry phase, and in your present lives—is how virtues are constructed. "Virtue describes a specific strength that is maturing into a *constant* and *consistent* ability."[47] Marriage and mission are two lifestyles that elevate our capacities to engage in effective communication, compromise, accommodation, prioritizing, etc. Being a spouse *and* a missioner are vocations for the valiant, for the courageous, for the virtuous. It is in the making of virtues—the frequent and aptly handled encounters of each crisis (*Christ-is*)—that God abides in us.

40 Ken Wiggers, personal e-mail, April 16, 2015.
41 Kenny, "Married Missioner/Volunteer Survey," 29.
42 Kenny, "Married Missioner/Volunteer Survey," 39.
43 Kenny, "Married Missioner/Volunteer Survey," 30.
44 Kenny, "Married Missioner/Volunteer Survey," 33.
45 Kenny, "Married Missioner/Volunteer Survey," 29.
46 Kenny, "Married Missioner/Volunteer Survey," 34.
47 Whitehead and Whitehead, *Marrying Well*, 192.

Word Cloud
Duration: 30–45 minutes

A word cloud is an image composed of randomly positioned words that reference a partic-ular theme or topic. When constructing such an image on a word-cloud generating website, individuals have the option to repeat the number of certain terms used or increase their font size. Altering words in this way indicates their importance. Word clouds, as powerful, con-cise, and innovative visualizations, have the ability to capture the essence of your service ex-perience. The following activity is a concrete way of artistically summarizing how you and your partner are integrating your overseas ministry with your life in your passport country.

STEP 1: Past Words. Each spouse will need a pen or a pencil, two pieces of paper, and one sheet to share. As individuals, take ten minutes to reflect on your mission work. What words present themselves when you think about your time in (insert host country)? Write down whatever comes to mind, as these words can be both meaningful and silly. Include common nouns, proper nouns, verbs, and adjectives. (The more words you think of, the larger and more detailed your word cloud will appear.) Once you both have finished brain-storming, share what words you wrote with each other.

STEP 2: Present Words. Next, return to your own pieces of paper. Take another ten minutes to think about your current home life. What terms surface now? Write those underneath the "past words" you came up with in the previous step. After you and your spouse have completed ten minutes of reflection and recording, come together and share the "present words" each of you wrote down.

STEP 3: Overlapping Words. Place your lists side by side and circle all of the words that ap-pear on both of your pieces of paper. You can also circle terms that are similar in meaning.

STEP 4: Integrated Words. As partners, brainstorm new words that incorporate or blend the ideas/words found in the two lists each of you has made. My husband and I wrote down "orphans" and "family" on our past and present word lists, so the "integrated word" we came up with together was "adoption". Both spouses do not necessarily need to have the same words written on their respective sheets of paper in order to create an integrated word. Record the terms that you think of as a couple.

STEP 5: Categorize. Write down all of the words you circled at the beginning of STEP 3 and the words you thought of together in STEP 4 on your third sheet of paper. These will be your integrated words. In creating your word cloud, depending on what website you use, the two of you will either (a) manually adjust these words to make them larger, (b) increase the number of times these words are used, or (c) do a mixture of both.

STEP 6: Upload. Take the initial list of words you each made in STEP 1 and STEP 2, the "overlapping words" you identified in STEP 3, and the list of integrated words you created in STEP 4, and plug them into any one of the following word cloud generating websites:

- Wordle: wordle.net/
- WordItOut: worditout.com
- Word Cloud Generator—Jason Davies: https://www.jasondavies.com/word-cloud/#%2F%2Fwww.jasondavies.com%2Fwordcloud%2Fabout%2F

As you and your spouse begin constructing your word cloud online, either of you can add more words to any "category" you wish. See **Figure 7.1** as an abbreviated example of what your finished product should look like.

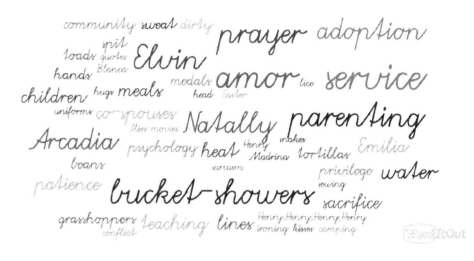

Figure 7.1

STEP 7: Placement. Once you and your partner have generated your word cloud, print it and frame it. Put your word cloud in a place in your home where you both will come across it on a daily basis. This word cloud can act as a tangible reminder of what you learned and loved during your time serving overseas, the realities of your life at present, and how these two worlds meet.

STEP 8: Extra Project. If you or your spouse is tech savvy and/or artistically inclined, you may want to check out the websites of free digital storytelling tools below:

- ZooBurst: zooburst.com
- Storybird: storybird.com
- Utellstory: utellstory.com
- StoryJumper: storyjumper.com
- Slidestory: slidestory.com
- ACMI Generator: generator.acmi.net.au/storyboard
- Picture a Story: artofstorytelling.org/write-a-story

You can combine narration, photos, animation, and video using these story generators, to produce yet another noteworthy portrayal of your shared service experience.

Mission-In-Reverse

"Our years in mission gave us perspective and taught us to lean on and trust the people God placed in our lives—we experienced our humanity."[48] Like this former volunteer, each of you has presumably broadened and deepened your own sense of humanity during your time overseas. (Humanity defined here as *the quality of being a person for others*.) The growth in and expansion of one's humanity makes "room for life, for others, and for God."[49] Consider the following analogy and its corresponding figures:

At the beginning of your ministry, you were like an edged rock—providing people what little comfort you could.

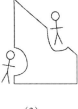

(1)

As your service experience began to unfold, you were touched by those to whom you ministered.

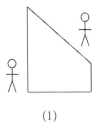

(2)

Their impact on you formed hollowed (and hallowed) spaces into which others could lean.

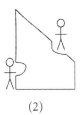

(3)

---

48 Kenny, "Married Missioner/Volunteer Survey," 30.
49 Thomas, *Christian Marriage*, 94.

Toward the end of your ministry, your deepened slopes became respites—places of shelter for still other people to seek relief.

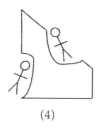

(4)

As illustrated, your mission work was a process of making room. Those you served were also serving you. They tempered the curves of your corners and softened your hard spots, transforming the edged rock you once were, into a smooth and gentle boulder—a person with more space for life, for others, and for God. This is mission-in-reverse. "The mission-in-reverse approach teaches that the minister can and should learn from the people ministered to—including, and perhaps especially, from the poor and marginal people."[50] As Pope Francis wrote in *Evangelii Gaudium*, "The Church does not evangelize unless she constantly lets herself be evangelized. ... It is a wonderful thing to be God's faithful people. We achieve fulfillment when we break down walls and our heart is filled with faces and names!"[51]

God did not call us to be religious; he called us to be human—to be a people for others. Being human means not only seeing the inherent value in your self and in those around you, but also assisting in the fruition of each person's worth. And that is what you and your spouse assumedly aspired to do, to help those at your volunteer site(s) recognize and actualize their dignity. But something extra occurred. In your efforts to make a difference, both of you were fortunate enough to reap exactly what you sought to sow, only tenfold. One former program director articulated this paradox well:

> One of the key lessons of mission work is the realization that we have come to benefit from, and have even been "evangelized" by those among whom we lived and shared our lives. We thought we were going to "do" something, but often end up receiving so much more than we ever gave. This is a great gift and not something that may have originally motivated us. However, the reality is that we, in the West, have something to learn from the poor and the marginalized. We are lacking and they have something to offer us, but only if we have the humility to accept and the courage to engage. The mission experience is one example of us moving out of our "comfort zones" because we need to; because we do not have all the answers. The process of mission, of being uncomfortable and accepting that we do not know it all, leads us to grow and become better, more whole individuals.[52]

50 Claude Marie Barbour, "Seeking Justice and Shalom in the City," *International Review of Mission* 72, no. 291 (July 1984): 304.
51 Francis, *Evangelii Gaudium* (2013), nos. 174, 274, http://w2.vatican.va/content/francesco/en/apost_exhortations/documents/papa-francesco_esortazione-ap_20131124_evangelii-gaudium.html.
52 Gerry Doran, personal e-mail, April 10, 2015.

The retrospection granted during the integration phase is a means by which you and your partner can become more aware of and grateful for the gift of humanity you have been given by those with whom you shared the vocation of service.

Enduring Service

Your volunteer experience may have inspired you and your spouse to pursue similar types of mission opportunities abroad. Several survey participants reported that they continued (or desired) to serve overseas as a couple after their first ministerial term:

- "We met at our mission site before we got married and returned there as a married couple. Service is the reason we are married."[53]
- "It gave us great memories and made us want to volunteer again."[54]
- "We kept serving after our year was over. … We led other couples in their service year together."[55]

In the same vein, your time overseas could have prompted the two of you to seek out a more general vocation of volunteerism, as shared by one survey participant, "Service together is the very expression of marriage in motion. We would be handicapped without the opportunity to improve that learned skill."[56] Another former missioner wrote, "Serving is partly what defines our marriage. Our sending church pastor taught us that marriage was all about communication, cooperation, and compromise. Serving together gives us additional 'c-word' opportunities in building the Kingdom of God together."[57] To have a shared calling as a married couple, or as individuals within a marriage, is a wonderful thing. To have that driving purpose rooted in your faith tradition, and inspired by your relationship with God can be even more of a blessing.

Closeness and Accountability

Many returned married missioners stated that their service experience brought them closer together and made them more appreciative of one another—thereby strengthening their overall marital partnership:

- "We have a healthy marriage and a strong commitment to each other because of our shared vision and experience."[58]
- "We learned to rely on each other and value the quantity and quality of time we spent together."[59]
- "Usually the hardest, most out-of-box experiences are the ones that have the potential to strengthen your relationship the most. That is what our year of service did for us."[60]

---

53 Kenny, "Married Missioner/Volunteer Survey," 40.
54 Kenny, "Married Missioner/Volunteer Survey," 36.
55 Kenny, "Married Missioner/Volunteer Survey," 26.
56 Kenny, "Married Missioner/Volunteer Survey," 38.
57 Kenny, "Married Missioner/Volunteer Survey," 38.
58 Kenny, "Married Missioner/Volunteer Survey," 38.
59 Kenny, "Married Missioner/Volunteer Survey," 31.
60 Kenny, "Married Missioner/Volunteer Survey," 42.

- "It drew us closer and helped us appreciate each other more."[61]
- "Our marriage and family is more faithful and stronger because of this service together."[62]

The natural construction of a check-and-balance system within your marriage is yet another benefit of having served abroad as a couple. As former volunteers with shared ministry-inspired values, you and your spouse are able to hold each other accountable for your actions. If either of you "relapses" and begins buying too many clothes, taking water for granted, or not being present enough in your interactions with others, you can remind each other of the lessons learned while in your host country. One survey participant attested to this in summarizing: "No matter how far we sometimes feel our lives have strayed from that time of intense service and connection to God, now that we have so many added distractions (kids and their lives and activities), we can both instantly connect to our shared experience as a reference of reprioritizing."[63] Having a constant companion in continuing to consciously live out your integrated goals and principles is of inestimable value.

Home

In closing, I would like to write about the notion of home, a topic put forth at the beginning of this chapter. "In experience, the meaning of space often merges with that of place. But 'space' is more abstract than 'place.' What begins as undifferentiated space becomes place as we get to know it better and endow it with value."[64] This phenomenon is illustrated by the concept of a *house* becoming a *home*. Home is not a purely geographical locale; it is not merely what we do, nor is it a situation totally inside ourselves. Our *space* in this world becomes our *place,* firstly, because of God and his love, and secondly, because of how we as Christian disciples—but perhaps even more importantly, how we as human beings—choose to follow God. Home is our return to Providence, a journey during which we become the person God wills us to be—simply, someone to love another. As a husband and as a wife, your "another" is each other. As missioners your "another" are all others. In marriage and in mission, you are both at home and headed there.

---

61 Kenny, "Married Missioner/Volunteer Survey," 38.
62 Kenny, "Married Missioner/Volunteer Survey," 39.
63 Kenny, "Married Missioner/Volunteer Survey," 39.
64 Yi-Fu Tuan, *Space and Place: The Perspective of Experience* (Minneapolis: University of Minnesota Press, 1977), 6.

Appendix

Blog Sites: Chapter 2

- Blogger.com: www.blogger.com
- Ghost: https://ghost.org/
- LiveJournal: www.livejournal.com
- Medium: https://medium.com/
- Pen.io: https://pen.io
- Penzu: https://penzu.com
- Postach.io: https://postach.io/site
- SquareSpace: www.squarespace.com/
- Svbtle: https://svbtle.com/
- Tumblr: http://www.tumblr.com
- Webs: www.webs.com
- Wix: http://www.wix.com/
- WordPress: https://wordpress.com/

Hints for Packing: Chapter 2

- Kohls, Robert L. "Appendix D." In *Survival Kit for Overseas Living: For Americans Planning to Live and Work Abroad*, 90-95. Yarmouth, ME: Intercultural Press, Inc., 1984.
- Her Packing List: http://herpackinglist.com/2013/03/mission-trip-packing-list/
- Missionary Travel Checklist: www.hccmis.com/missionary-travel-checklist/
- Packing Pro: application in iTunes priced at $2.99
- Projects Abroad: www.projects-abroad.co.uk/blog/?content=2014/ultimate-travel-checklist/
- U.S. Passport and International Travel: travel.state.gov/content/passports/english/go.html
- Additional items to consider packing: bungee cords, camping laundry line, a handheld fan, lice treatment, portable speakers, S-hooks, a small mirror, tupperware, a world map, and as many airplane blankets you can stuff in your carry-on

Information Sharing: Chapter 6

- Catholic Volunteer Network: https://catholicvolunteernetwork.org/sites/default/files/Whats Next Notebook v.1.pdf (page 18)
- Christianity Today: http://www.christianitytoday.com/le/2012/august-online-only/telling-great-story.html
- Goins, Writer: http://goinswriter.com/tell-story/
- Network for Good: http://www.fundraising123.org/article/5-tips-help-you-tell-better-stories
- Peace Corps: http://www.peacecorps.gov/resources/returned/thirdgoal/
- Storyteller: http://www.storyteller.net/articles/296
- Talkingstick: http://shiftingcareers.blogs.nytimes.com/2008/08/03/5-tips-for-telling-better-stories/?_r=0

References

Children/Family: Literature

Andrews, Leslie A. and Ted Ward. *The Family in Mission: Understanding and Caring for Those Who Serve.* Palmer Lake, CO: Mission Training International, 2004.

Barclay, John Stanley. *Families in Cross-Cultural Ministry: A Comprehensive Guide and Manual for Families, Administrators, and Supporters.* Melbourne, Australia: Bible College of Victoria, 2010.

Blomberg, Janet and David Brooks. *Fitted Pieces: A Guide for Parent's Educating Children Overseas.* Adrian, MI: SHARE Education Services, 2001.

Collins Burga, Lori. *Moving with Kids: 25 Ways to Ease Your Family's Transition to a New Home.* United States: ReadHowYouWant.com, 2010.

Knell, Marion. *Families on the Move: Growing Up Overseas – And Loving It!* Grand Rapids: Kregel Publications, 2001.

Lonely Planet. *Travel with Children: Your Complete Resource.* Australia: Lonely Planet Publications, 2009.

Miller, Susan. *But Mom, I Don't Want To Move!* Colorado Springs: Focus on the Family, 2004.

Pollock, David C. and Ruth E. Van Reken. *Third Culture Kids: Growing Up Among Worlds.* Boston: Intercultural Press, 1999.

Children/Family: Internet

A Life Overseas
www.alifeoverseas.com/to-the-parents-of-third-culture-kids/

Daraja
www.daraja.us

Denizen
www.denizenmag.com/about/

Families in Global Transition
www.figt.org

iCHED
www.iched.org/cms/scripts/page.php?site_id=iched

180

Interaction International
www.interactionintl.org/home.asp

MK Planet
mkplanet.com

MU Kappa International
mukappa.org

TCK World
www.tckworld.com

Youth Compass
youthcompass.org

Cross-Cultural: Literature

Austin, Clyde N. *Cross-Cultural Reentry: An Annotated Bibliography.* Abilene, TX: Abilene Christian University, 1986.

———. *Cross-Cultural Reentry: A Book of Readings.* Abilene, TX: Abilene Christian University, 1986.

Bridges, William. *Managing Transitions: Making The Most of Change.* Cambridge: Da Capo Press, 2003.

———. *Transitions: Making Sense of Life's Changes.* New York: Addison-Wesley, 1980.

Knell, Marion. *Burn Up or Splash Down: Surviving the Culture Shock of Re-Entry.* Mill Hill, London: Monarch Books, 2007.

Kohls, L. Robert. *Survival Kit for Overseas Living: For Americans Planning to Live and Work Abroad.* Yarmouth, ME: Intercultural Press, 1984.

Mitchell, Kenneth R. and Herbert Anderson. *All Our Losses, All Our Griefs: Resources for Pastoral Care.* Philadelphia: Westminster Press, 1983.

Storti, Craig. *The Art of Coming Home.* Yarmouth, ME: Intercultural Press, 1997.

———. *The Art of Crossing Cultures.* Boston: Intercultural Press, 1989.

Cross-Cultural: Internet

Escape Artist
www.escapeartist.com

Expatriate Connection
expatriateconnection.com

Exploring Culture
lifelearner.org/culture/

Culture Concepts Consulting
cultureconceptsconsulting.com

Insurance Services of America
www.missionaryhealth.net

Lessons From Abroad
www.lessonsfromabroad.org

Mental Health Resources for Cross Cultural Workers
www.crossculturalworkers. com/ebooks.htm

My World Abroad
myworldabroad.com

The Culture Test
theculturetest.com

Transitions Abroad
www.transitionsabroad.com/index.shtml

Transition Dynamics
www.transition-dynamics.com/links.html

What's Up With Culture
www2.pacific.edu/sis/culture/

Marriage: Literature

Anderson, Herbert and Robert Cotton Fite. *Becoming Married.* Louisville: Westminster John Knox Press, 1993.

Anderson, Herbert and Kenneth R. Mitchell. *Leaving Home.* Louisville: Westminster John Knox Press, 1993.

Anderson, Herbert and Freda A. Gardner. *Living Alone.* Louisville: Westminster John Knox Press, 1997.

Anderson, Herbert, David Hogue, and Marie Mccarthy. *Promising Again.* Louisville: Westminster John Knox Press, 1995.

Anderson, Herbert and Susan B. W. Johnson. *Regarding Children.* Louisville: Westminster John Knox Press, 1994.

Gottman, John M., Julie Schwartz Gottman, and Joan DeClaire. *Ten Lessons to Transform Your Marriage.* New York: Crown Publishers, 2006.

Gottman, John M. and Nan Silver. *The Seven Principles for Making Marriage Work.* New York: Crown Publishers, 1999.

Gottman, John M. and Nan Silver. *Why Marriages Succeed or Fail.* New York: Simon & Schuster, 1994.

Thomas, David M. *Christian Marriage: A Journey Together.* Collegeville, MN: Liturgical Press, 1983.

Whitehead, Evelyn Eaton, and James D. Whitehead. *Marrying Well: Possibilities in Christian Marriage Today.* Garden City, NY: Doubleday & Co., 1981.

Marriage: Internet

Couple Power
http://couplepower.com

For Your Marriage
www.foryourmarriage.org

Imago Relationships
http://www.imagorelationships.org

Marriage Builders
http://marriagebuilders.com

National Healthy Marriage Resource Center
www.healthymarriageinfo.org/index.aspx

Omega Institute
http://www.eomega.org

PREP
https://www.prepinc.com

Purpose Built Families
http://www.pairs.com

Stronger Marriage
strongermarriage.org

The Gottman Relationship Blog
www.gottmanblog.com

Service/Mission: Literature

Dodds, Lois A. and Laura Mae Gardner. *Global Servants: Cross-cultural Humanitarian Heroes, Vol. 1, Formation and Development of These Heroes.* Liverpool, PA: Heartstream Resources, 2011.

———. *Global Servants: Cross-cultural Humanitarian Heroes, Vol. 2, 12 Factors in Effectiveness and Longevity.* Liverpool, PA: Heartstream Resources, 2011.

———. *Global Servants: Cross-Cultural Humanitarian Heroes, Vol. 3, The Art and Heart of Agency Care.* Liverpool, PA: Heartstream Resources, 2011.

Gardner, Laura Mae. *Healthy, Resilient, and Effective in Cross-Cultural Ministry.* Fort Washington, PA: WEC International, 2015.

O'Donnell, Kelly. *Missionary Care.* Pasadena, CA: William Carey Library, 1992.

———. *Doing Member Care Well.* Pasadena, CA: William Carey Library, 2002.

Jordan, Peter. *Re-Entry: Making the Transition from Missions to Life at Home.* Seattle: YWAM Publishing, 1992.

Pirolo, Neal. *The Reentry Team: Caring for Your Returning Missionaries.* San Diego: Emmaus Road International, 2000.

Tiessen, Julie A. *The Trailing Spouse in Mission Leadership: Stewarded Commodity Or Lost Resource?* Charlotte, NC: Gordon-Conwell Theological Seminary, 2008.

Service/Mission: Internet

Barnabas International
www.barnabas.org/index.php

Brigada
www.brigada.org

Catholic Apostolic Center
www.catholicapostolatecenter.org

Catholic Volunteer Network
catholicvolunteernetwork.org

From Mission to Mission
www.missiontomission.org

Global Member Care Network
www.globalmembercare.org/index.php?id=40

Godspeed Resources Connection
godspeedresources.org

MisLinks
www.mislinks.org

Missionary Care
www.missionarycare.com

Mission Training International
www.mti.org

Oscar
www.oscar.org.uk/index.htm

United States Catholic Mission Association
www.uscatholicmission.org

Watt's Your Pathway
www.wattsyourpathway.co.uk/about.html

Bibliography

Anderson, Herbert and Robert Cotton Fite. *Becoming Married.* Louisville: Westminster John Knox Press, 1993.

Arbuckle, Gerald A., SM. *Culture, Inculturation, and Theologians: A Postmodern Critique.* Collegeville, MN: Liturgical Press, 2010.

Aronson, Elliot. *The Social Animal.* 10th ed. New York: Worth Publishers, 2008.

Austin, Clyde N. "Appendix E: Moving On." In *Cross-Cultural Reentry: A Book of Readings,* edited by Clyde N. Austin, 269–70. Abilene, TX: Abilene Christian University, 1986.

———. "Overview of Reentry." In *Cross-Cultural Reentry: A Book of Readings,* edited by Clyde N. Austin, 2–4. Abilene, TX: Abilene Christian University, 1986.

———. "Reentry Stress: The Pain of Coming Home." In *Cross-Cultural Reentry: A Book of Readings,* edited by Clyde N. Austin, 123–31. Abilene, TX: Abilene Christian University, 1986.

Barbour, Claude Marie. "Seeking Justice and Shalom in the City." *International Review of Mission.*" 73, no. 291 (July 1984): 304.

Bridges, William. *Managing Transitions: Making the Most of Change.* Cambridge, MA: Da Capo Press, 2003.

———. *Transitions: Making Sense of Life's Changes.* New York: Addison-Wesley, 1980.

Cambas, Chris. "Overcoming Infidelity." *National Marriage Seminars.* February 10, 2014. http://www.nationalmarriageseminars.com/aboutus/blog/2014/02/11/overcoming-infidelity/.

Catholic Church. "The Paschal Mystery in the Church's Sacraments." In *Catechism of the Catholic Church: Revised in Accordance with the Official Latin Text Promulgated by Pope John II.* New York: Doubleday, 1995.

Chapman, Gary. *The Five Love Languages: How to Express Heartfelt Commitment to Your Mate.* Northfield: Northfield Publishing, 1992.

Cherry, Kendra. "Erikson's Stages of Psychosocial Development: Psychosocial Development in Young Adulthood, Middle Age, and Old Age." *About Education.* http://psychology.about.com/od/psychosocialtheories/a/psychosocial_3.htm.

———. "What Is Social Psychology?" *About Education.* http://psychology.about.com/od/socialpsychology/f/socialpsych.htm.

Dodds, Lois A. and Lawrence E. Dodds. "Caring for People in Missions: Just Surviving—or Thriving? Optimal Care for the Long Haul." *Heartstream Resources for Cross-Cultural Workers.* Liverpool, PA: Heartstream Resources, 1997.http://www.heartstreamresources.org/media/Membercare.pdf.

Donovan, Melissa. "Seven Different Types of Journal Writing." *Writing Forward.* http://www.writingforward.com/news-announcements/journal-writing/journal-writing-styles.

"Do You See What I See?" Series: The Faith Hall of Fame. Lesson 3. *threethirtyministries.org.* January 2011. http://threethirtyministries.org/2011/01/lesson-3-do-you-see-what-i-see/.

Fifth General Conference of the Latin American and Caribbean Bishops. *Aparecida* Document, no. 360. May 12, 2007. http://www.celam.org/aparecida/Ingles.pdf.

Fontaine, Coralyn, M. "International Relocation: A Comprehensive Psychosocial Approach." In *Cross-Cultural Reentry: A Book of Readings,* edited by Clyde N. Austin, 39-47. Abilene: Abilene Christian University, 1986.

Freedman, Art. "A Strategy for Managing 'Cultural' Transitions: Re-Entry from Training." In *Cross-Cultural Reentry: A Book of Readings,* edited by Clyde N. Austin, 19-27. Abilene, TX: Abilene Christian University, 1986.

Gittins, Anthony J. *Bread for the Journey: The Mission of Transformation and The Transformation of Mission.* Maryknoll, NY: Orbis Books, 1993.

Gottman, John M. and Julie Schwartz Gottman. "How to Keep Love Going Strong." *YES! Magazine.* January 3, 2011. http://www.yesmagazine.org/issues/what-happy-families-know/how-to-keep-love-going-strong.

Gottman, John M. "John Gottman on Trust and Betrayal." *Greater Good: The Science of a Meaningful Life.* October 29, 2011. http://greatergood.berkeley.edu/article/item/john_gottman_on_trust_and_betrayal.

Gottman, John M, Julie Schwartz Gottman, and Joan DeClaire. *Ten Lessons to Transform Your Marriage.* New York: Crown, 2006.

Gottman, John M. and Nan Silver. *The Seven Principles for Making Marriage Work.* New York: Crown, 1999.

———. *Why Marriages Succeed or Fail.* New York: Simon & Schuster, 1994.

Guither, Harold D. and William N. Thompson. "Return, Readjustment, and Reminiscence." In *Cross-Cultural Reentry: A Book of Readings,* edited by Clyde N. Austin, 207-218. Abilene: Abilene Christian University, 1986.

Hansen, Randall S. "The Five-Step Plan for Creating Personal Mission Statement." *Quintessential Careers.* http://www.quintcareers.com/creating_personal_mission_statements.html.

Herh, Kristen. Introduction to *Living & Working Abroad: A Parent's Guide,* edited by Robin Pascoe. London: Kuperard, 1994.

"How Emotional Intelligence Can Improve Decision-Making." *The Huffington Post.* November 22, 2013. http://www.huffingtonpost.com/2013/11/22/emotional-intelligence-decision-making_n_4310192.html.

Hunter, Victor L. "Closure and Commencement: The Stress of Finding Home." In *Cross-Cultural Reentry: A Book of Readings,* edited by Clyde N. Austin, 179-189. Abilene, TX: Abilene Christian University, 1986.

Jansson, Diane P. "Return to Society: Problematic Features of the Re-entry Process." In *Cross-Cultural Reentry: A Book of Readings,* edited by Clyde N. Austin, 49–57. Abilene, TX: Abilene Christian University, 1986.

Jeffreys, Mary Ann. "Divided by the Great Commission." In *Survival Guide: Strengthening the Marriage of Missionary Couples,* 1–4. Carol Stream, IL: Christianity Today International, 2005.

Kaplan, Abraham. "The Life of Dialogue." In *The Reach of Dialogue: Confirmation, Voice, and Community,* edited by Robert Anderson, Kenneth N. Cissna, and Ronald C. Arnett, 34. New Jersey: Hampton Press, 1994. Quoted in Michelle Maiese. "The Life of Dialogue." Conflict Research Consortium. http://www.colorado.edu/conflict/peace/example/lifeofdialogue.htm.

Kasper, Walter. *Theology of Christian Marriage.* New York: Crossroad, 1981.

Kenny, Alexis C. "Married Missioner/Volunteer Survey." Master's thesis survey, Catholic Theological Union, 2015.

———. "Program Staff: Married Missioners/Volunteers Survey." Master's thesis survey, Catholic Theological Union, 2015.

Killen, Patricia O'Connell and John de Beer. *The Art of Theological Reflection.* New York: Crossroad, 1994.

Kinast, Robert L. *What Are They Saying About Theological Reflection?* New York: Paulist Press, 2000.

Kleinke, Chris L. *Common Principles of Psychotherapy.* Pacific Grove, CA: Brooks/Cole, 1994.

Kohls, L. Robert. *Survival Kit for Overseas Living: For Americans Planning to Live and Work Abroad.* Yarmouth, ME: Intercultural Press, 1984.

Koteskey, Ronald L. "Before You Get 'Home': Preparing for Reentry." *Missionary Care: Resources for Missions and Mental Health.* 2008. http://www.missionarycare.com/ebooks/Preparing_for_Reentry_Book.pdf.

———. "Missionary Marriage Issues." *Missionary Care: Resources for Missions and Mental Health.* January 2010. http://missionarycare.com/ebooks/Missionary_Marriage_Book.pdf.

Krauss Whitbourne, Susan. "The Definitive Guide to Guilt." *Psychology Today.* August 11, 2012. https://www.psychologytoday.com/blog/fulfillment-any-age/201208/the-definitive-guide-guilt

LaCugna, Catherine Mowry. *God for Us: The Trinity & Christian Life.* New York: Harper-Collins, 1973.

Lawler, Michael G. *Marriage and Sacrament: A Theology of Christian Marriage.* Collegeville, MN: Liturgical Press, 1993.

Limberger, Samantha. "The Break-Up Equation." *Let's Ask Violet.* April 19, 2013. http://www.letsaskviolet.com/2013/04/19/the-break-up-equation/.

Loewenthal, Nessa P. and Nancy L. Snedden. "Managing the Overseas Assignment Process." In *Cross-Cultural Reentry: A Book of Readings,* edited by Clyde N. Austin, 29–37. Abilene: Abilene Christian University, 1986.

Longsworth, Sam. "The Returned Volunteer: A Perspective." In *Cross-Cultural Reentry: A Book of Readings,* edited by Clyde N. Austin, 83–88. Abilene, TX: Abilene Christian University, 1986.

"Love Languages Study Guide." *Utah Education Network.* http://www.uen.org/Lessonplan/downloadFile.cgi?file=28905-2-35976-Love_Language_StudyGuide.pdf&filename=Love_Language_StudyGuide.pdf.

Lupien, Julie. "Hand Prayer." Presentation at the From Mission to Mission Workshop, Chicago, Illinois, October 24–26, 2014.

———. "How to Manage the Transition Experience." From Mission to Mission Workshop.

———. "Self-Care Stars." From Mission to Mission Workshop.

———. "Storytelling." From Mission to Mission Workshop.

Martin, Ryan. "Five Questions with Forgiveness Expert, Dr. Everett Worthington." *All the Rage: Commentary and Resources on the Science of Anger and Violence.* April 29, 2011. http://blog.uwgb.edu/alltherage/five-questions-with-forgiveness-expert-dr-everett-worthington/.

McAlpin, Kathleen, RSM. *Ministry That Transforms: A Contemplative Process of Theological Reflection.* Collegeville, MN: Liturgical Press, 2009.

McCaffrey, Jo Ann. *At Home in the Journey: Theological Reflection for Missioners in Transition.* Chicago: CCGM Publications, 2005.

Meyer, Cathy. "Types of Infidelity." *About Divorce.* March 1, 2015. http://divorcesupport.about.com/od/infidelity/p/infidelity_type.htm.

"Mission Statement Builder." *Franklin Covey.* http://www.franklincovey.com/msb/missions/family .

Mitchell, Kenneth R. and Herbert Anderson. *All Our Losses, All Our Griefs: Resources for Pastoral Care.* Philadelphia: Westminster Press, 1983.

Pascoe, Robin. *Culture Shock! Successful Living Abroad: A Wife's Guide.* Portland: Graphic Arts Center Publishing Company, 1992.

———. *Living & Working Abroad: A Parent's Guide.* London: Kuperard, 1994.

Rad, Michelle Roya. "The Positive Psychological Effects of Prayer." *The Huffington Post: Healthy Living.* April, 11, 2013. http://www.huffingtonpost.com/roya-r-rad-ma-psyd/prayer_b_3055127.html.

Rahner, Karl, SJ. *Leading a Christian Life.* Denville, NJ: Dimension Books, 1970.

Razak, B. *Peace Corps Close of Service Workshop: Trainer Guidelines and Workshop Materials.* Washington, DC: Peace Corps Office of Programming and Training Coordination, 1981. Quoted in Clyde N. Austin, "Appendix E: Moving On," in *Cross-Cultural Reentry: A Book of Readings,* edited by Clyde N. Austin, 269–70. Abilene, TX: Abilene Christian University, 1986.

"Re-entry." *IES Abroad.* http://www.iesabroad.org/study-abroad/parents/re-entry.

"Research FAQs." *The Gottman Institute.* http://www.gottman.com/research/research-faqs/.

Routledge, Clay. "5 Scientifically-Supported Benefits of Prayer." *Psychology Today.* June 23, 2014. https://www.psychologytoday.com/blog/more-mortal/201406/5-scientifically-supported-benefits-prayer.

Rutledge, Pamela B. "The Psychological Power of Storytelling." *Psychology Today.* January 16, 2011. https://www.psychologytoday.com/blog/positively-media/201101/the-psychological-power-storytelling.

Schreiter, Robert, CPPS. "The Ministry of Forgiveness in a Praxis of Reconciliation." Presentation at the International Seminar on Reconciliation, Lima, Peru, August 21, 2006.

———. *The Ministry of Reconciliation: Spirituality & Strategies.* New York: Orbis, 1998.

Searle, Mark. "The Journey of Conversion." *Worship* 54 (1980): 35–55.

Selig, Meg. "Routines: Comforting or Confining?" *Psychology Today.* September 14, 2010. https://www.psychologytoday.com/blog/changepower/201009/routines-comforting-or-confining.

Smithstein, Samantha. "(Re)defining Infidelity." *Psychology Today.* June 23, 2011. https://www.psychologytoday.com/blog/what-the-wild-things-are/201106/redefining-infidelity.

Staik, Athena. "How to Create a Timeline: The Power of Re-working Your Life's Story, 1 of 2." *PsychCentral.* January 5, 2013. http://blogs.psychcentral.com/relationships/%20 2012/04/the-power-of-creating-a-timeline-of-your-lifes-story/.

Storti, Craig. *The Art of Coming Home.* Yarmouth, ME: Intercultural, 1997.

———. *The Art of Crossing Cultures.* Boston: Intercultural Press, 1989.

Thogersen, Kristen. "Afterword: Self-Esteem and a New Environment." In *Homeward Bound: A Spouse's Guide to Repatriation,* edited by Robin Pascoe. Vancouver: Expatriate Press, 2000.

Thomas, David, M. *Christian Marriage: The New Challenge.* Collegeville, MN: Liturgical Press, 2007.

Thomas, Gary. "The Transforming Miracle of Marriage." *Psychology for Living: Narramore Christian Foundation.* http://www.ncfliving.org/miracle_marriage1.php.

Thompson, Dennis, Jr. "Gender Differences in Emotional Health." *Everyday Health.* July 14, 2010. http://www.everydayhealth.com/emotional-health/gender-differences-in-emotional-health.aspx.

Treat, Stephen and Larry Hoff. *Pastoral Marital Therapy: A Practical Primer for Ministry to Couples.* New York: Integration Books, 1987.

Tuan, Yi-Fu. *Space and Place: The Perspective of Experience.* Minneapolis: University of Minnesota Press, 1977.

Turner, Victor. "Betwixt and Between: The Liminal Period in Rites of Passage." In *Betwixt and Between: Patterns of Masculine and Feminine Imitation,* edited by Louise Carus Mahdi, Steven Foster, and Meredith Little. La Salle, IL: Open Court, 1987.

"25 Ways to Fill a Journal Page." *HubPages.* December 2, 2014. http://createthespark.hubpages.com/hub/25-Ways-to-Fill-a-Journal-Page.

United States Conference of Catholic Bishops Committee on Laity, Marriage, Family Life, and Youth. *Marriage: Love and Life in the Divine Plan.* Washington, DC: United States Conference of Catholic Bishops, 2010.

Werkman, Sidney L. "Coming Home: Adjustment of Americans to the United States after Living Abroad." In *Cross-Cultural Reentry: A Book of Readings,* edited by Clyde N. Austin, 5–17. Abilene: Abilene Christian University, 1986.

Whitehead, Evelyn Eaton and James D. Whitehead. *Marrying Well: Possibilities in Christian Marriage Today.* Garden City, NY: Doubleday & Co., 1981.

Made in the USA
Charleston, SC
30 October 2015